Seeking The Praise Of God

SEEKING THE PRAISE OF GOD

An Exegetical Commentary on First Corinthians Four

BY

SPIROS ZODHIATES, TH.D.

AMG PUBLISHERS
Chattanooga, TN 37422

Seeking the Praise of God
An Exegetical Commentary on
First Corinthians Four

ISBN 0-89957-443-2

Printed in the United States of America
03 02 01 00 99 98 –B– 6 5 4 3 2 1

To George Constantinides
who for years labored with me in the
publication of gospel messages
in almost the entire Greek press
enabling millions to hear the claims
of the Lord Jesus Christ
and
To S. John David
who in my estimation is a perfect example
of a sacrificing disciple of Jesus Christ for
and among his suffering fellow people of India.

Contents

Preface

"For they loved the praise of men more than the praise of God" (John 12:43). ". . . then shall every man have praise of God" (1 Cor. 4:5).

Most judgments between persons are praises or blames. Very few are neutral like "Bob is six feet tall," but even fewer are positive like "Bob is the most wonderful person I have ever met!" More frequently we hear, "Bob's a wreck!" or "Bob's nasty" or "Bob's an alcoholic!" When we don't hear such things about ourselves from others (since they hide most of it), we can always listen to the ongoing broadcasts about others in our own minds! By nature, we are creatures who habitually watch, measure, and compare every word, action, attitude, and choice of others as well as of ourselves. We look for consistency and hypocrisy, for praise or blame; and we do this most of the time mentally, if not verbally. Our natural tendency is to find fault, so we delight more in hypocrisy; at least that's what seems to sell the most newspapers and magazines.

Some critics in our world are unbelievers, which raises interesting questions. To what extent should we react to their criticisms or flatteries? Are all judgments of unbelievers false because their consciences are seared or do some accidentally line up with the Word of God? Even if they do line up, just how guilty should we feel when an unbeliever catches us somewhat short of the perfect will of God? Should we dish out retaliative flattery to unbelievers or just dispense intimidating truth? Is moral compromise with an unbeliever possible? Are there times when we should just keep silent?

Other critics are believers, introducing a whole new set of queries. When two regenerate consciences disagree over some ethical matter, what should be done? Can we always trust our consciences? Is every ethical issue settled in the Scripture? Are there higher principles to appeal to if a specific issue is not discussed in the Bible? What latitude do we have in these decisions? Are doctrinal issues ethical issues and is every ethical issue a doctrinal issue? Can we fellowship with those we disagree with?

Paul faced these problems with the Corinthians and even with his co-worker, Apollos, with whom he did not always see eye to eye. At times Paul seemed overly concessive as, for example, when he said he would never again eat meat if it offended his brother. At other times, he stood his ground with a depictive hyperbole like "I wish that those who were troubling you [with circumcision] would mutilate themselves (i.e., literally 'cut them off')." Were Paul's accommodations to certain beliefs or circumstances compromises? When is conceding to someone Christ-like obedience and when is it satanic compromise? Did Paul compromise principles? Was he able to live in peace with co-workers? How did he get along with unbelievers?

All these questions are subordinate to the main question: "Whose praise, ultimately, should we seek?" Of course, the simple answer is "The Lord!" but somehow when we expand that simple answer to "The Lord who said 'sell all you have and give to the poor and you will have treasure in heaven' and 'he that will be the greatest among you, let him become the servant of all,' " a disturbing, inner resistance seems to ascend out of our souls like the Beast out of the Abyss. Much of 1 Corinthians deals with compromises the believers in this church had made with the world to quell these ascending convictions.

Accordingly, we have entitled our work not the rhetorical "Whose praise do we seek?" but rather "Seeking the praise of God." We already know the **simple** answer; it's the **complex** one we want to deal with; and we believe the best way to do this is to examine the very seeking itself, the how, the content of seeking God's praise over and against man's. We know "**Who**?"; we need to learn more about the "**How**?"—the "**What** (should we be doing)?" to please the most important Critic, our most important Critic.

The "How?", the seeking, may be defined in terms of scriptural, holy actions and reactions with three major environments.

The first environment is the **world of unbelievers**, the alien and hostile society of unbelief. What does seeking the praise of God have to do with the praise and censure of unbelievers? When do we regard their opinion, when do we compromise, when do we disregard?

The second environment is the **new world created by Jesus Christ**, the church, the congregation of those who have been made "to differ from one another" by the Lord Himself (1 Cor. 4:7). Believers have different talents by creation and redemption, different spiritual gifts by regeneration, and different consciences by sanctification and experience. What does seeking the praise of God have to do with being free in Christ and yet a servant of all men? How do we handle local divisions? Is there a place for godly jealousy or does all jealousy lead to faction and rivalry? Is there a time when we can disregard the counsel of other believers? Where do we draw the doctrinal lines; what's fundamental and what's trivial?

The third environment is the **world of things**. What does seeking the praise of God have to do with our fundamental attitudes toward the things of this world—its possessions and status? How much of our time, status and fame, and possessions should we place at God's disposal? Is there a greater joy in sacrifice and deprivation? What can we learn from the lives of Jesus and the apostle Paul?

It is my prayer that this volume will, with the Spirit's guidance, help you to determine **how**, that is, **what to do**, to seek the praise of the Living God as your very first priority.

An Overview of First Corinthians

Author:	Paul the apostle, author of thirteen other epistles to various individuals and congregations.
Date:	About A.D. 55.
Recipients:	The congregation Paul had established in Corinth.
Place:	From Ephesus
Theme:	Paul had received news about the Corinthian brethren from several sources (1 Cor. 1:11; 7:1; 16:17). The church was afflicted with many of the problems that face young churches and new converts. The apostle, under the inspiration of the Holy Spirit, decided to write this urgent letter to admonish and instruct the church. Among other topics he discussed: the necessity of church discipline (5:1–13); divisions and disputes among Christians (1:10–16; 6:1–11); matters of conscience (8:1–13; 10:19–33); the support of preachers (9:1–27); abuses of the Lord's Supper (10:16–17, 21; 11:17–34); the misuse of spiritual gifts (12:1—14:40); and the importance of the resurrection of Jesus Christ (15:1–58).

An Outline of First Corinthians

In the days of the apostle Paul, Corinth was the capital city of the Roman province of Achaia and the glory of Greece. Though its great ancient splendor had been destroyed by the Romans in 120 B.C., the city was rebuilt under Julius Caesar and restored to wealth and luxury under Augustus. Among all the cities of the world, however, it was most well known for its lewdness. The apostle Paul lived in Corinth for eighteen months (Acts 18:11). After his departure, Paul went to Ephesus. During his three-year stay there, he heard reports of wickedness and division within the Corinthian church. In an effort to correct these evils, Paul wrote several letters to them, including the epistle of First Corinthians.

1:1–9	The introductory remarks of Paul.
1:10–16	Paul condemns the divisions in the church and exhorts its members to unity.
1:17—2:16	Paul defends his ministry. He has preached the wisdom of Christ crucified. This wisdom is foolishness to the world, but is the glory of all those to whom the Spirit of God has revealed the truthfulness of it.
3:1–5	Paul declares that the simplicity of his teaching was due to the carnal state of the Corinthians, which state is clearly evidenced by their divisions.
3:6–23	Jesus Christ is the only foundation. Ministers are mere servants; the work is God's.
4:1–6	The duty of ministers is faithfulness.
4:6–21	Paul contrasts the arrogance and conceit of the false teachers to the humility and sacrifice of the apostles. Using his unique position as their spiritual father, Paul calls on the Corinthian believers to be discerning.
5:1–13	Flagrant, sexual immorality was being practiced by one of the members of the congregation. Paul reproves

	their lack of discipline and calls for expulsion of the guilty party.
6:1–11	Christians should not bring their legal disputes before heathen judges.
6:12–20	Paul reprimands the perversion of the principle of Christian liberty to excuse fornication. Our bodies belong to the Lord and should be devoted to His glory.
7:1–17	Paul answers questions about marriage.
7:18–24	Paul advises that, provided they are not immoral or unlawful, our social positions should remain intact after coming to Christ.
7:25–40	Paul answers questions about virgins and widows.
8:1–13	Christian liberty and conscience: was it lawful to eat meat that had been sacrificed to false gods?
9:1–23	Paul declares the right of ministers to be faithfully supported by their congregation.
9:24—10:13	Exhortations to self-denial.
10:14—11:1	While the purchase of meat offered to idols is a matter of conscience, attendance at the heathen feasts of sacrifice is idolatry, even if such was not their intention.
11:2–16	Men and women should take care to conform to the customs of dress in their community that assure modesty and properly reflect the man to be "the glory of God" and the woman to be "the glory of the man."
11:17–34	Paul exhorts the Corinthians to properly partake of the Lord's Supper.
12:1–31	Paul answers their questions about spiritual gifts. He reminds them that they are all members of one body. God has distributed these gifts so that each member may perform the function it is designed for.

13:1–13	Love [*agápē* {26}] is superior to all other gifts.
14:1–25	The gift of prophecy is more valuable than the gift of tongues.
14:26–40	Principles for orderly public worship.
15:1–34	Paul proves the resurrection of Christ is fact. It is the foundation of our faith and the surety of our resurrection.
15:35–58	Paul explains the nature of our resurrection.
16:1–9	Paul's specific instructions for the collection of monies from several Greek congregations for the poverty-stricken saints in Palestine.
16:10–12	Recommendations for Timothy and Apollos to be accepted by the Corinthians.
16:13–24	Paul's final admonition to them to stand firm in the faith. Salutation.

1 Cor. 4:1 | *Your Personal Accountability to God*

Let a man so account of us, as of the ministers of Christ, and stewards of the mysteries of God.

Submission to Christ

"Is your father home?" someone asked a child on the doorstep of the village doctor.

"No," he said, "he's away."

"Where do you think I could find him?"

"Well," he said with a considering air, "you've got to look for some place where people are sick or hurt, or something like that. I don't know where he is, but he's helping somewhere."

Isn't that what people should be able to say about every follower of Christ? That's what Paul implied when he wrote, "Who then is Paul, and who is Apollos, but ministers by whom ye believed?" (1 Cor. 3:5).

The Greek word translated "ministers" here is *diákonoi,* which might more literally be translated "deacons." A *diákonos* or "deacon" is a minister or attendant. In Ephesians 3:7, 8, for instance, Paul calls himself "a minister [*diákonos*], according to the gift of the grace of God . . . that I should preach among the Gentiles." In Colossians 1:23 he calls himself a "minister" of the gospel. The attendants at a feast are called *diákonoi,* "ministers," as in John 2:5

and Matthew 22:13. Paul then in 1 Corinthians 3:5 speaks of himself and Apollos as "ministers" by whom the Corinthians believed. He was declaring their devotion to the gospel and its preaching.

In 1 Corinthians 4:1 he goes on to tell them how every man should view them. "Let a man so account of us, as of the ministers of Christ." The word he uses here, which is translated "ministers," is not *diákonoi,* "deacons," but *hupērétas* (*hupērétēs,* singular nominative), "servants," though it is of course related to *diákonoi,* but with a distinction in the meaning.

This is the only place in Paul's writings that he uses the word *hupērétēs.* It's possible that it's a derivative of *erettṓ,* meaning "to row." And of course with the preposition *hupó,* "under," it means one serving or rowing under someone else. Rowing was his function, but the important thing about this under-rower was not simply that he acted as a rower but that in doing so he received directions from a superior officer.

Furthermore, he could be distinguished from a *doúlos,* "slave," a term Paul repeatedly uses in his epistles. This is the bondman who has a permanent relation of servitude to his master. He couldn't exercise freedom even if he wanted to. The word *hupērétēs,* which Paul used in

Corinthians 4:1, indicates inferiority to a superior one and a relationship that is voluntary.

How earnestly Paul wanted men to know him and Apollos, and generally all those who preached the gospel in Corinth, as *hupērétas Christoú,* "servants of Christ." He wanted them to recognize not only their function as preachers of the gospel but also their relationship as servant to Master, to Jesus Christ. Two things should characterize a preacher: the proclamation of the gospel, serving out the grace of God to others, and a voluntary submissive relationship to the Lord Jesus Christ.

It is difficult to tell which is more important, the proclamation of the grace of God or submission to the Lord Jesus Christ, since the two are so interrelated. Anne Sullivan, who tutored young Helen Keller who was blind, deaf, and dumb, said, "I saw clearly that it was useless to try to teach her language or anything else until she learned to obey me. I have thought about it a great deal, and the more I think, the more certain I am that obedience is the gateway through which knowledge, yes, and love, too, enter the mind of a child."

The word *hupērétēs* in classical Greek was used of the messenger of the gods, who was called by that name. In the context, this can only mean that such a messenger, as a servant, was executing the will of Zeus, and thus had behind him the power and authority of Zeus as chief of the ancient mythological gods of the Greeks. The men of Delphi, for instance, were called *hupērétai*, "servants," of Apollo in the same sense, since in his name they proclaimed the will of him who declared himself in the oracle.

Paul is still concerned in the 4th chapter about the factionalism in the Corinthian church. He conceives of the Christian Church as a ship, of which Christ is the Pilot, and all His ministers are rowers under His command. They are so subordinate to Him that they can do nothing and be nothing in their ministerial character except as He gives the word.

It is noteworthy that Paul says "servants of *Christ.*" He does not use the human name, "Jesus," but the anointed human one, "Christ," the Anointed One, the One in whom are concentrated all the power and authority of heaven and earth (Matt. 28:18). Actually, in this verse, when commissioning His disciples to go and preach the gospel to all nations, Christ does not impart unlimited and inherent authority to them, but declares that He is going to keep it. "Unto *me* has been given all authority in heaven and on earth"—not to you. They were to be subservient to Him, as under-rowers.

Helen Keller recognized this when she wrote, "If we trust, and if we relinquish our will and yield to the divine will, then we find that we are afloat on a buoyant sea of peace, and under us are the everlasting arms."

A Great and High Calling

When Christ commissioned His Twelve Disciples to go out and preach, we read that He gave them power and authority to heal all diseases and cast out demons (Luke 9:1). This was only relative power, however, for He remains *the* Power and Authority. There's nothing more important for the servants of Christ to realize than that our power, our authority, are proportionate to the closeness of our relationship with Him. We have no business being separate lords and leaders; founders of schools, parties, or churches in our own name. The very highest of us, including Paul, are only servants, "under-rowers." "Whosoever will be chief among you," said our Lord, "let him be your minister" (Matt. 20:27).

Nevertheless, it is a great and high calling to be a servant of Christ, to be called to row the ship of salvation, to be entrusted with the working of the oars that propel the vessel of which Christ is the Owner and Pilot. Not even the apostles are independent heads and leaders. They are all underworkmen, hand-laborers, dependent servants, who must look to Christ for their authority and orders in all they undertake and do.

Paul feels that when others look at us they must realize we are servants, not of other men, or of an organization or church, but of Christ Himself. "As servants of Christ," he says. We are not to show servility to any man, but take our paramount direct orders from Christ Himself. The servant of Christ must maintain a direct line of communication, so to speak, through prayer and obedient study of the Word of God. "Ye are bought with a price; be not ye the servants of men" (1 Cor. 7:23).

The word for servants here is *doúloi,* which is opposed to *eleútheroi, "free."* It refers to a permanent relation of servitude to another. The will of a *doúlos* is swallowed up in the will of another. And in 2 Corinthians 4:5 Paul says, "For we preach not ourselves, but Christ Jesus the Lord; and ourselves your servants [*doúlos*] for Jesus' sake." In other words, when it comes to making Christ known, we don't mind losing our will to subject the will of others to Christ. But we must remember at all times that Christ in His redemptive purpose and work is Master. The preeminence and exaltation of Christ come first in the life and ministry of a servant of Christ.

Paul also tells us in this verse that we are being watched by other people. They are trying to figure us out, especially if we are preachers. The word Paul uses to express this is *logizésthō* which basically means "figure out." It comes from *logízomai,* "to reckon." *Logistḗs* is "an accountant." The word is derived from the substantive *lógos,* meaning "logic, thought, intelligence," as well as "expression that is the result of thought." Do you have any doubt that "man," *ánthrōpos* (meaning here mankind, all men and women), has his eyes upon us trying to figure us out?

Someone asked an elderly Scotswoman what she thought of Robert Murray McCheyne's preaching. She hesitated for a moment, then replied, "He preaches as if he was a-dying to have you saved." Is that our spirit? Those who watch us will know. How appropriate was Spurgeon's advice to a young minister who complained of the smallness of his congregation: "It is as large a one as you will want to give account for in the Day of Judgment."

The first thing others should discern in us, Paul says, is that we are servants of Christ—subservient, obedient to Him; that He is Master and we listen to what He says and do what He commands.

An unemployed laborer applied to a banker, saying that he was ready to do anything that would bring him an honest living. The banker took him to his farm and said, "All right, you take that pile of stones that you see in the end of the lot, and carry them to the other side and pile them up in the same manner that they are now." The man did his job and received a day's wages.

The next morning he reappeared and was sent by his strange employer to replace the stones as he first found them. So the laborer worked faithfully every day for a week, carrying stones from one place to another without complaint or question.

On Saturday night the eccentric banker said, "I like you. There is no nonsense about you; you do what you're told. Many men would have objected to doing the work over and over. You shall have work as long as I have anything for anybody to do." It is such servants the Lord wants.

Go, labor on; spend and be spent,
Thy joy to do the Father's will;
It is the way the Master went;
Should not the servant tread it still?

Go, labor on; 'tis not for naught;
Thine earthly loss is heavenly gain;
Men heed thee, love thee, praise thee not;
The Master praises—what are men?

Go, labor on; your hands are weak;
Your knees are faint, your soul cast down;
Yet falter not; the prize you seek
Is near—a kingdom and a crown!
—Horatius Bonar

To Whom Are You Accountable?

The apostle Paul tells us in 1 Corinthians 4:1 that not only must Christians discern their high calling as servants of Christ, but they must also realize that they are "stewards of the mysteries of God." First comes subordination and then stewardship.

What is involved in being a steward? The Greek word is *oikonómous* (singular, *oikonómos*). It is derived from the substantive *oíkos* meaning "house," and the verb *némō* meaning "to dispense, to distribute." It denotes the person who manages a house or dispenses what belongs to a house. It's the word from which we derive the English word "economist." A steward, then, is a business manager or treasurer.

What this implies is that none of us who proclaim the gospel are actually owners of what we manage. We are placed in trust with it. How true this is of all of life. It is not really ours. We have been placed in trust with it by God. The same holds true of salvation in Jesus Christ. It needs to be managed and expended. The realization that we are not owners of all that we have and are is very important. If we insist on regarding ourselves as owners instead of stewards, we cannot really be followers of Christ.

Scripture gives us the illustration of a young man who came to Jesus to ask what he should do to obtain eternal life. The Lord told him to go sell all that he had and give the proceeds to the poor. Why? Because for one thing Christ wanted him to realize that he really was not the owner of what he possessed, much or little though that might be. But the rich man turned away sorrowfully, because he wanted to retain his right of ownership rather than be a steward (Matt. 19:16–22). That you cannot do, for when you decide to follow Christ you resign your ownership and become a steward. This is clearly shown in 1 Corinthians 4:7, where Paul asks: "What hast thou that thou didst not receive?"

Stewardship is a distinct characteristic of a saved, redeemed person. A man whose whole attitude is geared to a materialistic philosophy of life is not likely to lose any sleep over the fact that many remote jungle tribes in South America have never once heard the gospel. He doesn't feel guilty that the money he spends on cigarettes and liquor is far greater than what he puts in the collection plate on Sunday (if he even goes to church), or gives to the relief of famine areas of the world, or any other charitable cause.

The non-spiritual man has no more sense of guilt in this matter of ignoring God's directions and requirements for stewardship than a newborn baby has over its imperious demands for food and comfort. His own needs and interests come first, and these do not include a sense of accountability to God for what he does with his time, talents, or money.

Just as our orders as servants of Christ are received directly from Christ, so our stewardship is directly reportable to Christ. Daily accounting to Him is necessary. Paul speaks later on of our accounting to Him in that day when all our work will be made manifest, but there must also be a daily accounting to see whether we are daily pleasing to Him.

Sometimes we take it for granted that what we are doing is perfectly satisfactory. You recall the story of the steward in Luke 16:1–9 who was called in directly for an accounting with his master. Every day we should go to the Lord for an appraisal of our lives and work. The Christian has a tremendous advantage here, in that the Master is always available and within call. If you work for someone in a high position, you may discover that accessibility to him can be a real problem. But the Lord's ear is always attuned to the words of His stewards.

Every Christian should daily come to Christ to give an account and to take orders. We should not hesitate to bring to Him in detail what has transpired. Sometimes we will have to confess, "Lord, there were many minutes and hours when I goofed and wasted time when I should have been working." Though we might never think of stealing money, we often waste time and miss opportunities that should uplift Christ (see C. H. Spurgeon, *An All-Round Ministry*, pp. 252–81).

What is the basis of stewardship? It is the recognition of the sovereignty of God. He is supreme He possesses all, He created all. He, through the second birth, brought you and me into existence. First as a human entity, by the creative act of God. How does anyone come into existence? First, as a human entity, by the creative act of God. How does anyone come into existence as a child of God, as a Christian? By God's gift, by His favor, by His sacrifice. As Christians we had nothing to do with it. Hence we are in existence by His favor, by His gift, by His sovereign love. All that we possess He gave. We do not own one single thing. We cannot claim proprietary rights over anything. It is God's, not ours. He gave it to us because of His favor, because of His sovereign grace, because of His love, because of His willingness to dispense to us what He possesses.

What Will God Hold You Responsible For?

Why must every large charitable organization, in order to secure tax exemption, first of all have its accounts audited by a Certified Public Accountant? It's because the Treasury Department wants to be satisfied with the organization's accountability.

What the Treasury Department requires in financial matters, the Word of God requires in spiritual matters. The apostle Paul tells us that Christians must regard themselves as "stewards of the mysteries of God." We are not originators of these mysteries, mind you. We are simply the recipients of them, holding them in trust under God.

Paul wants to remind us by this expression that we are accountable. He has just finished speaking of that day when the work of each one will be made manifest. Just imagine how careless a treasurer might be if he knew that he would never have to give an accounting of the funds entrusted to him. As Christians, we are to live constantly in view of the day of accounting that is coming. We will have to give an accounting for everything God has given us.

Christian stewardship is indeed a privilege, but it is also a grave responsibility. The doctrine of stewardship is a great regulative principle of life. The moment we lose a sense of personal responsibility we tend to become lax and indifferent. Stewardship and accounting keep us on our toes (see Luke 12:42; 16:2; 1 Tim. 1:11; Heb. 13:17; 1 Pet. 4:10). J. H. B. Masterman breaks down this stewardship for us:

> There are three tribunals before which every man's life is brought to judgment. First there is the tribunal of public opinion [of which Paul speaks in 1 Corinthians 4:1 when he says, "Thus let every man take account of us"]. The verdict of some of the Corinthians on S. Paul had not been very favourable. But his purpose was not to please men (Gal. 1:10) (J. H. B. Masterman, *Sunday Teachings: The Collects, Epistles, and Gospels,* 17).

There were two things, however, of which no one could accuse Paul: 1) that he was not a good servant of Christ—subject to Christ in his relationship to Him; and 2) that he was not a faithful steward of the mysteries of God—declaring His forgiveness and grace, which resulted in the miraculous transformation of those who heard and believed. He calls these miracles resulting from the preaching of the gospel "mysteries," because there could be no human explanation for them.

Paul's purpose was not to please men (Gal. 1:10). He knew that popularity might be a snare. No man likes to feel that public opinion is against him, but our standard of right must never be the popular opinion of the moment if that is contrary to God's Word. If we are wise, we will neither seek popularity nor shun it. Our Lord said of those who sought the approval of their fellow men, "They have their reward" (Matt. 6:2). Masterman continues his analysis with the second and third tribunals:

> Then there is the tribunal of the conscience. "I do not claim to judge myself, I know nothing against myself." S. Paul does not mean that he is conscious of no sin, but that he does not feel guilty of the misuse of his stewardship of which some Corinthian enemies were accusing him. But S. Paul had the best of reasons for knowing that even the conscience is not an infallible guide (Acts 26:9, 1 Tim. 1:13). The mere fact that a man's conscience is silent does not always prove that he is acquitted of all blame. There is a court of appeal above conscience—a court that is always sitting—"He who is summoning me to judgment is the Lord."
>
> Paul thinks of his life as always on trial before the divine judgment bar (1 Pet. 1:17; 4:5). The third tribunal, then, is that final judgment of which Paul spoke in chapter 3. The early Christians looked forward to final judgment that should vindicate them from the charges that the world made against them (1 Pet. 4:19) (*Ibid.*, 17, 18).

What are some of the things for which we must possess a sense of stewardship? *Time.* We did not create it. God has loaned it to us. There is a mystery about it. To some He allots much and to others little. Each of us must ask himself, What am I doing with my time? Am I killing it? Would I welcome a review of how I used every moment of it? While we are spending time, we should project ourselves to the day when we shall have to give an accounting for it.

Then there are *talents.* Although in the Bible this word denotes money, we can also take it as referring to abilities. Each of us possesses some abilities. It is an unfathomable mystery why God has chosen to give one person ten talents, another five, and another one. Why doesn't He give everyone an equal amount? For that matter, why does He make some persons more beautiful? We humans strive for equality, thinking it to be the ideal. But we are faced with the mystery of God's unequal gifts to men.

However, God doesn't want us to be known as interpreters of His mysteries but as stewards of them. And He wants us to use them without questioning. The world will be impressed by the way we make full use of whatever He gives. One thing is certain: if God gives us one talent, He expects us to produce two, not ten. But if He gives us five, He does expect us to produce a proportionate yield.

The Mystery of Suffering

We have seen in previous studies that God will hold us responsible for the use of our time and talents. But another mysterious trust God places upon us is various tribulations. These, too, must be viewed as gifts of God, strange as that may seem. We shall have to give an account to Him of how we reacted to them one day. The world will also judge us by the way we use these mysterious endowments of God.

We remember that when Job's wife turned from her husband in disgust and unbelief over his terrible afflictions, she told him to "curse God, and die" (Job 2:9). But Job's attitude was revealed in the words, "Though he slay me, yet will I trust him" (Job 13:15). He proved a faithful steward of the sufferings God had bestowed upon him. The world is a keen observer of how we live up to our profession of faith under affliction.

We have already noted the inequality with which God apportions time and talents to men. We also find that His endowments of material goods are unequally distributed. The Scriptures clearly teach that what we have is not really ours, but His. Therefore our responsibility in managing it is all the greater. It doesn't matter how much or how little we have—though we find God's providences mysterious here also and may wonder why He trusts some with much and others with little. The world is not going to judge us for what we think God should have given us, but for how we use what He does give us. If we call ourselves servants of Christ, yet are wasteful and extravagant, they will condemn us for it. They will also take note of how much we return to God of what He has given us.

God, too, will require an accounting from us of all that has been wasted. But we mustn't think it's the person who has much who is more likely to be unfaithful and unfruitful. In the Parable of the Talents, it was the person who received only one talent who buried it and produced nothing. The stewardship of even the little entrusted to us is a tremendous responsibility.

Baylor University is a fine institution in Beaumont, Texas. The Christian who gave the money for building that school later lost all his property. Men of the world asked him, "Don't you wish you had the money back that you put into that school?" He replied, "Not at all. It is all that I have saved. If I had kept that money, I would have lost it too. I am thankful that I gave that building when I did." The world will judge us by what we do with the property God has placed in our keeping.

Now why does Paul call all that God bestows upon us "mysteries"? Not because they are myths, but because they are facts that we can neither understand nor explain. As Joseph Parker points out:

> We know how easy it is to reduce everything to the mystery of darkness and to suppose that, because we can't see, therefore all things that are declared to be in existence cannot possibly be where they are said to be. When night comes down upon us, and the sea is covered, and the great rocks around our coast are all hidden, what would you think of a man who said, "There is no sea; there are no rocks; there are no mountains. I deny it; I swear there is no sea! . . . Why, if there was an ocean, should I not see it? If there were rocks, would I not behold them?" He forgets that he is surrounded by conditions that have obliterated to his vision the facts which he so emphatically denies (Joseph Parker, *Detached Links,* 180).

It should not surprise us that God's actions and providences are mysteries to us. It is natural; it could not be otherwise. "The great must always be a mystery to the little," continues Parker. "The arch must always be a mystery to the column; God must always be a mystery to His creatures. If I could understand all, I should be all. Only the whole can comprehend the whole. Only God can understand God."

And then Parker says:

> There is a mystery about religion, but there is ten thousand times more mystery without it. There is mystery with the Bible, but there is nothing but mystery without it. There is a mystery of *grace*; yes, and there is mystery of *sin*. Life is a mystery. All that is great touches the mysterious. In proportion as a thing rises from vulgarity and the commonplace, it rises into wondrousness—and wondrousness is but the first round in the ladder whose head rests upon the infinite mysteries (*Ibid.*, 30).

Blessed art thou, O child of God, who sufferest,
  And canst not understand
The reason for thy pain, yet gladly leavest
  Thy life in His blest hand.
Yea, blessed art thou whose faith is "not offended"
  By trials unexplained,
By mysteries unsolved, past understanding,
  Until the goal is gained.
—Freda Hanbury Allen

LESSONS:

1. We are personally accountable as subordinate servants or, literally, underrowers (*hupērétas*) or oarsmen, to our superior, the Lord Jesus Christ. We neither own nor pilot the ship of salvation.
2. By using Christ's anointed name, *Christoú*, Paul highlights the anointing of the Holy Spirit or Christ's perfect, sinless humanity. This anointing "without measure" in Christ (John 3:34) is measured out to us for service.
3. The most important truth for believers to retain is that their power to service Christ is directly proportionate to their relationship with Him.
4. Indirectly, Paul commends the church to understand the apostles as slaves and managers of God's mysteries.

5. The Lord entrusts the gospel to us as managers (*oikonómous*). We do not own the gospel; it owns us.
6. When we decide for Christ, we disown our possessions for His glory.
7. We receive orders directly from Jesus Christ, the God-Man, and we are also directly reportable to Him. He is eternally accessible. We should seek His praise and His new orders daily.
8. Believers will give an account of every talent, gift, and possession God has given them. We should live constantly with this in mind. If we do not, we drift naturally into apathy and irresponsibility.
9. Every man's life is judged at three tribunals: the tribunal of "all men" (i.e., the world), the tribunal of conscience, and the tribunal of the final judgment. Only the latter is infallible. Neither other sinners nor our own seared consciences match the Word of God as infallible guides to right and wrong.
10. Christian stewardship encompasses the spiritual use of time and talents. God gives more of these to some than to others, according to His sovereign good pleasure, but to those to whom more is given, more is required.
11. Trials, sufferings, and pain are all gifts from God, strange as this may seem. As Paul says, it was "granted" (*echarísthē*, literally "it has been graced") us to suffer for Christ's sake (Phil. 1:29).
12. Wasteful, extravagant living is alignment with the unrestrained luxury of the Whore of Babylon (see Revelation 17 and 18) and a bad witness to Christ who identified with the poor.
13. The Parable of the Talents proves that even the poor can waste what God has given them.
14. There are mysteries surrounding God's providential dealings with men, but without God life is universally meaningless.

1 Cor. 4:1 | *Facing Up to Life's Mysteries*

Let a man so account of us, as of the ministers of Christ, and stewards of the mysteries of God.

Truths That Defy Comprehension

When we read the epistles of Paul, we can't help being impressed by his intelligence. He was a highly educated man. He was also a "Hebrew of the Hebrews," who had persecuted Christianity. But after his encounter with Christ on the Damascus road, he preached Christianity, though he saw much that was mysterious in it. Just what is the meaning of the word "mystery" as used in Scripture?

Etymologically the Greek word *mustḗrion* is derived from the verb *muéō,* which means "to close the eyes or the mouth or any other gap." The word *mustḗrion,* "mystery," as a noun, is derived from a supposed verbal adjective that does not occur in use, *mústos* which means "closed, covered." Perhaps in the very beginning it referred to sacred objects that were covered, so that no one was permitted to see them.

In Greece for many centuries, a mystery meant a religious or sacred secret into which, after due preparation, men were initiated by solemn rites. At Eleusis, near Athens, for example, there were many mysteries of this description for centuries. They were designed to preserve and hand on certain supposed truths that formed part of the earliest religion of Greece—doctrines that were lost sight of or denied or denounced by the popular religion of a later day. A tenet thus concealed and thus disclosed was called a "mystery" for several reasons: 1) because after disclosure, it was still concealed from the general public; 2) because it had been concealed even from the initiated up to the moment of initiation; and 3) because it was of a character to suggest that, however much truth it might convey, there was more to which it pointed but which still remained unknown.

This was the general sense that the word had acquired at the time the New Testament was written. The meaning given by the apostle Paul is that certain Christian doctrines, after having been hidden for long ages in the mind of God, were at last revealed by men taught by the Spirit of God.

Thus Paul writes to the Romans, "According to my gospel, and the preaching of Jesus Christ, according to the revelation of the mystery, which was kept secret since the world began" (Rom. 16:25). And in Ephesians 3:3, 4, Paul writes: "How that by revelation he made known unto me the mystery; (as I wrote afore in few words, whereby, when ye read, ye may understand my knowledge in the mystery of Christ)." The mystery here was the call of the Gentiles along with the Jews into the Church of Christ. And speaking of the inward presence of Christ in the souls of those who once were heathen, Paul describes it as "the mystery which hath been hid from ages and from generations, but now is made manifest to his saints" (Col. 1:26).

Consider what Liddon says about the biblical sense of mystery:

> Mystery in the biblical sense, then, is used to describe not a fancy, not a contradiction, not an impossibility, but always a truth, yet a truth which has been or which is more or less hidden. A mystery is a truth, a

fact . . . never [applicable] to any shadowy sort of unreality. But it is a partially hidden fact or truth.

Truths are of two kinds, both of them truths, and, as such, equally certain, but they differ in that they are differently apprehended by us. There are some truths on which the mind's eye rests directly, just as the bodily eye rests on the sun in a cloudless sky; and there are other truths of the reality of which the mind is assured by seeing something else which satisfies it that they are there, just as the bodily eye sees the strong ray which pours forth in a stream of brilliancy from behind the cloud and reports to the understanding that if only the cloud were to be removed the sun itself would be seen.

Now mysteries in religion, as we commonly use the word, are of this description; we see enough to know that there is more which we do not see, and while in this state of existence, we shall not directly see, the ray which implies the sun behind the cloud. And thus to look upon the apparent truth, which certainly implies truth that is not apparent, is to be in the presence of.

Science does not exorcise mystery out of nature; it only removes its frontier, in most cases, a step farther back. Those who know most of nature are most impressed, not by the facts which they can explain and reason on, but by the facts which they cannot explain and which they know to lie beyond the range of explanation (H. P. Liddon, *Sermon Outline Bible, Acts 7—1 Corinthians*, 291, 292).

"If we could see, if we could know,"
    We often say,
But God in love a veil doth throw
    Across our way.
We cannot see what lies before,
    And so we cling to Him the more.
He leads us till this life is o'er:
    Trust and obey.

You Can't Live without Faith

When the apostle Paul spoke of "the mysteries of God," he recognized that he himself was a product of such a mystery. Like Moses, he received a direct revelation from God—not in a burning bush but in a unique and unexplainable way on the road to Damascus. "Suddenly there shined round about him a light from heaven: and he fell to the earth, and heard a voice saying unto him, Saul, Saul, why persecutest thou me?" (Acts 9:3, 4).

Who can explain what this light was, this power that struck Saul the persecutor to the ground? No one. But in this mysterious experience Saul found God through Christ. How many others have found God through mystery! We are to look at the mysterious experiences of life as places where we can meet God, speak with Him, see His glory, and exchange our fear of Him for love. God uses mysteries to wake us up from our slumber, to make us realize we are not the "masters of our fate."

As preachers and teachers we are not to minimize the fact that the gospel is beyond our full human comprehension. We are stewards of God's mysteries. In 1 Corinthians 2:7 Paul referred to the hidden wisdom of God as being designed for our glory: "But we speak the wisdom of God in a mystery, even the hidden wisdom, which God ordained before the world unto our glory." And in Proverbs 25:2 we read, "It is the glory of God to conceal a thing." Deuteronomy 29:29 tells us, "The secret things belong unto the Lord our God: but those things which are revealed belong unto us and to our children forever."

There you have it. Mysteries are nothing that bring shame to God or to us who accept them by faith as demonstrations of His wisdom. "For now we see through a glass, darkly"; we know only "in part" (1 Cor. 13:12). We are not to act as if we know it all when we proclaim the gospel, but the gospel is true knowledge to the extent it is revealed to us.

Nevertheless, we can't evade the question of why God has so arranged His revelation to us that much remains hidden from our knowledge. Look at it this way. There's a parallel between the material, natural world and the spiritual. Physical and spiritual laws have the same Author. Why, then, should we accept the mystery of much that is in the natural world but balk at the mystery of the spiritual?

Take the rationalist. He's the person who says that all must be discovered by the process of reason. Yet there are facts that the rationalist accepts even as he confesses his inability to comprehend them. If these facts in the natural world were to be rejected because they are mysterious, the whole basis of human knowledge and truth would be upset. In fact, as knowledge increases, mysteries increase rather than diminish. The more we know the more we know we don't know.

> The peasant that turns up the ground, and casts in the seed perceives no mystery in its growth, but the philosopher who understands the wonderful process of vegetation is conscious of difficulties which he cannot solve, in its several stages towards maturity (Samuel Sumner, "Christian Mysteries," *Samuel Sumner Sermons*, 92).

The farmer doesn't refuse to sow the seed because he can't see the actual wheat or corn in it. A sperm cell is almost invisible, yet it contains the full potential for a perfect human organism. Think of the mystery in such natural phenomena. We accept them because we can't live without them. God hasn't given us the freedom to reject natural laws and mysterious phenomena in connection with our physical lives. But He has chosen to give us the ability to reject His spiritual laws and not *immediately* feel the consequences.

If we refuse to eat, we'll die. There are no two ways about it. But in the spiritual realm we feel no immediate physical impact of disobedience to God's laws. There is a spiritual consequence, but those who have no spiritual sensibility or life don't feel it. It would be just like inflicting punishment on a corpse; it could not feel it. Just so the spiritually dead can't feel the spiritual consequences of their disobedience.

This is aptly illustrated in our Lord's account of the rich man and Lazarus in Luke 16:19–31. While the rich man lived, he had a good time, dressed in rich apparel, and dined sumptuously. He never gave a thought to the suffering beggar Lazarus at his doorstep. He was totally insensitive to his sin. But the day came, after his death, that he found himself in torment in Hades. Just as we cannot escape the consequence of disobeying physical law in this life, we cannot escape the consequence of disobeying spiritual law in the world to come.

We accept physical law out of necessity, whether we can explain it or not. We can't live otherwise. In the same manner we can't live spiritually unless we accept spiritual truth by faith, without fully understanding it. Let's not balk at that word "faith." Our daily lives depend on it. Every step we take is based on faith. We proceed on the assumption that the law of gravitation will work today as it did yesterday, and that the food we eat will continue to turn into life-giving blood in our body. Only a fool will say he can live without exercising faith.

Living by Truths You Cannot Comprehend

In the third chapter of John's Gospel, we have the account of a Pharisee named Nicodemus who came to Jesus by night and addressed Him as "a teacher come from God." Jesus' answer to that was, "Ye must be born again." It startled His visitor. What? Me, an old man, go back into my mother's womb? Instead of accepting the fact on the authority of Jesus, he inquired, "How can these things be?"

Where would the human race be if people refused to bow to the laws governing procreation? Imagine men and women saying, "We can't understand how this works, so we won't believe it or act on it." The human race would die out in one generation. Yet Nicodemus said, "How can these things be?" Note the Lord's answer: "If I have told you earthly things, and ye believe not, how shall ye believe, if I tell you of heavenly things?" (v. 12).

Jesus was referring to a fact that was going to take place on earth—His substitutionary atonement that would make the new birth possible for sinful men and women. Those who looked with faith at the crucified Christ who took their place would become new creatures. Some people don't believe that can happen, but it's happening all the time. Spiritual babies and adults are just as much an evidence of the miracle birth as physical babies and adults are of natural birth.

The facts speak for themselves, and only the willfully blind can deny them. A class of people exists today—and has existed in every age of the Christian era—who have been born again. The unbeliever may not be aware of, or understand, or even care, how they became what they are, but the twice-born are here just as truly as these who have only been born physically.

A psychiatrist who visited a rescue mission listened intently to the testimonies of many converts. The superintendent asked him if he would like to say a word. This is what he said: "Tonight I have been given an opportunity to observe something I did not know existed anywhere. It has been my privilege to listen to the testimony of men who were glad to witness to what Christ had done for them. I know nothing about that, but I confess I cannot otherwise explain what has taken place in their lives. A few of these men I recognize. As drunkards, even as dope addicts, some of them have come under my observation at the hospital. But here they are, alive, well-dressed, delivered, and in their right minds. I do not know how the miracle has been wrought, but of one thing I am confident—nothing in science can account for this change in them. That kind of gospel is worth preaching to anyone, anywhere."

The new birth—a fact though a mystery—is to be proclaimed as such. The Lord told Nicodemus in effect, if I have told you of things that can happen on earth, however mysterious, and you don't believe them, how will you believe if I tell you heavenly truths? If the fact of the new birth is to be rejected because it transcends your reason, what reception can I expect to be given to those higher truths and mysteries that will only be developed in the heavenly world? If the new birth confounds you, how will you be able to receive a truth still more difficult of comprehension, that I, who now speak with you and who came down from heaven, am still in heaven—in heaven and on earth at the same moment of time? (John 3:13).

This is a great mystery. By this language our Lord suggests that the superior sublimity of heavenly things produces an obscurity comparable to that which attaches to the phenomena of earth.

The reason we should not hide the mysteriousness of the Christian revelation is that we would then be hiding the very nature of this revelation. The truths of the gospel, according to Paul, seem foolishness to the human mind because they are beyond its comprehension. They are a striking commentary on God's nature. God help us if we preach a humanistic, easily explainable gospel instead of a divine gospel and therefore a mysterious and unexplainable gospel!

God is an infinite Being without limit to His essence. "Canst thou by searching find out God? canst thou find out the Almighty unto perfection?" (Job 11:7). If divine mysteries were intended to make us acquainted with any other being, they might achieve their end. But God is the first cause of all, the self-existent Jehovah. The prototype of all existence is in His mind. He is a universe in Himself. Such things cannot be crowded into a finite mind. The most exalted creature throughout eternity will only perceive a part of God's ways.

Our narrow intellect can never measure the perfection of the divine nature. We stumble at the very threshold of inquiry. We are lost in that part of His nature that is made known to us. The splendor of this outer court of the temple of truth is too dazzling for our feeble vision. How, then, shall we enter into its recesses? How can we penetrate the holiest of holies? The doctrines of the gospel, simple in the terms of their annunciation, are associated with the difficulties we cannot solve, with depths we cannot fathom.

"O the depth of the riches both of the wisdom and knowledge of God! how unsearchable are his judgments, and his ways past finding out!" (Rom. 11:33).

The First Concern of a Christian

In 1 Corinthians 4:1, the apostle Paul stated that the world expects a Christian to be a servant of God and a steward of divine mysteries. Now in verse 2 he goes on to tell us the basic characteristic of a steward: "Moreover it is required in stewards, that a man be found faithful."

The Greek word translated "moreover" is *hṓde,* which means "here," that is, "on earth and in human life," or perhaps "in these circumstances." The reason a Christian is called a steward, a keeper and dispenser of the mysteries of God, is that he is expected to be faithful to the gospel with which he has been put in trust. If he isn't faithful he can't be counted a steward; and conversely, if he is a steward, he is expected to be faithful.

It is interesting to note that Paul applies the word "faithful" here only to stewards and not to servants (ministers, in the King James Version). Literally, verse 2 might read, "In these circumstances, therefore, it is expected of the stewards to be found faithful." Why doesn't Paul include servants here also? Because the servant, *hupērétēs,* is constantly under surveillance, while the steward is given liberty to act on behalf of his employer without such close supervision. This makes it easier for him to become lax, since he is given such discretionary powers.

Isn't this the same with us as Christians? We enjoy great freedom in Christ as we handle His mysteries, His truth. But since His visible presence is not with us, we are not always conscious of His surveillance or control. What have we done with His mysteries? Have we tried to reduce them to a system of do's and don'ts, of types and physical acts, or have we faithfully proclaimed them in a manner that preserves the mystery of the gospel? Let's try to analyze the Church of today—what Christians say and do—to see whether we have proven faithful stewards or not.

The whole context of First Corinthians is based on the fact that a day of accounting is coming. But meanwhile, here and now, our first concern is to be found faithful. We must not try to demythologize the gospel, to dismiss its complexities such as the Trinity, the Virgin birth of Christ, His resurrection, and His coming again. We are not to make the divine human or natural. Far too many have done just that. They have reduced the mysteries of God to a humanistic religion of performances in the realm of the physical and natural. The liberty inherent in stewardship has been misused as license to depart from the mysteries of God.

As Paul J. Hallinan once said, "The greatest challenge to Christianity today is a popular, bland, respectable faith termed secular humanism . . . It equates the Christian moral code with such terms as decency, brotherhood—the Golden Rule. It is the orthodoxy of the non-believer, but it is a ready refuge for the half-believer too. . . . It simply says, 'Take up your credit card and follow me.' "

I don't believe it was by accident that Paul left out the word "servants" in verse 2. It is not those simple Christians under the direct supervision of the Master who have departed from the faith, but the "big shots," the leaders, who have proven faithless as keepers and dispensers of the mysteries of God. Nothing is sadder, as one reviews the history of the past century, than to note how many who once were staunch defenders of the faith once delivered to the saints, have become wise in their own conceits and have forsaken the historic Christian faith for a watered-down version of their devising. They are no longer faithful stewards, for they have misused the liberty Christ gave them by lowering His revelation to a humanistic religion instead of maintaining the inherent glory of its mysteriousness.

The Greek verb translated "it is required" *is zēteítai.* The root verb *zētéō* means "to seek," and especially to seek what is lost, as in Luke 19:10. A shepherd looks for his lost sheep (Matt. 18:12) or a woman for her lost coin (Luke 15:8). But the same term can also be used of God's holy "demand" that requires much of him to whom He has given much (Luke 12:48), and that expects fruit from the tree (Luke 13:6f.) (see Heinrich Greenven, "*Zetéō,*" *Theological Dictionary of the New Testament,* edited by Gerhard Kittel, vol. II, 892).

Here in 1 Corinthians 4:2, Paul tells us what God demands from the steward. God is represented as patiently and hopefully expecting His stewards to be found faithful (*Ibid.*). Faithfulness, therefore, is inherent in stewardship.

In verse 1 we saw what a man expects of a Christian: that he be a servant and a steward. The very *zēteítai,* "*is* required," is in the present tense, indicating that this is a constant demand. God requires that we be found faithfully discharging our duties of stewardship at all times. How profitable it would be for each of us, at the end of the day, to ask ourselves, "Have I been a faithful steward today?"

Checking Up on Yourself

When you and I come to the end of the day, it is a good idea for us to stop and think of what our actions, thoughts, and dispositions have been, to examine them in detail. Honest appraisal and confession will wipe the slate clean before we retire, and strengthen our resolve to do better.

God requires of His stewards that we "be found faithful." The Greek verb *heurethḗ*, "be found," is in the aorist passive tense, subjunctive mood. The present active indicative is *heurískō,* which refers to a particular time in the future. A day is coming when we shall all appear before the Lord, who will find us faithful or unfaithful. That is the day Paul spoke of in 1 Corinthians 3:13 when he said, "Every man's work shall be made manifest: for the day shall declare it." That is a specific day in the future, and it is surely coming. But God wants us to examine ourselves every day—today while we have the opportunity of making amends—instead of waiting for the day of judgment and the point of no return.

Obviously the reference here is to the stewards of the mysteries of God of whom Paul spoke in 1 Corinthians 4:1. "In the stewards" is the literal translation. I'm intrigued by the preposition here. The Greek word is *en,* the primary meaning of which is "in," which would indicate that faithfulness is an inward trait that expresses itself outwardly. It is an attitude; it is a character. The word *pistós,* "faithful," is never used in connection with things or machines, but only with reference to people. A machine can't be faithful, because it can't think or will. But a human can or cannot be faithful. What he does depends on what he wills to do. The Lord is not going to examine every act of ours to see whether it is characterized by faithfulness. After all, we are human and can't be one hundred percent perfect. There are times when, because of circumstances, we could have done better. None of us can truthfully state that we have always done our best. But that doesn't mean that we shall be classified as unfaithful stewards. It is the will to be faithful, the attitude, the character that counts. We don't need to examine all the thoughts and actions of a person, and find him perfect, in order to declare him a faithful person.

We don't declare a woman a poor mother if she is loving and patient with her children most of the time, but occasionally loses her patience with them. We don't expect our employer never to show a moment's irritation when people take up his time with trivial complaints. We don't think the less of our spouses if occasionally they forget some minor duty we expected them to perform. In all such instances our regard for those we love or respect is based on their habitual acts and attitudes, not on their occasional lapses.

Not that we should condone our own lapses of conduct or attitude, nor does God. But we must recognize our inability to be one-hundred percent perfect in this life, and in humility confess it and seek God's strength to do better. And on His part, when God sees such an attitude in us, He still counts us faithful stewards, because our wills are one with His and habitually produce right actions.

One more observation on the structure of this verse: "In these circumstances (there)," it is required in the stewards that *one* be found faithful. First it is "the stewards," plural, all of them. The definite article *tois* in this instance leads us to conclude that reference is made to the particular stewards who are entrusted with the mysteries of God. But when Paul goes on to speak of the judgment of the stewards he says, "so that *a man* be found faithful." Actually the word in Greek is *tis,* singular, which means any one of these stewards. The idea is that in the day of judgment there will be an individual assessment. Each one will be judged on his own faithfulness.

This is necessary, of course, if there are to be individual rewards. In the keeping and dispensing of the mysteries of God, each of us bears an individual responsibility. None of us can hide behind the fact of our denomination or church. For instance, if your church, of which you are a minister or adherent, is not a faithful steward of the mysteries of God—if it denies the Triunity of God, the Virgin birth of Christ, His miracles, His substitutionary atonement on the cross, or His physical resurrection—you will be held accountable for choosing to submit to the orders of your superiors who are not faithful stewards of the mysteries of God.

All these truths are unexplainable mysteries that you must faithfully hold as a sacred trust. In that day you cannot say, "I had to be indirectly unfaithful because I was raised in that church, because it was my tradition." "Any *one*" of the stewards is expected to be found faithful. Will that include you? Is your first allegiance to Christ or to a church or a bishop or a denominational leader? Remember that this was the general context in which Paul was writing this epistle. The Corinthian Christians had become possessed of a party spirit. Some were of Paul, some of Cephas, and some of Apollos. It's perilously easy to slip into the error of being a steward of an apostle, a saint, a church, or a denomination, instead of being a steward of the mysteries of God, directly responsible to Him.

LESSONS:

1. Some New Testament truths are referred to as mysteries—revelation from God that had previously been hidden even from His people.
2. One of these mysteries is the church which engrafts Gentiles, along with the Jews, into the kingdom of God, making the two classes one new man in Christ.
3. We never comprehend Christian mysteries as God does. But what He does reveal of them is truth and therefore knowable.
4. By revealing only part of the full understanding of our course through life, God chastens our ambitions and strengthens us.
5. Our goal of conformity to Christ is clear, but the way to it, the complexity of events that makes up our lives, is not fully disclosed. To this

extent, life itself is mysterious. We discover "the Way" along the way, that is, in the traveling.

6. We must not act as if we "know it all" or be ashamed because we don't. Not only are the mysteries part of the whole truth of God, but our very understanding of them is partial. The apostle Paul includes himself in this assessment.
7. It is no less arrogant to claim comprehension of the natural world than it is of the spiritual world. Science is equally confronted with mysteries it cannot comprehend. It produces alot of "that's" (existences) but few answers to "why's?", "how's?", or "what's?" (explanations).
8. Christians should eat "every word that proceedeth out of the mouth of God" (Matt. 4:4) as conscientiously as they feed on bread. The long-term impacts of disobedience are just not felt as quickly as starvation. But they are known intuitively at death.
9. The new birth is a fact and a mystery. The same Jesus who said "unless a man be born again" also said "you know not where it is come from or where it is going" (John 3:7, 8). The mystery of the new birth, however, does not negate its facticity.
10. Truths of the gospel are also considered foolishness by unbelievers because of the blinding effect of sin on their minds (1 Cor. 1:18; John 12:40).
11. A primary requirement for stewardship is faithfulness. This is implicit in the trust that is committed. The main "trust" committed to the Christian believer is the gospel.
12. Stewards (*hupērétēs*) compare with servants (*doúloi*) by the amount of supervision they need: the former is entrusted with a "long rope," while the latter is closely watched or supervised.
13. God has entrusted us with the "true riches" which include mysteries like the Trinity, the Incarnation, and the Resurrection from the dead. We must not use our liberty to reduce these complex truths to contradiction, mythological status, or humanism, that is, watered-down human creations.
14. The nature of God as three persons containing a single essence or set of attributes is a mystery, defying human comprehension. Nevertheless, it is a revealed truth from God Himself.
15. Faithfulness is something God seeks (*zētéō*) in us. It is sought after by God, Paul tells us in the second verse.
16. Though mysterious from the standpoint of comprehension, Christian revelation is sufficient to secure eternal life and growth in holiness.

17. The death of an innocent man, the Lord Jesus, for guilty, evil enemies is another mystery, yet it is the heart of the gospel. Repugnant to the ethics of the natural man, God's gift of Jesus Christ is above the humanism of the world.
18. We should examine ourselves daily to confess sin and to repent. This will best prepare us for the Lord's imminent return when He will judge the degree of our faithfulness to Him.
19. The willingness to be faithful counts in those instances where opportunities to act are denied. The thief on the cross might have served the Lord whom He confessed, had he been given the opportunity to live out his days.
20. In judging us, the Lord takes into account our lack of perfection. Neither our actions nor our motives are perfect. We do not always serve the Lord, and when we do we rarely do it with a perfectly motivated heart.
21. The Lord will judge each man's faithfulness in stewardship. There is no corporate judgment; individuals will account for their own lives.

1 Cor. 4:2 | How to Meet Criticism

Moreover it is required in stewards, that a man be found faithful.

How Dependable Are You?

Our troubles in this life come from many sources: we may bring them on ourselves; others may cause them; or they may come from completely impersonal sources such as the inexorable laws of cause and effect in nature. How we react to them, however, represents the test of our character. And this testing may come from two sources: God or Satan.

In 1 Corinthians 4:2 we read, "Moreover it is required in stewards that a man be found faithful." The Greek conjunction *hína,* translated "that," is telic, indicating that it is God's conscious desire that on the day of judgment each individual steward may be found faithful. God may give us opportunities to test our faithfulness to Him here and now and often, so that His desire that each one of us may be found faithful may be fulfilled.

Again we discern God's attitude and desire toward us in testing us. His testings (*dokimasíai*) must be discerned as having as their goal approval and promotion—passing the test instead of failing. This is diametrically different from Satan's tempting (*peírasmoi*) whose purpose is to make us sin (see pertinent discussion in author's book, *Getting the Most Out of Life,* in the section on 1 Cor. 3:13).

What does it mean to be faithful? How can we judge whether we are faithful or not? In 1 Corinthians 1:9 Paul made a sweeping statement about the character and conduct of God. He said (literally translated), "Faithful the God." In my book, *A Richer Life for You in Christ,* I give a detailed examination of the word *pistós,* "faithful." When *pistós* refers to God, for the most part it has the passive sense, meaning "worthy of trust, or trustworthy, dependable." You and I can trust God. His laws are consistent. There is no variableness in Him; He is absolutely dependable. When the word is used of man, it is generally used in the active sense, denoting an active or constant trust and obedience. A man is said to be faithful when he trusts God, or obeys his superiors, or executes the duties he is supposed to perform.

In connection with 1 Corinthians 4:2, where Paul speaks of believers as stewards of the mysteries of God, we must understand the word *pistós,* "faithful," as being possessed of the character of God, being trustworthy and dependable. That's what the world looks for in a Christian. In the first years of Christianity the believers were called *christophóroi,* "Christophers," which means "the bearers of Christ." We bear His image and character. The world looks for the same dependability in us as it sees in Him.

So as we seek at the end of each day to find out whether we have been faithful or not, we should ask ourselves the very specific question, "Have I been dependable today?" And we should proceed to make the application practical by asking, "Have I been carelessly late for any appointment? Did I take advantage of every opportunity to tell others of Christ? Did I feed the hungry as Christ did? Did I speak a word of comfort to those who needed it? Was I consistent in my attitude? How much time did

I waste when I was supposed to be working?" Our goal should be to be as dependable as God.

The mysteries of God in this verse are compared to great treasures since they require stewards to administer them faithfully. A steward keeps and manages his master's assets. He must be absolutely dependable. If he loses his sense of stewardship, he may be tempted to speculate with his master's wealth. There's a very thin line between speculating and managing. In the Parable of the Talents in Matthew 25:14–30 and that of the Pounds in Luke 19:11–27, our Lord indicates that He expects us to put to work and multiply whatever He places in our hands. He doesn't forbid speculating in so many words, but this is implied in that every servant or steward is expected to increase the original investment. We are told that the ten talents yielded another ten, the five another five, and so forth. Speculation involves the risk of loss by using, but in these parables what was invested was not speculated with and lost but was increased. And the one who refused to use what was committed to him, and kept it hidden and idle for safety's sake, was reprimanded. Both misuse and disuse should be avoided by a faithful steward.

We are not to speculate with God's mysterious revelation, lest we lose it by trying to explain it through human rationalization. We must accept His unexplainable truth as fact and proclaim it as such. On the other hand, we are not to hide it and keep it to ourselves for fear that when used and proclaimed it may be lost or wasted on others.

Perhaps we cannot understand how a truth that we cannot fully explain can change lives, but let us remember that it changed us and therefore can change others. Let us proclaim it as the truth—not of man but of God—as the mysteries of God.

Sir Walter Scott felt the force of this when he penned these lines about the Bible:

Within this ample volume lies
The mystery of mysteries.
Happiest they of human race
To whom their God has given grace
To read, to fear, to hope, to pray,
To lift the latch, to force the way;
But better had they ne'er been born
That read to doubt, or read to scorn.

Who Is the Judge of Your Life?

Many people in this world—and regrettably many so-called Christians among them—want "the name without the game." They want the reputation of being faithful Christians without a willingness to accept the responsibility and work involved. It is only in accepting them that we are faithful stewards and servants, including taking the risk which that involves. For when our Lord makes the servant in His parable say, "I was afraid," and confess that he buried his talent instead of using it, He indicates that in faithfulness there is the element of courage.

Who decides whether we are faithful stewards of the mysteries of God or not? That's the problem that confronted the apostle Paul. He faced an evaluation of himself. He said that men expect the Christian to be a servant or steward who is faithful and dependable. You are judging me, Paul seems to be telling the Corinthian Christians. Am I going to accept your judgment?

As Christians we face this problem every day of our lives. Others among whom we live and to whom we declare God's revelation are passing judgment on us. We know they expect us to be servants and stewards of God (1 Cor. 4:1). But God expects faithfulness in our stewardship, and who is competent to judge us in this matter?

"But with me it is a very small thing that I should be judged of you, or of man's judgment," says Paul in verse 3. He declares in no uncertain terms that he is not bowing to the authority of the Corinthians or to any human tribunal. Since everyone is going to be judged as an individual, as we saw in verse 2, Paul says it behooves him to examine himself. That's what everyone of us should do. I am responsible for myself. No one can demonstrate the concern that I should demonstrate for my own self. I must determine what God expects of me as a steward and then turn my scrutiny upon my own self.

What does Paul mean when he says, "It is a very small thing?" The Greek expression is *eis eláchiston estín,* literally, "It amounts to very little." In fact, *eláchiston is* the superlative of *mikrós,* meaning "small." The very least, the most insignificant thing for me, is to be judged by you, says Paul in effect, as to whether I am a faithful steward or not. He doesn't say their opinion counted for nothing, but for very little indeed.

Of course, he was speaking of the effect their judgment had on himself subjectively. What does the criticism of others do to our inner self? Take the case of Col. George Washington Goethals. While contending with the manifold problems of geography and climate in the building of the Panama Canal, he had to endure the carping criticism of countless busybodies back home who freely predicted he would never complete his task. But he pressed steadily forward in his work and said nothing. "Aren't you going to answer your critics?" a subordinate inquired. "In time," Goethals replied. "How?" The great engineer smiled. "With the canal," he said.

Paul was concerned, of course, with what the criticism of the Corinthian Christians was doing to others. In Romans 14 we see him deeply concerned about how our own lives, and the criticism we offer and receive, affect others. It's not what such criticism does to us subjectively, but what it does objectively, that matters. "For none of us liveth to himself, and no man dieth to himself" (Rom. 14:7).

What Paul opposes here is the assumption by the Corinthians that they have a right to act as sole judges of him and his ministry among them. This is what we think of you; therefore that's what you are. That is intolerable, says Paul. What you think of me doesn't end the matter as to what I really am. It is the least of my worries. But what you say about me may have a ruinous affect on others, and that's serious. That's why he defends himself.

This was an attack on Paul's character. These same Corinthians also took it upon themselves to attack his apostolic office. But office is not everything in an apostle; besides and beyond it is character and motive. These same people who were now attacking his character by branding him unfaithful insisted that he was not even an apostle because he had not seen the Lord Himself during His earthly life, as had the Twelve. And Paul wished to be thought of as what he really was, Christ's apostle by the will of God.

When he said, "With me it is a very small thing that I should be judged of you, or of man's judgment," he wasn't being indifferent as to whether men thought rightly or wrongly about his apostolic credentials or his character. What they were saying about him affected the spiritual condition of all those to whom he was ministering, and that's why he spent a great deal of effort to convince the Corinthians that his apostleship was authoritative. Regarding the accusations against him, he really didn't care what people thought of him as an individual. But what they thought of him as an apostle was extremely important to him, because he didn't want to bring any offense to the gospel he was preaching. When the criticism of others is unjust, and affects our ministry, we have a right and a duty to defend ourselves.

Respecting the Opinions of Others

It's typical of human nature to be fond of judging others. But how many of us feel that others are truly capable of passing judgment on us? Shouldn't that make us stop and think whether we are capable of passing judgment on them either?

Of course, there are times when we have a responsibility to make such judgments as are necessary for the conduct of our business and other practical matters. But putting aside such legitimate exercises of judgment, we know quite well that we often form and express judgments on the actions and characters of others quite unnecessarily. And if we are candid, we'll have to confess that these judgments are often arrived at on insufficient evidence—and we don't always err on the side of charity.

We know how our Lord treated this habit. He denounced it as a sin, one of the sins of the Pharisees. "Judge not, that ye be not judged," He said. "First cast out the beam out of thine own eye; and then shalt thou see clearly to cast out the mote out of thy brother's eye" (Matt. 7:1, 5).

We know that the judgment of others upon our acts and characters is an inevitable fact of life. But the one who criticizes may harm himself more than the one he criticizes. Much of the criticism aimed at us is unjustified and shouldn't disturb us so much that it becomes a crippling obsession. If we answer all our critics, we won't have time or energy left to do what is really important in life.

This is what unjust criticism often seeks to accomplish. Hardly anyone who has served Christ in sincerity and truth has escaped it. We're in good company when others misjudge us. That men will go on judging each other must be taken for granted. The question for Christians is, how are we to conduct ourselves with reference to these judgments?

Paul wasn't indifferent to the opinions of others on all questions of conduct. Not all criticism is worthless, and Paul recognized this. Some criticism is necessary and even providential. It acts in the world of thought and conduct as does the policeman on the street—to be the protector of a conventional standard of conduct. The majority of the people agree on such conduct, and the policeman will arrest anyone who violates it.

But there are always those who disagree with conventional conduct and will criticize and even assault the policeman who tries to uphold those standards the majority has agreed are right. Paul in his writings often shows respect to such public opinion. That's why in 1 Timothy 3:7 he bids Christians take care to "have a good report of them which are without," that is, those outside the Church. He wants Christians to stand well in the opinion of their pagan and Jewish neighbors in all lawful matters. He recognizes there are some truths that are as much a part of man's natural constitution as his imagination or memory, since they are implanted by the Creator in the depths of every human soul. There are certain truths of God that are common to all people. As Christians we must recognize that they exist even in those who haven't been regenerated by the special saving grace of God.

For instance, most unredeemed people have a concept of a Supreme Being who is the Author of the distinction between right and wrong and has decreed that wrong be followed by punishment, whether in this life or the next. In Romans 1:20 Paul states the limits of God-consciousness in unredeemed men: "The invisible things of him [God] from the creation of the world are clearly seen, being understood by the things that are made, even his eternal power and Godhead."

Here is an original deposit of truth attributable to God. But even this can be dissipated by sin. Such was the case with the heathen who, "when they knew God, they glorified him not as God" (Rom. 1:21). Even then, enough of this truth remains to secure to human opinion a certain element of truth. It is like the ruin of a once beautiful edifice; we must look at these moral ruins and realize what can yet be erected. Therefore, the

Christian must recognize both the remnant of truth and the potential of new creations.

What Paul was writing, however, in 1 Corinthians 4:3, was not a criticism of the unredeemed but of Christians. What should be our attitude toward the opinions of fellow Christians? They possess higher truth than that found in common nature. Thus when public opinion emanates from Christians it ought to be viewed differently. They have had their consciences imbued with a new set of principles. We ought to listen to them with the thought that through them Christ Himself may be speaking to us.

And that is how we should view our own responsibility when we express opinions of others. Of course, we recognize that Christians are still human, and in their language there may be much that is yet of the flesh. But, since the light of heaven has been poured upon them, it would be wrong to treat the general judgment of Christians with disrespect. We are not to conclude, then, that Paul was heedless of the opinions of his fellow Christians.

Let's carefully evaluate the criticisms and opinions of our fellow Christians in the light of God's Word, and be humble enough to profit by them.

How Valid Are Your Opinions?

Public opinion is practically unanimous in condemning certain acts as criminal. Unbelievers and believers alike are opposed to such evil deeds as murder, rape, robbery, and the like. Such actions are repugnant to the natural conscience of man as well as to persons who have been enlightened by the principles of the gospel of Christ.

When we consider of the more private acts of an individual, however, we must weigh them carefully. David's adultery and murder of Uriah (2 Sam. 11:2–27) would be as thoroughly condemned by man's natural conscience as it is in David's own inspired language of penitence in Psalm 51. The betrayal of our Lord by Judas Iscariot has made his name despicable to all. And the judgment against Nero, with all his murders, is general and indelible throughout history.

But what about the adverse judgments we make on our own when we don't have conclusive scriptural condemnation? These would include judgments upon the character of a person—something we can arrive at only by carefully following and analyzing their actions. A case in point would be Constantine the Great, who became the first Roman Emperor to recognize and accept Christianity as the official religion of the state. Yet he murdered his own son. How shall we then assess his character? Liddon observes:

> The truth is, that, in estimating character, the judgment of men can only be certain in rare cases, and seldom or ever during the lifetime of the person judged. Posterity may decide where we can only hesitate. In order to estimate character, you require time and distance. You can not measure a hill while you are standing at its base, or climbing the side of it; you must move to a distance, and see how it looks on the horizon, against the sky.
>
> And thus it is that, in respect of the characters of the great majority of those who have filled a foremost place in history, men are constantly reviewing the verdicts at which they have arrived; constantly modifying, supplementing, retracting, explaining; rehabilitating those who have been condemned, and condemning those who have been unduly praised. But all this shows how uncertain such judgments are; how tentative and partial; how liable to be reversed by a higher Judgment that will be pronounced t hereafter (H. P. Liddon, *Advent in St. Paul's,* vol. I, 408).

Having said all this, and recognizing the possibility of the rightness or wrongness of public opinion, we are now ready to examine Paul's reason for saying that the opinions of the Corinthian Christians about him were "a very small thing."

First of all, their judgment was inadequate because they hadn't had enough time with Paul. He had stayed with them only a year and a half. Their judgment of him ". . . was like a portrait-painter's sketch at a first sitting" (*Ibid.*, 409). When we are tempted to pass a hasty judgment on someone, it's a good idea to ask ourselves, "Have I known him or her long enough?" Or when we hear adverse criticism of ourselves, to say, "They haven't known me long and well enough."

Liddon gives us another reason:

> Secondly, this Corinthian estimate of St. Paul was a strongly biased one. The Corinthians were largely influenced by some teachers who wished to bring into the Church as much as they could of the old Jewish Law, and who were opposed to the apostle because he would not allow this (*Ibid.*).

When they spoke of Paul as not being faithful, perhaps this was what they had in mind. They wanted him to adhere scrupulously to the Law.

When people pronounce us unfaithful, let's examine what yardstick they are using to measure us by. And when we call others unfaithful, let's be very careful that the yardstick we're using is not just our own opinion, or a denominational rule, but is really God's absolute and unmistakable expectation of all believers, as set forth in His Word. It's perilously easy to hold divergent opinions and interpretations of the divine precepts and expectations. Let's beware of making our personal interpretation the law, and of pronouncing all who disagree with us unfaithful. Interpretation of truth and truth itself are not always the same thing, and we must be careful about this when judging fellow Christians. If this distinction were carefully observed, there would be less disruption of unity in the body of Christ.

Paul was misjudged in this fashion by the Judaizers at Corinth. What they called a judgment was actually a formulated prejudice. He knew it and that's why he rejected their verdict of unfaithfulness as "a very small thing." We, too, can reject men's condemnation of us on such grounds. If our actions square with God's revealed will in His Word, we are clearly following an apostolic example in ignoring biased criticism. But we must be very sure that we know how to distinguish between truth and prejudice in such matters.

Shakespeare said, "This above all: to thine own self be true, and it must follow as the night the day, thou canst not then be false to any man." But the Christian has a higher standard than that. He is called to be true to Christ; to be true to God's Word; to be true to the leading of the Holy Spirit; and to deal truly with his neighbor as a result.

Beware of Hasty Judgments

Have you ever passed judgment on something you had no real means of investigating? We've probably all been guilty of that at some time or other. That's what certain of the Corinthian Christians did with regard to the apostle Paul.

> They could decide whether he was or was not a true apostle by examining the sources and nature of the apostolic authority on the one hand, and the events of his life on the other. But how could they decide whether he was or was not a faithful steward of God's mysteries—faithful in intention as well as in act? . . . Single acts, which his Corinthian critics might deem unfaithful, did not show that his life as a whole was an unfaithful life (Liddon, *Advent*, vol. 1, 409).

The critics couldn't know the motives of certain isolated acts. And, unless we know why some people act as they do, we lack the ability to pronounce judgment on their character. An excellent principle is not to judge character from isolated acts, or to judge when we are ignorant of motives. A godly man in a moment of great stress may let slip an exclamation that is at variance with his whole manner of life. He will regret it immediately afterward, and be in a self-condemning spirit and penitential mood the rest of the day. Are we to form an opinion of his character on the utterance of a single hasty or unseemly word? "He that is without sin among you, let him first cast a stone" (John 8:7).

God alone knows the inner motives of a man's actions. Just as we shrug off the adverse criticisms of others who don't know our motives, so we should abstain from criticizing someone without knowing his motives. A man may be criticized as miserly, when in reality he is having a hard time meeting the needs of an invalid wife, mother, or child.

How could the Corinthians know Paul's motives, which always lie below the surface? When someone criticizes us, before we get all upset about it, let's consider who it is that is making the criticism. If it's a church or a group of people, we should feel free to examine their background. Public opinion is not all the same, nor is it infallible. Much depends on the nature of our critics as to how much importance we should attach to their judgments.

When we examine Paul's first Corinthian epistle, we find out that among Christians of Jewish background there was not only a tendency to revive the Judaic Law, but there were also gross immoralities that they tried to rationalize. Paul couldn't remain silent about these. Had he done so, there might have been less criticism of him. He had to defend the true faith of Christ and a standard of conduct that would bring glory to Christ. Compromise may save us present trouble, but it will pile up accusations against us that we'll have to answer in the day of judgment. Paul wouldn't compromise; therefore he was severely criticized. He was faithful to the Lord, but he was accused of being unfaithful because he wouldn't go along with the commonly accepted norm of conduct or Christian public opinion.

Here are some of the wrongs that were evident in the Corinthian Church:

1) A case of incest, in which a son took his father's wife, something not countenanced even among the heathen (1 Cor. 5:1–5).

2) A disbelief, derived from Greek philosophy, of the cardinal Christian doctrine of the resurrection (1 Cor. 15:35ff.). Paul patiently proved the fact of the resurrection to indicate the error of these philosophical presuppositions that the dead could not rise. His argument was conclusive, and it was natural that some Corinthians wouldn't like him for that.

3) Gross irreverence at the celebration of the Lord's Supper (1 Cor. 11:17–22).

4) So-called free love, that is, love outside the God-ordained bond of marriage (1 Cor. 7). That's what many are advocating today, doing away with marriage and giving vent to their instincts. Paul couldn't stand for that. No wonder Paul felt it was a small thing to be criticized by them. If the public is morally rotten, naturally it will criticize the chaste and moral individual.

5) Pride in supposed spiritual gifts, such as speaking with tongues. More than likely they had borrowed the practice of the priestesses of Delphi, who, having gone off into a trance, would make strange incoherent utterances that were "interpreted" to the anxious and often puzzled inquirers who consulted them by a so-called prophet.

Undoubtedly they tried to impress Paul and others that what they were doing was a repetition of the Pentecostal experience, when the Holy Spirit enabled the disciples to speak in other languages understood by those who heard them as their own native tongues. When Paul told them in 1 Corinthians 14 that their practice was not the same as that of Pentecost (Acts 2), Caesarea (Acts 10), or Ephesus (Acts 19), they accused him of unfaithfulness. He rejected this accusation and told them it was a very small matter for him to be criticized by them (see author's book, *Tongues!?*).

Paul didn't hesitate to exercise his God-given authority to correct error, and this will always arouse opposition in some.

<u>LESSONS</u>:

1. God tests our faithfulness in order to produce a more godly character within us. To be faithful is to be possessed of the character of God. Accordingly, early Christians were called *christophóroi*, "bearers of Christ."
2. In the Parable of the Talents, we are taught to invest—not speculate or waste—the talents the Lord has given us. He expects spiritual returns on His investments (trusts) to us.
3. God owns all things and sometimes reminds us by attacking property itself. We borrow but own nothing of God's creation in an ultimate sense.
4. Other peoples' opinions of us pale in comparison with the Lord's judgment which is and will be based on absolute truth.
5. No one person or group of persons can judge another believer as the Lord does. What we think of others is not necessarily what they are. The Corinthians, for example, adversely judged Paul's apostolic authority and character, but this was not a true judgment. Paul's motives and character were pure before God.
6. As we labor for the Lord especially, we will be criticized. Paul endured criticism, sometimes very harsh criticism.
7. Although their judgment of Paul had little significant impact on him, he was validly concerned for the impact on the church. If the church had rejected his authority altogether, it would have been rejecting inspired scripture.
8. Do not allow the opinions of others to bind you to habits and patterns of living that God has not ordained for His people.
9. We judge others to entertain ourselves, but we do so most often unnecessarily, with insufficient evidence, and not on the side of charity.
10. Our lack of charity is certainly attested in the Lord's observation that we tend to ignore the beams in our own eyes as we try to remove specks from the eyes of others (Matt. 7:3).

11. Negative judgments harm the judger as well as the "judgee." The judger may advance in depravity while the judgee becomes paralyzed with guilt and self-reflection that may not be objectively justified.
12. Even unbelievers, Paul says in Romans 1, "knew God" and currently know that His formal differentiation between right and wrong is true and just. But they apply this premise inconsistently, alternately condemning others and justifying themselves for the same acts.
13. So, on the scale we should value regenerate criticism—if we can find such a thing—above that of the unregenerate, seared conscience. And among believers, we should value more highly the opinion of those who walk closest to the Lord.
14. Character generalizations in either direction are a severe and unfair form of judgment, because they conclude (fallaciously) from a number of instances the very state or nature of a person. While the Scriptures teach that we are all naturally depraved, we should avoid making these experiential pronouncements in our heads and especially with our mouths.
15. Historians constantly revise their interpretations of history, showing just how tenuous these judgments are. Knowing how frequently and quickly we change our own opinions, we should be very cautious.
16. The Corinthians' evaluation of Paul was inadequate because of the limited time they had known him directly and because of the bias of their "informants."
17. In plain language, such judgments are a form of prejudice. When we are prejudiced, we stop giving "hearings"; we hang people without evidence and trial.
18. Negative judgments without investigations are morally evil.
19. Not only are character generalizations fallacious, but judgments on discreet acts are defective simply because motives are not publicly accessible. If a person does not reveal his or her motive in any particular action, there is no way, short of being God, to uncover it.
20. It is best to withhold condemnation as often as we can.
21. Godly people may sin verbally and publicly but then confess and repent out of earshot. We should be very slow to judge "explosive" words.
22. We cannot compromise essential doctrinal and ethical truths to hostile critics. In doing so, we face answering to the Lord.

1 Cor. 4:3, 4 | Is Public Opinion a Safe Guide for Christians?

But with me it is a very small thing that I should be judged of you, or of man's judgment. . . . but he that judgeth me is the Lord.

How Far Should You Be Influenced by Public Opinion?

How much do other people's opinions weigh with you? Whenever a certain wise Christian pastor listened to complaints against himself or others, he would say, "Consider the source." If it were someone given to negative attitudes and a gossiping tongue, he would discount the criticism heavily.

In Corinth as well as in Galatia, the critics of the apostle Paul were active and unscrupulous. They suggested that he had no true apostolic commission (1 Cor. 9:1, 2); that he was working with no such credentials as the great apostles at Jerusalem (2 Cor. 11:5); and that these apostles were really opposed to him (Gal. 2:7–9).

They played off against him at one time the authority of Peter, whom they called for the sake of greater veneration by his Syriac name of Cephas. At another they lauded the Alexandrian learning and eloquence of Apollos, to Paul's disparagement; at another the most sacred name of all, that of the Lord Himself (1 Cor. 1:12).

They succeeded, it would seem, in creating a body of public opinion against Paul in the Corinthian Church which, by the time the Second Epistle to the Corinthians was written, had become really formidable, and at this earlier date was already troublesome.

No wonder so many of the members of that church had set themselves against the one who had originally brought the gospel to them. Gossip about him was rampant; criticism was constant, as is evident from what he says in 1 Corinthians 4:3–6. Paul was perfectly aware of all that was going on. That's why, in discussing his claims and right as an apostle of Christ to receive the obedience and love of Christians, he had laid stress upon faithfulness as the first requisite of a steward of the Christian mysteries. He felt instinctively that this quality of faithfulness was exactly what a great many busybodies at Corinth were denying him. And he told them, "With me it is a very small thing that I should be judged of you, or of man's judgment." As Liddon puts it, "St. Paul did not, therefore, feel or affect indifference to the question whether he was or was not faithful; he wished it to be tried before a competent tribunal" (Liddon, *Advent*, vol. 1, 410). This was the same principle he applied when certain men wanted to try him before a provincial magistrate: he appealed to a higher court, to Caesar himself (Acts 25:10). "He that judgeth me is the Lord," he told the Corinthians.

There are certain things in which we must not allow criticism to affect us, even when it comes from fellow Christians. If we do our work as faithfully as we know how, in dependence on God's revealed will in His Word, we can rest in the fact that the Lord, who knows us inside out, including our motives, will judge us rightly.

What should be our attitude, then, toward public opinion, inside the Church and out? First, let's recognize that public opinion is a mixture of viewpoints. It is formed by those who love the Lord and those who don't. The Christian, therefore, should not accept public opinion as the infallible guide of his actions and life. Public opinion has its own valid functions, but it is inappropriate and insufficient in guiding a Christian worker. Liddon notes:

> It is no disparagement to a broom to say that it is not adapted to clean an oil-painting. It has its own function, that of cleaning a wall or a passage floor, and it discharges this much more efficiently than would be the case if it were a paintbrush (*Ibid.*).

How disastrous it would be if a body of well-meaning and earnest persons, armed with brooms, were to burst into an art gallery with a view to improving the paintings. The best intentions won't enable a rough instrument to do work for which it is unfit. Liddon concludes that:

> . . . public opinion, by reason of its grandeur and massive force, is unfitted to deal with the secrets of the kingdom of heaven, with the sanctities and exigencies of the conscience of man. The apostle says of the natural man, it cannot know the things of the Spirit of God because they are spiritually discerned [1 Cor. 2:14]. It has an eye for material grandeur, political grandeur, for social grandeur, for intellectual grandeur, but it either does not recognize moral and spiritual grandeur, or recognizes them only to be conscious of a secret hostility.
>
> Certainly a public opinion which should have combined the petty sectarianisms of the Corinthian Christians with the proud indifference to religious and moral considerations prevailing in the Imperial courts at Rome would not have commanded the homage of St. Paul. It would have appeared to him "a very small thing" had he been judged, however severely, by such a tribunal (*Ibid.*, 411).

Who can say with Paul that public opinion is a very small thing to him? Two kinds of people: a very evil person or a mature saint like Paul. An evil person is morally insensitive to all that is good in public opinion; he has burnt out the sensitive nerve of his conscience (1 Tim. 4:2). On the other hand, a mature saint like Paul is insulated by the presence of God from the provocations of men (Ps. 31:20).

But most of us are between the two—neither so bad that we don't care, nor so good that we can leave the whole matter with the Lord and not be affected by it. Let's beware of fearing the tongue of men more than the eye of God.

Who Is Qualified to Judge?

When you know you're right, can you hold out against those who try to persuade you to the contrary? The apostle Paul didn't fall into line with the public opinion of the church in Corinth. He maintained the independence of his own opinion under God. Yet, though he expressed his convictions in no uncertain terms, he maintained his sympathy toward these people as individuals. When writing to the Galatians under similar circumstances, Paul said, "Brethren, I beseech you, be as I am; for I am as ye are: ye have not injured me at all. . . . My little children, of whom I travail in birth again until Christ be formed in you, I desire to be present with you now, and to change my voice; for I stand in doubt of you" (Gal. 4:12, 19, 20).

Observe how lovingly he addresses them as "brethren" and "my little children." He travailed in soul for them. But when he was accused by the Corinthians of unfaithfulness, he brushed feeling aside and told them they were prejudiced, and that their public opinion would not affect him.

Let's not assume, however, that whenever a man chooses to defy public opinion he is right. The defiance of an eccentric person may merely be an evidence of his sick nature. A criminal may also be at war with public opinion. Murderers, thieves, and forgers defy the public opinion of any civilized community as much as they defy the law of God. Where such people are concerned, God's law and public opinion are, for the time being, in harmony. As Liddon points out, believers should prophetically contend with public opinion only on the basis of truth:

> Some individuals seem to think that, because the divine Prophet of Nazareth was in conflict with the dominant opinion of His day and country, therefore all modern forms of antagonism to social institutions are probably right. If that were true, Barabbas was already entitled to an encomium in the pages of the Evangelists. . . . No brethren, St. Paul was not right *because* he was opposed to Corinthian opinion; he opposed Corinthian opinion because as against it, he was right (Liddon, *Advent*, vol. 1, 271).

Another category of beliefs is classified in the Greek as *antilegómena,* things that are contrary to basic truth. Church historian Eusebius used the term to indicate the spurious books of the New Testament. This term stands in opposition to the *homologoúmena,* truths commonly confessed. Paul refuses to be criticized about his faithfulness to basic truth. Man, he says, cannot judge him about that.

> The truth is, ordinary public opinion, looked at on its moral or religious side, is, from the nature of the case, a compromise. It affirms just so much moral or religious truth as, in a given state of things, will keep society together; so much and no more. It affirms not the whole law of God, but an abstract from it; just so much of it . . . as is likely to be useful for social purposes (*Ibid.,* 271, 272).

Take the punishment for murder as an example. God's law says, "Whoso sheddeth man's blood, by man shall his blood be shed" (Gen. 9:6). But a large segment of public opinion nowadays is generally against capital punishment. Or take marriage: public opinion about that is also in large measure contrary to God's law. Liddon concludes,

> Thus, you observe, public opinion strikes an average between the impulses which it receives from above and from below, from the good and bad elements in society. And as the criminal makes war with it, because

he is below it; so the true Christian takes issue with it because he is above it.

> Paul was opposed to public opinion in the church at Corinth because it was below him. . . . had it succeeded [it] would have taken the heart out of Christianity, by virtually denying the all-sufficient virtue of the Redeemer's sacrifice (*Ibid.*).

Paul didn't really care how he was judged by public opinion such as that which would have stripped Christianity of the living Christ. We, too, should follow his example when church public opinion is so situational and relative that it denies the eternal and absolute teachings of God's Word. No wonder Paul wrote to the Corinthians that it was a very small matter to be judged by them.

This was not a thoughtless disregard of church opinion in Corinth. Paul examined the Corinthian accusations against him and found them baseless. What he told them in essence is that they were not qualified to judge him.

The verb translated "judge" here is *anakrínō,* made up of *aná* (*ánō*), "up," and *krínō,* which primarily denotes "to separate, select, choose." A judge or an examiner picks up something, lifts it up out of all that is going on, to examine it. The translation of *anakrínō* as "judge" is likely to be confused with *krínō,* "judge or condemn," as in John 12:48, Acts 13:27, and Romans 2:27; or *katakrínō,* "to condemn," as in Matthew 20:18, Mark 10:33; 16:16, 1 Corinthians 11:32, etc.

Anakrínō in 1 Corinthians 4:3, 4 basically means "to investigate." It is used of judicial investigation, especially before the hearing proper. So Paul is actually saying, "It is a very small thing for me to be investigated by you," meaning they were not competent to do it, and he would wait for the hearing proper—God's final judgment.

Man's Day of Judgment and God's

Sometimes the literal translation of a Bible passage from the Greek text sheds more light on the meaning than the King James Version. An instance of this is found in 1 Corinthians 4:3, where Paul says, "But with me it is a very small thing that I should be judged of you, or of man's judgment." Actually "man's judgment" in Greek is "human day." The translators took the liberty of paraphrasing it as "man's judgment." But I believe, if we translate it this way, we miss the antithesis that Paul is drawing between 1 Corinthians 3:13, "Every man's work shall be made manifest: for the day shall declare it," and 1 Corinthians 4:3. The same word *hēméra*, "day," is used in both verses. This word is translated correctly in 1 Corinthians 3:13 and refers to the day of the coming of the Lord, when He will reward each believer according to his work. That's God's day of reckoning with all His redeemed.

But man thinks he has his day when he passes judgment on Christians. There is a distinction between God's judgment and man's. Paul declares that he is not concerned with man's judgment, with man's day. If we study 1 Corinthians 3:13 carefully we will see how everything man has done and said will be made manifest and tried by fire. God can't be fooled in His judgment of man. But man can't fully discern the worth or lack of worth of anyone. Man's judgment, therefore, can neither be final nor complete.

When it comes to judging our own selves, such judgments are also inadequate. In nine cases out of ten a man may be too lenient with himself, and perhaps in the tenth case he will be too severe in his self-condemnation and plunge himself into despair. For that reason a man can't be his own judge. He can't get outside himself and see himself in perspective. He looks at everything from his own point of view and judges by his own standard. He is biased by his personal tastes and prejudices. And in his folly he is infringing on the prerogatives of God by making the attempt. Joseph Seiss comments on man's self-appointed day in court:

> The time in which the apostle wrote, and the whole interval between that and the coming again of Christ to judge the world, is "*man's day*." Man's opinions and resolves now have the sway. All the governments, courts, judgments, and common enterprises of this world are of man's wisdom and making. The laws of society and the standing of men are mostly the aggregate of human opinion and adjudication. This age . . . is the period of the exercise and rule of human self-will, in which man is the chief actor, who judges things according to present interests and necessities, with very little regard to God or of what shall be hereafter. And, according to the wisdom and conclusions which now govern, there is scarcely anything that is rightly judged.
>
> "Man's day" is particularly unfair to the things of God and eternity. Its discernment does not seem to penetrate them or to have any capacity to decide upon them with justice. Judged by "man's day," the whole economy of God is reversed; the cross is a stumbling block and foolishness; and those who live and act with reference to eternity are looked upon as weak . . . fanatics (Joseph A. Seiss, *Lectures on the Epistles for Sundays and the Chief Festivals*, vol. 1, 50, 51).

Paul also declares in so many words that his own judgment of himself is inadequate: "Nor do I investigate [*anakrínō*] my own self." He didn't mean that he never examined himself to see whether he was pleasing the Lord or not. What he meant was, just as others weren't able to bring out all the truth about him, neither could he do it about himself. Human judgment is neither final nor complete; therefore Paul would not depend upon his own judgment about himself.

Nevertheless, Paul exercised enough judgment about himself to reject the accusation of the Corinthians that he was an unfaithful steward of the mysteries of God. He did not find it pleasant to disagree with their estimate. Social and ecclesiastical compromise can seem tempting sometimes. But when we agree with others in such instances, we cause them to presume that they are right. And Paul did not want to cause such a presumption on their part. He therefore declared himself in disagreement with them, and that's painful. However, the integrity of his apostolic office and ministry was at stake. He was not setting himself up as being exempt from the divine checkup he spoke of in 1 Corinthians 3:13, but he had to take a firm stand on his own self-evaluation of what he knew to be right conduct on his part. Obviously both sides could not be right, and he had to tell them in a spirit of love that they were in error and he was right.

Paul was deeply concerned that the Christians should not quarrel and disagree when there was no necessity for it. It was he who said, "So much as lieth in you, live peaceably with all men" (Rom. 12:18), and "Avoid even the appearance of evil" (Rom. 12:17). But to avoid it you must first recognize it. Avoiding it makes you different. It is a judgment on others and on yourself. All this means that when no higher interests are compromised a Christian will do his best to be and keep in harmony with the common opinion of his fellowmen, but not otherwise.

How to Regard the Judgments of Men

King Solomon was an excellent psychologist and judge of character, as we see in the book of Proverbs. One of his most astute observations about man is, "For as he thinketh in his heart, so is he" (Prov. 23:7). He was thinking especially of a deceitful man in this context. But isn't this true of all men? Many a smile hides an adverse opinion. We all wear the mask of good manners on occasions when we really don't feel cordial at all. And because society knows nothing of the thoughts and intents of our hearts, it is therefore incompetent to judge us.

To be blamed and denounced by the world is no proof of wrongdoing. And to be praised by the world is no proof of goodness.

The world has often blamed and denounced the very best. The "noble army of martyrs" is an army of witnesses to the world's tragic misjudgments. Which of the prophets has it not slain? Which of the apostles has it not persecuted? It numbered the Son of God among the criminals, and crucified Him between two thieves.

We would be foolish indeed to put our trust in popularity contests. The world has praised and applauded men whose wickedness has been obvious and flagrant. What are we to think of a society that rejected Christ and chose Barabbas? Society is not a competent court of judgment. Does it blame and criticize Christians as ignorant fanatics? We should think it a very small thing as long as we have Christ's approval. Does it praise and flatter us at times? We should be cautious about building upon it unless we know we are also "approved of God."

So far we have been thinking of the Shallow Way of regarding the judgments of society, of those few who know us best, of our own selves, and of God. Society's judgments, in the nature of the case, are bound to be shallow. But now we come to the "manly [note: generic man, not male] Way," described by James Stalker, which:

> . . . is to treat lightly the judgments passed on us by others, but to be anxiously and honourably sensitive about the judgments which we are compelled to pass on ourselves. This . . . will produce a manly character and a noble life. It's not difficult to meet the demands of the world. Its code of morality is mainly negative; all it requires of us is to be respectable. But he who keeps a strict watch upon his own spirit, and judges his own outer and inner life conscientiously and intelligently, must make great demands upon himself.
>
> There are few feelings more satisfying than amid public depreciation and obloquy to fall back on one's own sense of pure motives and right conduct. This, however, is a comparatively easy and comforting thing to do; it is a rarer manliness to acknowledge the faults which one's eye can detect even when others are applauding, and to pass through all the drama of moral feeling which the conscientious review

> of our conduct ought to excite, whether others know anything about it or not. This is an experience unknown to the shallow man; it is the manly Way.
>
> Yet I will show you a more excellent way—*the apostolic way*. . . . After man's judgment and our own judgment, there is another far more august—the judgment of God. It is only the recollection of this which will keep the manliest minded from becoming proud and Pharisaical (James Stalker, "Man's Self-Judgment," *Anglican Pulpit Library*, vol. 1, 171).

For myself, as I pass my day's work in review, I often see much to blame myself for. But when I submit it to God for review, I know His eye will detect a hundred more faults, perhaps, for each one I have noticed. And when I think of having to confront all my past life again, and hear His judgment on it from the great white throne, I know that I have nothing to depend on but His infinite mercy and the precious blood of His Son, Jesus Christ, that cleanses from all sin.

The apostle Paul felt that, in spite of the fact that he had a clear conscience and a good standing in the eyes of those whose consciences were as good judges as his (2 Cor. 4:2), he wasn't therefore justified (1 Cor. 4:4). What is the meaning of this verb *dedikaíōmai*, "justified"? The root verb *dikaioún* is always forensic, that is, having to do with courts of law. It means "to pronounce a verdict of acquittal." This has nothing to do with making anyone just. The Lord justifies the sinner by grace through faith in Christ (Rom. 5:1). That's quite different from simply not finding him guilty.

An earthly judge hears the case, weighs the evidence, and may pronounce the prisoner just. But he does not actually do anything to change the condition of the accused. That is the meaning of 1 Corinthians 4:4.

But when the Lord justifies us by faith through Christ, He has actually found us guilty of sin. He wants us to accept the fact of our guilt and confess it, and then to believe that the penalty for our sin was paid by Christ on the cross. We accept the punishment Christ bore on our behalf, and then God pronounces His verdict upon us as though we had never been guilty. We are justified freely, or by grace, by God through Christ.

The instrument that bridges our guilt and justification is faith. We can never justify ourselves in the sense that we can pronounce ourselves "not guilty," "For all have sinned, and come short of the glory of God" (Rom. 3:23).

Can You Trust Your Conscience?

The Bible tells us that all men are sinners and are helpless to make themselves righteous in the eyes of a holy God. "For all have sinned and come short of the glory of God" (Rom. 3:23). "Wherefore, as by one man sin entered into the world, and death by sin; and so death passed upon all men, for that all have sinned" (Rom. 5:12).

Not only is man unable and unfit to act as his own judge and pronounce himself "not guilty," but also, once he recognizes his guilt, he cannot make himself just. This can only be accomplished through the payment of an adequate sacrifice for his sin. He can't make this sacrifice himself, nor can another imperfect human being make it for him, because God will not accept the sacrifice of a sinner.

For you and me to be justified, this sacrifice had to be made by a sinless, perfect individual, and there was no one who could do this except Christ, the sinless, virgin-born Son of Man (Heb. 7:26; 9:25, 26; 10:5–7, 12). It is only by accepting Jesus Christ as our substitute that we can be restored to the position of one who is "not guilty," or better still "redeemed." In this case we are made just. We receive forgiveness of our past sins, a change of nature, and thus victory over sin now.

In 1 Corinthians 4:4, Paul doesn't use the verb *dedikaiōmai,* "justified," with the meaning of being made just, redeemed, but with the meaning of being declared not guilty. In other words, since the Corinthians had accused him of being unfaithful in dispensing the mysteries of God, it is in this regard that his conscience clears him. But more important than that is the unbiased and strict court of the Lord. Paul isn't hesitant about standing before the Lord as his Judge in regard to his conduct.

Note that the verb is in the passive voice, which means that Paul needs to be justified by someone other than himself. But this other judge is not society, public opinion, the Corinthians or his own conscience. It is the Lord. Furthermore, the verb is in the present perfect tense, indicating that he is now cleared, he is now guiltless. It is as if he took the matter before the Lord when the accusation of unfaithfulness was hurled against him, and the Lord pronounced him "not guilty." That verdict of the past stands in the present.

We must first take any accusation against us before our own conscience to be judged. But that's not enough. We must also take it to the Lord and ask Him for His verdict. If He impresses us with the fact that we are indeed guilty, we can confess our sin to Him, and He is faithful and just to forgive us our sins and to cleanse us (1 John 1:9). But if we are not guilty, let us be assured of this from Him and abide in the sunshine of His justice (see Hermann Cremer, *Biblico-Theological Lexicon of New Testament Greek,* 4th ed., pp. 193–98).

Again I call attention to the fact that the translation of the first statement of 1 Corinthians 4:4 is certainly unfortunate. Instead of "For I know nothing by myself," it should read, "For I am conscious of nothing against myself." This should be taken in conjunction with Paul's previous statement in the 3rd verse, "Neither do I investigate my own self."

The verb used throughout here is *anakrínō,* which refers to judicial examination. Such examination, through the taking of depositions, is for the purpose of finding out whether a case ought to be tried in court or dropped. But to reach the level of *anákrisis,* the judicial examination, there must be a suspicion of guilt. In other words, Paul maintains, "I know I am not guilty; therefore I am not going to submit myself to a judicial investigation to persuade myself I am guilty of what you are accusing me of."

"For I am conscious of nothing against myself." That is, I have examined myself, and, though I am not sinless, I find myself not guilty of this specific accusation; my conscience does not condemn me. As Joseph Parker so beautifully puts it, Paul is saying, "I know nothing of myself, by myself, against myself."

The verb used in the first clause of 1 Corinthians 4:4 is *súnoida,* made up of the conjunction *sún,* which means "together," and the verb *oída,* which means "to know." This verb is to be distinguished from *gignṓskō* which means to know by acquisition and experientially. *Oída* refers more to intuitive knowledge. It is knowing by virtue of what you are rather than by what you have learned through life from others. For instance, a child doesn't learn how to breathe or take nourishment. That's intuitive knowledge; it comes naturally by virtue of what a child is.

The substantive of the verb is *suneídēsis,* which means "conscience." It's the knowledge we have intuitively in common with God. The conscience of the natural man is different from the conscience of a spiritual, redeemed person. If God is not within us, if we are not what He is, we don't know what He has implanted in our hearts as intuitive knowledge. Conscience is a dependable faculty within believers and unbelievers only to the degree that God is present in them. In the unbeliever there is a very small cognizance of God's presence through the human spirit. But in the believer that human spirit is energized by the divine Spirit. Thus the conscience of the believer recognizes evil far more clearly and fully than the conscience of the unbeliever.

LESSONS:

1. We can afford to discount criticism from evil sources like gossips and bigots, confident that the Lord will judge according to truth. He knows our motives—the condition of our hearts. Without scorning public opinion, we should set our eyes constantly on the day of Christ's holy judgment.
2. We should also weigh our motives as the Lord does (Prov. 16:2) and pray for purer motives. This prayer will certainly be answered.
3. Since tares grow alongside the wheat until the time of the harvest (Matt. 13:30) and false teachers arise up among us (2 Pet. 2:1), we can safely assume that most of the "corporate" opinions of local churches are not infallible.
4. Secular opinion is worthless. Heathen are in no position before the Lord Jesus to judge His people or His church. No one can condemn what God elects (Rom. 8:33). In our moments of oversensitivity toward public opinion, we should remind ourselves of Jesus' words that "the world will hate you because I have chosen you out of the world" (John 15:19).
5. Secular families and societies require laws and shared opinions to prevent anarchy, bind together, and produce progress of one sort or another. But for the believer, none of these opinions are the Word of God, and they have no authority over the Word of God. God's revelation is our ultimate and final source for the ethics that alone produce stable and long-lasting society.
6. Consequently, we cannot sacrifice—for the sake of peace with secularism at any cost—the very doctrines without which the church comes apart at the seams.
7. Furthermore, like the apostle Paul, we should maintain our independence of even church opinion that is aligned against God's revelation.
8. Man has his "day in court" (something Paul calls "man's day") as prosecuting attorney, but this is short-lived and the believer should put it in perspective, like Paul, as the "small thing" that it is. The "big thing" is the Lord's Day.
9. Because we are prone to self-deception and self-justification, we are apt to be too lenient on ourselves in most cases, yet too severe with others. Self-judgment is extremely limited.
10. Because man's natural wisdom is unable to penetrate the wisdom and justice of God, those who live the life of the cross are adjudged weak and fanatical.

11. The Bible teaches that we are what we think (Prov. 23:7). Since God knows our thoughts (motives, etc.) but men cannot (unless, of course, we disclose them—assuming they're conscious to us), only God can judge us according to truth.
12. Jesus' ongoing reminder to the Pharisees that their fathers killed the prophets tells us something about what the natural man does with truth. In the end, he pins it on a cross and kills it. "We will not have this [Truth] to reign over us" (Luke 19:14).
13. People prefer thieves (like Barabbas) to benefactors (Jesus), liars ("your father the devil") to truth-tellers (Jesus), and suppression of truth to reception of it (Rom. 1:18). Opinions generated from such depravity are not valid.
14. We are not justified by clear consciences but by grace through faith in the Lord Jesus. It is always possible that secret sins (those below consciousness) are getting the better of us. This is why David prayed that such sins would not master him (see Ps. 19:13; 90:8).
15. While confession of sin is correlated with cleansing from all unrighteousness (1 John 1:9), it is still the blood of Jesus Christ that actually does it (1 John 1:7). Confession does not justify. Justification requires the sacrifice of a sinlessly perfect individual.
16. The perfect tense, *dedikaĩōma*, means we were justified in the past and the results continue to the present. The passive voice tells us that someone else (the Lord) did this.
17. We should bring accusations against us before the bar of our conscience and, more importantly, the bar of our transcendent God. If He impresses guilt, then we are free to confess and reinstate our freedom.
18. Our English word "conscience" is a composite of the Greek terms for "together" (*sun*) and "intuition" (*eídēsis*), a knowledge we have in common with God by virtue of our nature created in the image of God, regeneration, and the presence of God's Spirit of truth within us.
19. The conscience of the unbeliever is seared and therefore fallible, part of the ruined but not annihilated image of God. The renewed image and conscience in the believer, while not infallible, is trustworthy to the extent that it agrees with the Word of God.

1 Cor. 4:4 | *Conscience and Premature Judgments*

For I know nothing by myself; yet am I not hereby justified: but he that judgeth me is the Lord.

Is Conscience Always Right?

Henry L. Mencken once said, "Conscience is the inner voice that warns you someone may be looking." Though this was meant facetiously, there's some truth in it. Just spell "someone" with a capital "S" and you'll have a pretty good definition of conscience.

In the enlightened Christian, conscience is indeed that regulatory factor of conduct that makes us realize we are under the eye of God. It leads us to submit all our decisions to Him for His approval or disapproval. We go, as it were, into the supreme court of heaven to ask the Judge of all the earth for His ruling and verdict.

The apostle Paul appealed to his enlightened conscience as if it were a human court. When the Corinthians accused him of being an unfaithful steward of the mysteries of God, he felt no answering echo of accusation in his heart. Compared with the court of society, no doubt, the court of conscience is a higher one. Its judgments are far deeper and truer than those of society. In fact, if we could get an absolutely true conscience, its judgments would be absolutely valid. The judgments of such a conscience would agree with the judgments of God Himself. But J. D. Jones reminds us that:

> . . . no conscience is absolutely *sensitive or true*. Conscience has suffered in the general twist human nature received through sin. In some it has been seared and silenced; in all it has been dulled and blunted so that the judgments of Conscience can no longer be trusted as absolutely true judgments.
>
> Paul had a good conscience as he says in this text, "I know nothing against myself," and yet he was not going to put his trust in the verdict of approval pronounced by Conscience. "Yet," he knew his conscience was no infallible judge, he says "am I not hereby justified, but he that judgeth me is the Lord" (J. D. Jones, *The Unfettered Word*, 249).

Since our conscience is more often reliable when it tells us we're wrong, we ought to follow Paul's example in making sure that our conscience is as pure as possible. The more our human nature is brought into harmony with God's nature within us the more trustworthy our conscience will be. We only need to look back over our life's history to see how, as light increased, dark corners were revealed that were invisible in our less enlightened state.

How long it has taken the Christian Church to understand what Christ's gospel teaches about slavery, the relations of the sexes, drunkenness, war, and hundreds of other things we don't yet know, but which our successors may wonder that we failed to see. Inquisitors and martyrs have equally said, "We are serving God." Surely, nothing is more clearly seen in our individual experience than that we may do a wrong thing and think it right.

If we were like our Lord Jesus Christ, we would know intuitively as He knows. We would see and judge the world and ourselves as He does. But since the fallibility of human nature is impossible to eliminate as long as we are in the body, our conscience cannot be the ultimate judge of conduct.

True, we must bring everything to the bar of conscience, but we cannot accept its verdicts as infallible. As Principal Edwards puts it, "When conscience condemns, God condemns—but the silence of conscience does not imply that God absolves."

> It is a great thing to have a conscience void of offense, but no one must conclude from that that he is guiltless before God. In a word, if the world's judgment upon a man is faulty and untrustworthy, so is a man's judgment upon himself. For it is our man's natural tendency to judge himself leniently, to put all his actions in the most favourable light. He always tries to whittle down and explain away his blunders and folly. He always has excuses to offer for our sins (*Ibid.*, 249, 250).

"The woman tempted me, and I did eat," said Adam; and ever since mankind has found excuses for sin. Conscience is no longer the sharp, severe, inflexible judge. It has been bribed and drugged. And its judgments, as a result, are hesitating and uncertain and confused.

The hands of a clock indicate the time, but to be accurate the works must be in a good order and carry the hands forward just as fast as time itself goes. If the works are out of order, the clock may stop. Or, if it continues to run, it will give false information. Conscience is represented by the works of the clock, and consciousness by the hands. If it is an enlightened and true conscience, regulated by the Word of God, its judgments will be true. If it is disordered, it is altogether unreliable, and he who trusts it will be led into error. A false timepiece has caused many a man delay, with serious consequences. A disordered conscience can prevent a man from doing good and even from finding his way to heaven.

Present and Future Judgment

The only safe judge of whether we are doing right or wrong is not conscience but God. That's why, though the apostle Paul felt he was guiltless of the accusation of unfaithfulness leveled against him by certain members of the Corinthian Church, he added, "But he that judgeth me is the Lord."

Paul is not referring merely to the future judgment of the Lord, but to His judgment here and now. The final accounting will be in that day Paul referred to in 1 Corinthians 3:13. The verdict then will be irreversible. There will be nothing we can do to erase our earthly unfaithfulness. But, if we are open to God's constant examination here and now, we still have time to correct ourselves.

"The One who judges or investigates me is the Lord," says Paul. The verb used here is in the present participial form, which indicates continuity of action. It is *ho dé anakrínōn,* which would literally make this statement read, "But the One judging me or [to put it more accurately] investigating me is the Lord." There isn't a moment, Paul intimates, that I allow my conscience to be the final and only judge. I lay my life constantly before the Lord for His examination.

How careful we should be, when our conscience says, "You may do thus and so," to go to the Lord and ask, "May I'?"

Observe that Paul uses the word *Kúrios,* "Lord," here, meaning "the strong One." This is equivalent to the Jehovah of the Old Testament. Paul knows there is always the possibility of his being found guilty, and that his Judge is a strong One who will not be afraid to announce His verdict and demand the punishment required by His justice. God is not intimidated by the audacity of man. He is Lord. But Paul knew that, even if the Lord were to find him guilty, He was ever ready to forgive confessed sin. He wants truthfulness, not hypocrisy.

Conduct below God's standard is always possible for the Christian, even the best of us, but it should never lead to hypocrisy or an attempt to cover up, but to confession. We should never be satisfied with the judgments of conscience but go to the Lord to hear His verdict of "not guilty," or His verdict of "forgiven" if we have confessed our sin.

Achan in the Old Testament attempted to conceal his sin and was destroyed. Peter in the New Testament confessed his sin and was forgiven.

Paul uses the present tense of the verb *eimí,* "to be," in the third clause of 1 Corinthians 4:4: "But the one who is examining or investigating me is the Lord." It is the Lord who judges Paul here and now, not who will judge him in the future. Of course, in verse 5, Paul goes on to refer to the coming Lord who will reveal the hidden things of darkness. But we should allow Him to make these manifest to us here and now.

It's good that the Lord finds ways and means to reveal to us those things hidden from society, the churches, and from our own conscience. But the finality of His judgment is yet to come. We should not wait for that to amend our conduct, for then it will be too late. However, the knowledge that it is coming ought to make us willing to have God investigate us now for our good, while we have the opportunity of confessing our sins and receiving pardon as well as grace to mend our ways. Our Lord's judgment is our only safe guide. It is the only true judgment.

> He knows what is in man. He looks behind the outward act to the inner motive. He pierces through the external behavior to the thoughts and intents of the heart. He is not deceived by appearances—He looketh upon the heart [1 Sam. 16:7].
>
> Our Lord's faculty of moral judgment is perfect. *Our* capacity has been injured by sin. Conscience has lost some of its accuracy and sensitiveness because of the taint of evil that is present in human nature. But Jesus "did no sin, neither was guile found in his mouth" [1 Pet. 2:22]. In virtue of His sinlessness, He is the perfect judge.
>
> This is what makes our Lord's judgments true and His verdicts final—His faculty of judgment is flawless and perfect, for He is holy, harmless, undefiled, separate from sinners [Heb. 7:26] (Jones, *Unfettered Word*, 251).

The estimate of the Lord will cause the sentences of human courts (society, churches, or conscience) to dwindle into nothingness.

This judgment of God that persists all through our lives is preliminary to His future judgment and sentence. In 1 Corinthians 4:3, 4, Paul uses the word *anakrínō* three times. It means to investigate in view of the possibility of bringing a case to trial before a court. But in verse 5 the verb is *krínō:* "Therefore judge nothing before the time." *Krínō* means judging with the idea of already condemning. *Anakrínō* means preliminary examination, but *krínō* means the actual final trial and sentence.

What we are undergoing in this life is preliminary to that final judgment. The depositions are being written now by society, church, conscience, and the Lord. But the final decision is coming. How little of what the world and our fellow Christians have said about us will matter them. Let's submit to God's daily judgment now, that we may order our lives aright before Him while there is time.

The Peril of Judging Men's Motives

God alone has the right to judge men's hearts. Scripture makes this very plain. "Man looketh on the outward appearance, but the Lord looketh on the heart" (1 Sam. 16:7). "I the Lord search the heart, I try the reins, even to give every man according to his ways, and according to the fruit of his doings" (Jer. 17:10).

Since the knowledge of men's hearts is God's prerogative, for us to assume to know it is to invade His authority. When it comes to our own hearts, of course, we have direct access to them. Yet even so, it is no easy matter for us to know them. "He that trusteth in his own heart is a fool," said Solomon (Prov. 28:26). Since we can't even understand our own hearts completely, how presumptuous it is for us to draw hasty conclusions about the hearts of others, into which we can only look indirectly, by external indications.

Judas, one of Christ's Twelve Disciples, was quite evidently well thought of by the others. He was sent forth with them to preach the kingdom of God and to work miracles. They made him their steward, their treasurer. When a woman poured expensive ointment on Christ, Judas said, "Why was not this ointment sold for three hundred pence, and given to the poor?" (John 12:5). Such was his indignation that he roused the same spirit in his brethren. When Christ warned His disciples that one of them would betray Him, they each asked Him, "Lord, is it I?" (Matt. 26:22). Not one of them suspected Judas. Yet Judas was a thief, a traitor, a son of perdition. Here is an instance of a bad man who fooled many distinguished Christians.

Yet Scripture gives us an instance of how Christians showed great hesitancy in accepting a very good man, the apostle Paul. He had been for some time a violent persecutor of the Christian Church. On the road from Jerusalem to Damascus, where he was going with a commission to search out Christians and drag them back to stand trial and face death as heretics, Christ met him and wonderfully changed him in temper, heart, and views. He was completely brought over to the faith of the gospel.

Soon he became a zealous preacher of the faith he had once sought to destroy. Having preached for a time in Damascus, he returned to Jerusalem and tried to join himself to the disciples. But they couldn't accept him into their fellowship. "They were all afraid of him, and believed not that he was a disciple" (Acts. 9:26). Then Barnabas took him and brought him to the apostles, declaring to them how Paul had seen Christ in the way and had boldly preached in Christ's name. On this testimony he was received by the apostles and consequently by all the disciples.

Perhaps the memory of this had something to do with Paul's forbidding premature judgment of the motives, acts, and situations that involve ourselves and others. Human judgments must be made, but these must not be regarded as substitutes for that final judgment of God.

But what does Paul mean by that term of exclusion, "nothing," when he says, "Judge nothing before the time"? Actually, in Greek, this word is *ti,* which means "anything." "Do not judge anything before the time" would be a more accurate translation. No single case should be judged prematurely.

What Paul had in mind here is a certain class of situations in which we dare not prejudge as if we were exercising the judgment of Christ. He doesn't refer to all deeds and pronouncements; otherwise we'd be forbidden to say what is right and what is wrong. But within a certain category we have no right to presume Christ's judgment. What is this category?

Let's consider the case at hand. Some of the Corinthians were saying Paul was not faithful, was not sincere, in his stewardship of the mysteries of God. If they had merely said that he didn't teach the truth, he would have argued the matter out with them as he did with the Judaizers in Galatia. As it was, they undertook to decide the character and worth of his motives. That's why he bids them judge "nothing" before the time. By this he meant nothing of a purely internal character, "until the Lord come."

Our Lord is the one who will drag bad motives from obscurity and bring to light the hidden things of darkness. He will reveal in the full light of day the real motives upon which all before His throne had acted. He will "make manifest the counsels of the heart." The judgment that is forbidden by our Saviour and His apostles, therefore, is judgment of that which does not meet the eye, a judgment of character as distinct from acts.

If we witness a robbery, we must say that it is an act of theft, and that Almighty God will punish it. If we are asked to say further what is the moral condition of the thief before God, the answer is by no means that easy. There are serious reasons why we may hesitate to give any answer at all. The thief may already, like his penitent predecessor on the cross, be preparing for death in earnest by repentance, and thus be assured of the promise of paradise by the whisper of the Lord Himself in the innermost recesses of his soul.

Present Darkness and Future Light

All through the 3rd and 4th chapters of 1 Corinthians, the apostle Paul speaks of the light that will shine upon each man's work on the day of the Lord. In 1 Corinthians 3:13 he said, "The work of each one will be made manifest." The Greek word translated "made manifest" is *phanerón,* from the verb *phaínō,* which is a derivative of *phṓs,* meaning "light." *Phṓs is* the opposite of *skótos,* "darkness," in 1 Corinthians 4:5.

The gospel and Christ are presented in the New Testament as "light." John 1:5 says, "And the light shines in the darkness." The Greek word for "darkness" here is *skotía,* which refers primarily to the consequences of sin, while in 1 Corinthians 4:5 it is *skótos,* which stands more for sin itself (see author's book, *Was Christ God?,* p. 170; and Cremer's *Biblico-Theological Lexicon of New Testament Greek,* pp. 866, 867).

What John 1:5 says is that the light shines because of the darkness that has been brought about as a result of sin. "And," continues John, "the darkness [*skotía*] did not comprehend it," did not understand it. One reason we are unable to understand the secret things or mysteries of God is our sin. Had it not been for sin, God would probably be less of an enigma to us. Sin has thrown all around us a veil of moral darkness.

Therefore we may take darkness here to mean ignorance in nature and revelation, in the physical and spiritual realms, as a result of sin. When the Lord comes, this darkness of ignorance due to sin will disappear. 1 John 3:2 states it very clearly: "We know that, when he shall appear, we shall be like him; for we shall see him as he is." This has the meaning of understanding Him, translated in 1 Corinthians 4:5 as "will bring to light." As Heinrich Greeven says, "Darkness can denote that which is hidden and will be disclosed at the last judgment." (Heinrich Greeven, "*Skótos*," *Theological Dictionary of the New Testament*, vol. vii, p. 442).

The verb *phōtísei* usually has a good connotation. It is the same verb used in John 1:9, which speaks of Christ as the "Light, which lights [*phōtízei*] every man coming into the world." Man lies in darkness, and Christ is man's light. The verb *phōtízō* in its various tenses is found in John 1:9, 1 Corinthians 4:5, Ephesians 1:18; 2 Timothy 1:10, Hebrews 6:4; 10:32, and Revelation 18:1; 21:23; 22:5. In every case it is used of the benevolent light of God.

We could therefore paraphrase the clause in 1 Corinthians 4:5, "who [i.e., the Lord, the Mighty One] even [*kai*] will throw light [*phōtísei*] on the hidden things due to darkness or sin." Observe that I translated the Greek conjunction *kai* found after *hós* [who] as "even," which basically means "and." Here it is used for emphasis.

If you will examine 1 Corinthians 3:10–23, and the author's exegesis in his book, A *Revolutionary Mystery,* you will see that the day of judgment referred to there is not for the purpose of punishing the Christian but for the sake of rewarding him. That's the intrinsic meaning of the verb *dokimásei* in 1 Corinthians 3:13, "And the fire shall *try* every man's work of what sort it is." This "trying," *dokimḗ, is* not like *peirasmós,* "tempting," which means to make us fail. It is proving us worthy of the reward God is about to give us. He is going to throw light on what He has been hiding from us. He may have given us sickness or other afflictions on earth which men may have interpreted as an evidence of God's disfavor. But God is going to throw light on those afflictions to show us that they were for His glory and ours (see 1 Cor. 2:7).

Not only are we unable to comprehend or analyze God, but this also holds true when it comes to understanding our fellowmen. There are so many unknown elements in the lives of those who come within our sphere of observation. No matter how sincere any of us may be in our Christian faith and life, the residue of our sinful state causes us to keep certain things about ourselves secret. Could any one of us honestly say we've made a full disclosure of all our thoughts, intents, and acts to another human being? Even as we have secrets by virtue of our dual human-divine nature, so do other believers.

But the day of the Lord will disclose such matters about us and others. Sin causes us to hide things. The word expressing this in our text is *kruptá,* "the hidden things," an adjectival noun that means those things we consciously conceal because we are ashamed of them. But we could also apply this word to the things God has hidden from our knowledge. Go back to 1 Corinthians 2:6, 7, where Paul speaks of God's wisdom: "But we speak God's wisdom in a mystery, *the hidden one.*" Especially the word is the same as in the third clause of 1 Corinthians 4:5 (*apokekrumménēn* in 1 Cor. 2:7, and *kruptá* in 1 Cor. 4:5, from the verb *krúptō*).

God's wisdom is hidden. His secrets are also hidden. And this is because of the darkness, sin, which has enveloped the earth and man's understanding ever since the fall of man due to his disobedience to God. But praise God, one day we shall know, even as we are known (1 Cor. 13:12).

LESSONS:

1. The enlightened conscience of the believer reminds us of God's scrutiny, His "keeping an eye" on us. We can always believe, appeal to,

and hope in His perfect judgments, although we cannot fully trust our regenerated consciences because of the presence of unsanctified flesh. Conscience becomes more trustworthy as we live consistently with the Word of God.

2. That the enlightened conscience is still influenced by the flesh is evident from Paul's reflection that he is not justified simply because his conscience is clear. In this way he allows for sins below consciousness, buried under layers of self-deceit and rationalization.
3. Because of self-deception's bias toward evil, we can probably count more on our consciences when they condemn us than when they acquit. Even then we have to be on guard against watering down their testimonies to us.
4. God is always "The One judging [us, i.e., now]," according to Paul's use of the Greek present participle, *ho anakrínōn*, meaning He is always and everywhere perfectly bringing out into light the things cowering in darkness (especially evil motives), in anticipation of His final judgment.
5. This is a wonderful basis for security. It is not the threat of a rod so long as we confess the sin the Holy Spirit convicts us of and put to death the habitual deeds of the flesh under His lead and empowerment. Moreover, we can be assured that the Lord is presently condemning and judging every false accusation against us.
6. Only God can judge the human heart because only He can know it. We, by contrast, judge on appearance (Jer. 17:2). Self-reflection is futile according to Jeremiah 17:9 and self-trust is not only foolish (Prov. 28:26) but accursed (Jer. 17:5).
7. Our judgments, therefore, are severely handicapped, and totally blindsighted to mens' motives and, therefore, character.
8. Not a single thing (*ti*) should be judged before the time which Paul identifies as the coming of the Lord.
9. God will bring to light all concealed motives in His judgments—both in this age and in the final judgment.
10. The Lord will reveal the quality of our work on the Day of Judgment. Motives and other concealed thoughts will all be brought out into the open and tried by fire.
11. Because motives are hidden from view, we are unable to judge our brothers' words and actions. The day of the Lord will disclose these matters about us and others. Let us have grace, mercy, and contrite hearts in preparation for that Day.

1 Cor. 4:5 | *The Cure for Factions in the Church*

Therefore judge nothing before the time, until the Lord come, who both will bring to light the hidden things of darkness, and will make manifest the counsels of the hearts.

The Day When All Secrets Shall Be Known

We find it much easier to confess our secret sins to the Lord than to others—not only because we are ashamed of them, but also because we are always sure of God's longsuffering and His spirit of forgiveness. The reason we're so reluctant to confess our sins to others is that we instinctively know their understanding and forgiveness are not as great as God's. We protect our egos by keeping our "hidden things of darkness" safe from human judgment.

But a day is coming when we'll no longer be able to keep anything secret. In the day of God's judgment, not only will our own "hidden things of darkness" be made manifest, but everybody else's also. No one will be able to make a pretense of being better than he is. All our pretenses will be stripped from us, and we'll stand before God revealed for exactly what we are.

Let's not assume that those guilty of "the hidden things of darkness" are only the unconverted. I believe this whole passage has to do with Christians, as evidenced by the readiness of the Corinthians to criticize and condemn Paul. It is their "hidden things of darkness" that Paul is referring to. And lest anyone should feel that there are no "hidden things of darkness" in his life, Paul adds that God "will make manifest the counsels of the hearts." Would you like everything you're thinking made public?

The verb *phanerṓsei* (*phanerṓnō*), translated "he will make manifest," is related to *phōtísei* in the previous clause, but does not really have the same meaning. *Phōtízō* (present indicative of the verb) means to give help by giving light, to throw light when you try to find your way in the dark. But *phaneróō* (present indicative) means to make something visible that is invisible. To "make manifest the counsels of the hearts," therefore, means that God will make even our inmost thoughts visible.

The Greek word translated "counsels" is *boulás* (*boulḗ*, in the nominative case). There are two Greek words commonly translated "will, counsel"—*thélēma* (as in John 1:13; see author's book, *Was Christ God?*), and *boulḗ* (as here, in 1 Cor. 4:5). They occur together in Ephesians 1:11: "who [Christ] worketh all things after the counsel [*boulḗ*] of his own will [*thélēma*]." What's the difference between them? *Thélēma* signifies the will urging on to action, but *boulḗ is* the counsel preceding the resolve. In other words, *boulḗ is* something that is still in the mind, in the heart, that has not even decided the form of its outward manifestation.

Nobody can know the *boulás,* the counsels of God or of another man, for that matter! God is going to reveal His when Christ comes again. But Paul's argument here is that no one can or should judge another person's motives and character, because they never externalize themselves fully.

Of course, in speaking of "the hearts" (*kardíai,* nominative case) here, Paul is referring to man's soul or spirit, the seat and center of his personal life. Paul has spoken only of himself in verses 2 to 4 because he was the target of criticism. But here in verse 5 he uses the plural "hearts," meaning all hearts, including his own. This is a polite way of reminding the Corinthians that the Lord is not only going to judge Paul, but them also. They, too, were supposed to be faithful servants and stewards, and God is going to reveal this, just as He is in Paul's case.

"And then," Paul concludes, "shall every man have praise of God." This is an unfortunate translation. On the surface you would conclude that God will find every man praiseworthy. This is not the meaning here. The word translated "every man" is *hekástō* (*hékastos*), which means "each one as an individual." Herrick Johnson amplifies this thought:

> It is a distinguishing mark of the divine method that it individualises men. The tremendous emphasis of the gospel is on personality. God is . . . Person. And when He made man in His own image He made him a person. Personality is, therefore, the mightiest and the finest thing in the universe. God honours it as He honours nothing else. He never ignores it, never merges it in another, never loses recognition of it in any multitudinous company. We do, in human movements of magnitude; we can't help it. A general does not deal with his army man by man. Each soldier cannot be individualised in the vast armed host. Indeed, an army is at its best when individuality is lost in solidarity, when it is a mighty machine; an intelligent, thinking machine, indeed, but still a machine, held, marched, hurled, and fought to victory as one compact, and so resistless, force. But God doesn't deal with saints that way. Though they get to be ten thousand times ten thousand and thousands of thousands . . . the individuality of each is never lost in the record God keeps of them (Herrick Johnson, "God's Great Praising Day," *The Churchman's Pulpit*, vol. 1, 491).

Your Individual Worth before God

Herrick Johnson gives us some great incites into our personal worth before God:

> [God] enthrones personality as an indestructible unit in His moral universe, and through all His vast designs the personality of each is respected and dealt with as if there were no other personality to deal with. His approach to each soul is personal. His call to repentance is personal. His pardon is personal. . . . Every man must give an account of himself to God.
>
> Now carry this thought of the individuality of God's dealings into His praise-giving, and how it glorifies the matter. . . . [a] distinct and specific recognition of individual service; for each man shall have his praise from God. "He calleth his own sheep by name" [John 10:3] is Christ's own way of telling us of the tender shepherd's personal care. . . . each lowly disciple getting his individual need of honor for his own particular and personal fidelity (Johnson, "God's Great Praising Day," 491).

Paul was not seeking praise from the Corinthians, but neither was he about to accept their severe and unjustified condemnation of him as an unfaithful servant and steward. Just as their criticism was based on appearances, so would their commendations and praise be, if they offered any. Neither criticism nor praise should be taken at face value when others give it. They can't judge what's in our hearts, but God can and does. Therefore His praise is always genuine; there will be no flattery in it.

> God will not indulge in mere compliments. It is not thinkable that He would say other than what He means, or that He should mean what is not justified to the full by the conditions and facts. Praise from His lips will have the stamp of absolute sincerity.
>
> It is hard to find it so in human relationship. Partly because of love's bias. Partly because of social conventionalities. Our affections influence our judgments.
>
> God's praise, when He comes to give it, will . . . represent actual worth without exaggeration and without defect. It will measure up to the exact value of deed and character, and be utterly unaffected by partiality or prejudice (*Ibid.,* 490, 491).

The reward spoken of, which is here translated "praise," is *épainos,* which means approval or commendation of the whole life by God at the last judgment. It is based on the conduct of believers. It stands in contrast to the condemnation of the wicked. This approval and vindication by God is based on the fact that He is not limited in His judgments as we are, but He searches the human heart in all its depth and hiddenness. It signifies the acceptance or approval of the righteous by God alone. It is the definitively saving sentence of God in the last time, at the revelation of Jesus Christ (see 1 Pet. 1:7).

The tenses of the verbs in this verse, and in other passages referring to the coming of the Lord to judge the believers, indicate a definite future occurrence. An example is the verb *geńēsetai*, "shall be." It is the future of the verb *gínomai*, meaning "to become, or to be formed." The total life is taken into account. There will be degrees of praise. The Lord will give each one a "grade," so to speak, taking into account his failures and his acts of mercy, as indicated in James 2:12, 13, and the Beatitude pronounced on the merciful in Matthew 5:7. Our mercifulness, our compassion toward others, will counteract failures. Those who have been merciful on earth will find mercy at the judgment. Note how the last clause of 1 Corinthians 4:5 is worded: "and then" (*tóte*, an adverb of time). This is a specific time, when God Himself will "grade" His servants and stewards (see the author's two books: *The Behavior of Belief* on James 2:12, 13, and *The Beatitudes* on Matt. 5:7).

For many of us, God's estimate of our worth will come as the greatest surprise of our lives. He will reward faith and fidelity according to deed and doer. His thought of us, of each one of us, will be clearly read from the record, and things long forgotten will be recalled. Battles that seemed defeats will be found to have been set down by God as victories. A word of ours, spoken in love but also in great weakness, will be shown to have been winged by God's Spirit to win a soul to Christ. "Lowly deeds will be given undying honor. Gifts of love that went untrumpeted on earth . . . will shine out with transcendent beauty and glory by the divine estimate put upon them" (*Ibid.*, 492).

LESSONS:

1. The Judgment of God will be a day in which the Lord will make secret things public. Two Greek verbs bring this out: *phanerṓsei*, to make apparent, and *phōtísei*, to throw light upon an object that is in darkness.
2. The counsel (*boulḗ*) of hearts—the intentions, motives, and plans that are prior to words and actions—will all be revealed.
3. Not every (*pas*) but each (*hekástōs*) man will have praise from God according to the private counsel that was in his heart. Praise, like condemnation, is an individual, and therefore personal, thing. God does not judge, condemn or applaud "team-effort." The church will not be judged as a whole against the kingdom of the devil. Satan and his demons will not be judged as a group either; some will receive "greater condemnation," and "many [more] stripes."
4. Like Paul, we should neither elate over the praise of men nor sink under their condemnation. Both should be discounted from face value, taken with a grain of salt until the Lord comes.
5. God's judgments are genuine, divorced from (1) partiality, (2) prejudice, (3) emotion, (4) flattery, and (5) falsity. "[A]ll things are naked and opened unto the eyes of Him with whom we have to do" (Heb. 4:13).
6. The believer's greatest reward is *épainos*, God's approval or commendation. Unlike flattery, the praise of God contains no hidden agenda, no evilly contrived motive. It is wholly motivated by and based on Truth and Good.
7. God's perfect estimates of the entire sweep of our Christian lives will be scaled to the degree of grace, mercy, and compassion joining our actions. We will probably be quite surprised at the level of work not so much that we did for him but which **He** accomplished in us.

1 Cor. 4:6 | *Can We Alter Our Views without Compromising?*

And these things, brethren, I have in a figure transferred to myself and to Apollos for your sakes; that ye might learn in us not to think of men above that which is written, that no one of you be puffed up for one against another.

A Difficult Passage of Scripture

First Corinthians 4:6 is one of the most difficult verses in the New Testament, especially the first part. In my research, I found only two sermons on this verse. One was by Llynfi Davies, preached at Canaan Congregational Church in Swansea, Wales, in 1930 (recorded in the *Christian World Pulpit,* vol. 118, pp. 22, 23). The other was by I. M. Haldeman, who preached it in 1910 at the First Baptist Church of New York City, of which he was pastor for 51 years. The first sermon deals with the first part of the verse, and the second sermon deals with the last part of the verse. Much of what I shall expound will be expressive of the thoughts of these two preachers, who dared to tackle this unusual verse.

To make the meaning of this verse clear, we must first recall what preceded it. You remember that Paul was criticized by the Corinthian Christians as an unfaithful servant and steward of the mysteries of God. He defended himself (see 1 Cor. 4:3,

5) by saying that it mattered very little to him what others thought of him, whether it was the Corinthians, or any other man, or even what he thought of himself. He wasn't seeking the praise of the Corinthians, but the praise of God.

He then goes on to give them some straightforward advice that may seem like scolding. He closes this 4th chapter with the words, "What will ye? shall I come unto you with a rod, or in love, and in the spirit of meekness?" They sought to criticize him. He now tries to instruct them. He considers such instruction to be part of his apostolic mission if he is to be faithful, as he said every minister of Christ ought to be. The words "these things" in verse 6 must therefore be taken to mean the instructions that are to follow. And as usual, when he is about to reprimand them, he calls them "brethren," to assure them that he is doing it in love.

But he tells them something else, which is very difficult to interpret without a basic understanding of the Greek word Paul used. It is *meteschēmátisa* (*metaschēmatízō*), which in the King James Version is rendered "I have in a figure transferred to myself," and in the New International Version, "I have applied these things to myself."

Metaschēmatízō is made up of the preposition *metá*, meaning "after," implying a change from the present, and the verb *schēmatízō*, meaning "to assume a certain form, shape, figure, posture, or position." There is no doubt that the verb here is used transitively, transferring the action to Paul himself and to Apollos. It is as if he were saying, "I placed a different shape upon myself and Apollos." The tense is the first aorist, indicative mood, active voice, which means that this is something he decided to do once and for all. It was a philosophy of life that he adopted in dealing with the Corinthians.

Before we proceed to examine the specific meaning of Paul's word in this context, it is necessary for us to determine the true meaning of *metaschēmatízō* and the substantive from which it is derived, *schḗma,* as contrasted to another verb, *metamorphṓomai* or *metamorphóomai,* commonly translated "transfigure," which is derived from the substantive *morphḗ,* "figure." The distinction between these two words—*schḗma,* from which we get our English word "schematic," and *morphḗ,* from which the English word "metamorphosis" is derived—is very important.

The word *schḗma* is found in 1 Corinthians 7:31 and Philippians 2:8. In both instances it is correctly translated "fashion." "For the fashion of this world [*kósmou,* 'material universe'] passeth away." The image here is probably drawn from the shifting scenes of a theater. But the cosmos itself, the material universe, abides. In the New Testament we never read of "the end of the world," *télos toú kósmou,* that is, the material universe, but only of the age, eon or eons(*aiṓn* or *aiṓnos*). Thus the shape of the material universe changes, but not the universe itself.

The second use of the word *schḗma,* in Philippians 2:8, has serious theological implications, as distinguished from the word *morphḗ,* which occurs in Philippians 2:6, 7 and Mark 16:12. To bring out the distinction between the derivative compound verbs *metaschēmatízō* and *metamorphóomai,* it is necessary to examine the distinction between the two nouns *schḗma* and *morphḗ* especially in the Christological passage in Philippians 2:6–8. We will take this up in detail further on in this study.

"Refashioning": The Process by Which God Became Man

In this section we shall begin our examination of a number of Greek words that are essential to the understanding of 1 Corinthians 4:6.

In Philippians 2:6–8, speaking of the Lord Jesus Christ in His eternal state and His incarnation, Paul writes:

"Who [the eternal *Lógos,* Christ], being in the form [*morphḗ*] of God, thought it not robbery to be equal with God:

"But made himself of no reputation [in the Greek, emptied himself], and took upon him the form [*morphḗn*] of a servant, and was made in the likeness of men:

"And being found in fashion [*schḗmati*, the dative singular of *schḗma*] as a man, he humbled himself, and became obedient unto death, even the death of the cross."

Paul is telling us two important things here about the Lord Jesus Christ: 1) That in His eternal state He was in the form of God (*en morphḗ Theoú*); and 2) that in His incarnation He assumed the form of a servant (*morphḗn doúlou labṓn*).

The word *morphḗ* here is not explicitly *ousía*, "substance," or *phúsis*, "nature," as church fathers like Ambrose (Ep. 46), and Gregory of Nyssa (Con. Eunom. 4) used it against the Arians who rejected the deity of Christ. But implicitly it does refer to the divine nature of our Lord. No one could be in the form (*morphḗ*) of God who was not God. *Morphḗ* signifies the form as it is, the utterance of the inner life. Therefore it means "mode of existence." Only God could have the mode of existence of God. But the One who had been thus from eternity *en morphḗ*, in the form of God, as He Himself told us in John 17:5, took at His incarnation *morphḗn doúlou*, the form of a servant. The actuality of His incarnation is herein implied. It was not a mere appearance of humanity, as it was not an appearance of deity. It was true deity before His incarnation, and true humanity at His incarnation. There was nothing imaginary about it.

But His manner of existence in His incarnation was that of *doúlos*, "servant," a bondman, a slave. The Greek word *doúlos* refers to one who is in a permanent relation of servitude to another, his will swallowed up in the will of the other. Certainly this was not Christ's relationship toward man. That is why He is never referred to as a *doúlos anthrṓpōn*, "a servant or slave of men." He became identified with the human race in the capacity of *diákonos anthrṓpōn* (see John 13:4, 5, and Matt. 20:28), a servant of men in that this indicated His activity on behalf of the work He came to do. He did not subject His will to man; He worked on behalf of man.

Here in Philippians 2:7 we are told Christ became a servant, slave, *doúlos,* not of man but of God. Being equal with God, being in the form, *morphḗ,* of God, He emptied Himself of the glory of that form and took upon Himself the form of a servant or slave, *doúlos,* of God. The mode of His personal existence changed from that of God to that of a servant, a slave. As God He ruled; as God-Man He ministered. That was humiliation.

The next clause we consider is in Philippians 2:8 which says, "And being found in fashion [*Schḗmati*] as a man." The word is different here. *Schēma* here signifies Christ's whole outward presentation, His bodily form as a man.

First, we have His eternal deity.

Second, we have His true humanity, what He became in addition to what He was. The *Lógos* permanently took upon Himself true humanity.

Third, we have His shape perceived by men: "And being found [*heuretheís*] by men as man." In no way did Jesus appear to humans as any different from the other children of men. By the Father, He was recognized as being equal with Himself. By men He was recognized as being of the same fashion or shape as themselves.

When we come to the two verbs *metaschēmatízō* and *metamorphóō,* we find the distinction made even clearer. "If I were to change a Dutch garden into an Italian," says Trench, "this would be *metaschēmatismós,* refashioning. This would still be a garden but of a different style. But if I were to transform a garden into something wholly different, as into a city, this would be *metamórphōsis.* For instance Satan is said to *metaschēmatízesthai*—to take the shape of, or disguise himself as, an angel of light (2 Cor. 11:14). He can take the whole outward semblance of such. But to any such change of his it would be impossible to apply the *metamorphoústhai,* taking a different form: for this would imply a change not external but internal, not of appearances but of essence, which lies quite beyond his power.

"The two verbs are used in Romans 12:2, 'And be not conformed—*suschēmatízesthe*—become the same in fashion, outward appearance—to this world (*aiṓn*—age): but be ye transformed—*metamorphoústhe*—changed in form, essence—by the renewing of your mind. . . .' This is an abiding deep change in you as the Spirit of God alone can work in you (2 Cor. 3:18)" (R. C. Trench, *Synonyms of the New Testament,* 263, 264).

When a Dispute Arises between Christians

We conclude from our examination of the verb *meteschēmátisa* so far that it does not mean what the King James Version translates it as: "I have in a figure transferred to myself." This would infer that Paul was blaming himself and Apollos for the inconsistencies and divisions among the Corinthians. It would be as if he were saying, "None of you are to blame; I myself and Apollos are the culprits." But though Paul was a humble man, he never assumed a false humility. He was far too honest for that. He did not try to excuse the guilty but to correct them. And the only way he could correct was to place the blame where it belonged.

The verb *meteschēmátisa* means "to refashion." It is used by Paul alone in the New Testament, and on only three occasions: in our text, in 2 Corinthians 11:13–15, and Philippians 3:21. In the latter two instances it is used with reference to Satan fashioning himself into, or disguising himself as an angel of light, and in the Philippians reference with regard to the fact that Christ would change our body till it resembled the body of His glory.

Why should Paul mention Apollos along with himself in this context of 1 Corinthians 4:6? It doesn't seem to make sense. We know, however, that there were differences between himself and Apollos, even as the Corinthians had differences among themselves. He is trying to correct the Corinthian divisions. But how about the division between himself and Apollos? He has rejected the Corinthian criticism about unfaithfulness, but he confesses that he is willing to refashion his relationship with Apollos, even as he is pleading with the Corinthians to do among themselves.

"I am willing to do what I am asking you to do," he says in effect. He had just said that he did not judge himself; nevertheless he is ready to change certain outward appearances for the sake of the Corinthians. It was not actually his character that was involved, which would have been the case if the verb *metamorphóō* had been used. *Morphḗ,* as we saw earlier, refers to the inner self, and *schḗma* to the outward. His standing up against Apollos may in itself have been right and necessary, but his dispute with Apollos apparently was not a good example for the constantly disputing Corinthians.

We, too, must be willing to avoid even the appearance of evil, even if what we are doing may not be evil at all. A dispute with a brother may be fully justified in itself, but if it harms others it may be wise to change our ways. Truth is essential, but how we apply it in an ever-changing world should be subject to our constant scrutiny.

Refashioning our conduct need not involve change of or compromise with the truth, according to Llynfi Davies' perceptive analysis of the apostle Paul who, he claims, "was adapting the truth to the case in point with a view to saving a church so dear to him as the one church at Corinth, to which he had devoted eighteen months of his precious missionary labors" (Llynfi Davies, "Paul's Refashioning," *Christian World Pulpit*, vol. 118, 22, 23). He felt that none of his own interpersonal relationships should be allowed to harm the Church.

How wise we would be to follow Paul's gracious example. Let's ask ourselves the question: "What will my public dispute with another do to a local church or to the cause of Christ anywhere and everywhere?" And then let's be ready to refashion our conduct for the sake of the Church of Christ and our testimony before the world.

Now what were the matters in question between Paul and Apollos? Davies continues:

> That they had both ministered at Corinth we know. Paul had left Corinth at the end of his second missionary journey and had proceeded to Jerusalem. Before Paul had returned to Ephesus, Apollos, after about three months training in gospel truths in that city by Aquila and Priscilla, had proceeded to Corinth. We know nothing of the exact nature of his ministry there apart from a brief summary in the Acts; "He mightily convinced the Jews and that publicly, shewing by the scriptures that Jesus was Christ" [Acts 18:28]. But we know that by the time Paul had returned to Ephesus on his third journey Apollos had also reached that city with his ministry at Corinth over. We know further that he had barely reached Ephesus before the news was brought to Paul that the church at Corinth was the next thing to a wreck with factions.
>
> Now, in the face of these indisputable facts, we are bound to wonder whether the nature of Apollos' ministry at Corinth had had something to do with the deplorable condition of the church. That he showed that "Jesus was Christ" is manifest. But is it possible that his method of presenting the gospel had been such as to till the ground in which obnoxious weeds might grow? It is just like the case of a young and inexperienced minister, but full of enthusiasm and good intentions, following a veteran in the ministry of an important church, and things unaccountably to him, going wrong (*Ibid.*, 23).

What some of these problems may have been we shall consider next.

Did Paul Write the Epistle to the Hebrews, and Why?

In order to understand a man, we must know something of his background and how it affects his character. Thus, in seeking to understand the matters at issue between Paul and Apollos, we must ask ourselves just who this man Apollos was. Davies offers the following interesting thesis:

> It should not be forgotten either that he was an Alexandrian, and accordingly of a philosophical turn of mind [Acts 18:24]. Do his Alexandrian training and his necessarily imperfect knowledge of the gospel as preached by Paul justify us in assuming that the nature of his ministry at Corinth was such as to whet the philosophical appetite of the Corinthian and that, with the desire for speculation awakened, the ground had been unintentionally prepared for conflicting opinions regarding the Scriptures and the Christ?
>
> Did Apollos' Alexandrian training get the better of him in his preaching? Did he, an Alexandrian Jew, suggest a different view of the Law to Paul's view? How did he "mightily convince the Jews" at Corinth [Acts 18:28]? Was it by presenting them with a more acceptable view of the Law and of Christ's relation to it, such as we have in Hebrews, than Paul's usual view of the Law as a yoke intolerable?
>
> Why does Paul in this very epistle, before dealing with the question of the parties, state that when he was in Corinth he had determined not to know anything among them except Jesus Christ, and Him crucified [1 Cor. 2:2]? Is there here a suggestion that someone had followed him at Corinth, and had preached Christ in a different way? Is there, too, a suggestion that he himself could have preached the gospel in a philosophical way had he been so minded?
>
> Surely Paul's theology does not exclude such a possibility in given circumstances. In all this, was Paul quietly alluding to the nature of Apollos' ministry in the Corinthian church? And had he Apollos in mind, but not naming him, when he followed with his disapproval of the wisdom of the world in the same chapter [1 Cor. 2:4]? Is not Apollos' ministry somewhere in the background of things as Paul writes the second chapter of this epistle, which leads directly to the question of parties?
>
> Questions such as these cannot help coming to one's mind in the light of the fresh statement that Paul had refashioned some things that concerned himself and Apollos. That Apollos was not happy over what had happened at Corinth is manifest from the fact that he declined to return to Corinth at Paul's suggestion [1 Cor. 16:12] with, possibly, the refashioned matter for the church's consideration.

> . . . Paul deliberately cast that epistle into an Alexandrian mould in order to save the church at Corinth. . . . Scholars have hesitated to label the epistle Pauline. And yet there is much in it that is Pauline. But it differs from the Pauline conception of the law, and of Faith especially, though not in its thought of the pre-eminence of Christ. But is it an epistle that Paul could not have written it if he had made up his mind to "refashion"?
>
> I believe that in the epistle to the Hebrews we have in that epistle of Alexandrian mold the things "refashioned" between Paul and Apollos, the Alexandrian Jew. Briefly, my contention is this: things had unintentionally gone wrong with Apollos' ministry at Corinth. He had preached a view of the Scriptures and of Christ that was not in strict keeping with Paul's gospel of Christ crucified. So powerful was the party associated with Apollos' name that it dominated the Church and threatened its peace and unity.
>
> Comparing notes, so to speak, with Apollos at Ephesus, Paul embodied the result in a work that would indicate to the Church how far they could safely proceed on the lines suggested by Apollos' preaching. That work was the epistle known as Hebrews (*Ibid.*).

Study it with this in mind. That was Paul's method of refashioning. He practiced it also in what he wrote to the Corinthians concerning their speaking in tongues, a practice quite divergent from the historical instances. In those we have Jews (Acts 2), Gentiles (Acts 10), and the disciples of John (Acts 19), enabled by the Holy Spirit to speak instantly and temporarily in languages unknown to them but understood by those who heard them. This element of immediate comprehension was missing from the Corinthian practice, which was speaking in an incomprehensible so-called unknown tongue.

Paul refashions these things in saying to the Corinthians that the point of tolerance is if things are done decently and in order, not giving an impression to others that the one thus speaking is a maniac; and that others understand what is being said through an interpreter. Paul is a master at refashioning certain matters that do not affect the faith once delivered to the saints. In all this there was no compromise with truth; only a way of presenting truth in a way suited to the comprehension of those to whom he was addressing himself.

The Humility That Indicates True Greatness

In ascribing the authorship of the epistle to the Hebrews to Paul, we have seen that it was written as a refashioning of the truth to meet a specific need. Davies continues his commentary on this subject:

> We are not, accordingly, to look for Paul's usual doctrinal thoughts. . . . for it expresses not his own customary way of thinking, but his considered examination of Apollos' way of thinking. It was the veteran minister's way . . . of getting his younger colleague out of a very unpleasant situation.
>
> It follows from this that the usual considerations advanced against the Pauline origin of the epistle become ineffective, for we are not now called upon to account for the differences between this work and the usual work of Paul. It is definitely not a Pauline work in the usual sense of that word, but a Pauline work in the sense that it is Paul's considered examination of Apollos' general point of view, which the apostle considered safe for the church at Corinth to follow. Whatever differences of thought existed between Paul and Apollos, the apostle was great enough to talk matters over with Apollos at Ephesus, and humble enough to produce an epistle which, on the surface, appeared like yielding up the laurel to his rival! What a lesson for our own time! How we quibble about differences, heeding not the distressing fact that the Christian Church is divided into so many camps, and each one with its distinctive label like in Corinth of old. We have always condemned these parties at Corinth . . . but we have perpetuated their underlying fault in our eagerness to stress this and that view of the Scriptures and of Christ.
>
> Let us emulate the apostle by giving first heed to first things, the honor and glory of Christ, the souls of men, the welfare of the Christian Church, and do this by refashioning, if needs be . . . not altering the fundamental truths of the gospel (*Ibid.*).

The term *di humás*, "for your sakes," is very important. Commentator Lenski is somewhat inconsistent when he translates this expression in 1 Corinthians 4:6 as "for your sakes" in the text, but in his commentary as "on account of you" (R. C. H. Lenski, *The Interpretation of I and 2 Corinthians*, 174). This results from his endeavor to justify the traditional view of this verse, which holds that Paul and Apollos were free from the criticism that Paul was leveling at the Corinthians. Paul did not write about himself and Apollos "on account of" the Corinthians, but "for their sakes." He refashioned his position with Apollos to be a good example to the schismatic Corinthians. (It is to be noted, however, that *di humás* with an accusative may mean either "for your sakes" or "on account of you," but one of these two meanings must apply in this particular instance).

Robertson and Plumber are more accurate when they offer the following paraphrases: "I have transferred these warnings to myself and Apollos *for the purpose* of a covert allusion, *and that for* your sakes, that in our persons you may get instruction" (Archibald Robertson and Alfred Plumber, "A Critical and Exegetical Commentary on the Second Epistle of St. Paul to the Corinthians," *International Critical Commentary*, 79, 80). It is as if Paul were saying, "I want you to do not only what we say but what we ourselves do, as fellow-ministers of the gospel." Would to God that Christian ministers everywhere could turn to their people and say the same. What preachers proclaim in the pulpit, let them exemplify in their daily life and walk with Christ.

What follows in this verse is a telic clause introduced by the conjunction *hína*, "so that, for the purpose of"—so that in us you may learn. "Use us as examples" is the meaning here. That's exactly what Paul says later on in verse 16: "I beseech you, be ye followers of me," that is, become my imitators. That's quite an injunction from a mere man to a whole church. Without the meaning of refashioning in the verb *meteschēmátisa* in verse 1, it would be difficult to justify such a command. "Imitate me" is quite a thing to say, but Paul could say it because of what he did in his relationship to Apollos.

Observe that he doesn't include Apollos as an additional object for their imitation. Why? Because most of the refashioning was on his part, in spite of the fact that Apollos was the weaker of the two in his knowledge of God's revelation. After all, Paul defends his apostleship (1 Cor. 9:1), but he doesn't claim apostleship for Apollos. The refashioning of the greater for the sake of the lesser entitles him to become the object of imitation by others.

Sometimes when people come to us for advice, we know the correct course for them to follow, though we ourselves don't always abide by it. Somewhat humorously we may advise them, "Don't do as I do; do as I say." When this concerns a small matter like following a cooking recipe to the letter, the results may not be catastrophic. But when a Christian minister or teacher, or even a Christ professing layman, is asked for advice on the Christian life, he had better be pretty sure he practices what he preaches, if he doesn't want to disillusion those who look to him as an example.

Handling the Scriptures Carefully

An inherent danger in seeking to understand and interpret the Scriptures is to read into them more than God intended them to convey. This is not merely the danger of the unlearned, but also of those who have become so familiar with the Scriptures that they begin to take liberties with them, bending them to fit their own particular viewpoints or pet theories of interpretation.

Paul was particularly desirous of nipping any such tendency in the bud in the Corinthian church. The occasion of his concern was the matter of the relationship between him and Apollos which had been misunderstood by the Corinthians. The particular lesson he wanted them to learn as stated in the King James Version was "not to think of men above that which is written." But in the Greek, there is no verb; to say that the verb is "to think" is a conjecture. Since the maxim here is given in an elliptical form, without a verb, the insertion of a verb is at best arbitrary. It is equally arbitrary to translate the relative pronoun *há* primarily as "men." If Paul had thus meant "men" he should have used the relative pronoun in its masculine plural form *hoi.* In this case, the translation in the King James Version is incorrect. The relative pronoun *há* is in the neuter plural, which agrees with the demonstrative pronoun *taúta* (neuter plural of *hoútos*) in the first part of this verse, which refers to things, not persons.

The literal translation of this maxim that Paul proposes as basic and fundamental truth is "not more than or beyond what has been written." No one should go beyond what has been written when it comes to the revelation given by God. This is a slap in the face to speculative philosophical thought—a tendency to which the Corinthians were especially prone.

"So that in us ye may learn." Here the verb "learn" in the Greek text is *máthēte,* which is in the aorist tense. The word means to cause to know, with a moral bearing to it (see Hermann Cremer's *Biblico-Theological Lexicon of the New Testament Greek,* p. 410). It is as if Paul were saying to the Corinthians that what he is about to tell them to learn and practice is most important; it is basic.

The Greek word *gégraptai* is in the passive voice, which refers to what has been written, and which exists in written form. Paul was, of course, referring to the Old Testament Scriptures, to which he had already alluded in 1 Corinthians 1:19, 31; and 3:19, 20. To go beyond God's revelation, and add to it one's own elements, or to speculate about things not revealed, is a grave danger, leading to all sorts of fallacies.

This was obviously what was happening in Old Testament times with the false prophets, and it is happening today. What Paul is saying categorically here is that additions to the Scriptures are forbidden when made by unauthorized persons. The outward appearance or *schēma* of truth, the dress, so to speak, the way it is presented, especially in preaching, is flexible, but not the substance, *morphḗ*, itself. Paul had refashioned his thoughts, as he dealt with Apollos, for the sake of the Corinthians, in the interest of preserving unity among them. But he didn't do this at the price of sacrificing essential written truth.

Read Jeremiah 23:16–32 for its relevance in this connection. "Hearken not unto the words of the prophets that prophesy unto you: they make you vain: they speak a vision of their own heart, and not out of the mouth of the Lord. . . . I have not sent these prophets [saith the Lord], yet they ran: I have not spoken to them, yet they prophesied. . . . I have heard what the prophets said, that prophesy lies in my name, saying, I have dreamed, I have dreamed. How long shall this be in the heart of the prophets that prophesy lies? yea, they are prophets of the deceit of their own heart. . . . I am against the prophets, said the Lord, that steal my words every one from his neighbour . . . that use their tongues, and say, He saith. Behold, I am against them that prophesy false dreams, saith the Lord, and do tell them, and cause my people to err by their lies, and by their lightness; yet I sent them not, nor commanded them: therefore they shall not profit this people at all, saith the Lord."

What Paul is saying in 1 Corinthians 4:6 is that we must be careful to reject as false any religion or teaching that goes beyond what is written in the Word of God. Man's experiences, dreams, utterances in no matter what tongue, have no validity if they go beyond or against the Scriptures. That is axiomatic and admits of no exceptions. If anyone says that the Scriptures are not sufficient in themselves and need a supplement, we are to reject him. He can only lead us astray. Any religion that puts Scripture in any way in a secondary place, or on a par with other writings or sayings, and demands that it be interpreted according to a particular individual's ideas, is false and not worthy of our consideration.

The books of men have their day and grow obsolete. God's Word is like Himself, "the same yesterday, and to day, and forever" (Heb. 13:8).

"It Is Written"

The Christian has no quarrel with scholarship, science, or interpretations as such, when it comes to understanding the Bible. They have their place, but they are never to supplant the Scriptures.

Observe that it is not an ignoramus who advised the Corinthian church not to go beyond anything that has been written. If ever a man could have spoken in the words of human wisdom, and with scientific accent, it was the apostle Paul. He was a member of the Jewish Sanhedrin. He had sat at the feet of Gamaliel, the greatest teacher of his times. He was not only versed in the Hebrew Scriptures, he was thoroughly conversant with Hebrew literature and the Talmud. He knew Latin as well as Hebrew and Greek. When he said that he spoke in tongues more than all the Corinthians, he did not mean the unintelligible ecstatic utterances of the Corinthian church but real languages. He knew Roman philosophy, although it was taught by Greek professors. In fact, Paul had the highest possible education, and a mind second to none. He could analyze and synthesize. He was a logician whose conclusions were reached from premises stated with unfaltering precision.

But Paul didn't speak with the aim of making people admire him, but for the purpose of causing them to be transformed by the power of the cross. He knew the only wisdom worth having was God's not his. He warned the Colossians against those preachers who would seek to spoil them with philosophy and vain deceit, after the tradition of men (see Col. 2:8). He exhorted Timothy not to be seduced by the "oppositions of science falsely so called" (1 Tim. 6:20).

To Paul, the science of that day, the *gnṓsis,* "knowledge," of that hour, which laughed at the idea of miracles, tied God up in His own creation, and made Him the slave of the laws and forces that He Himself had created, was neither scientific nor knowledgeable. Such science turns the world into a vast chemical laboratory without a chemist, or a huge engine room with no suspicion of a supreme engineer behind it.

The science that denies the God of the Bible, robs the world of the Christ of the Bible, and finally—shredding the Bible apart page by page—discounts it and wrenches it loose from the pulpit as no longer the inerrant Word of God—that science to Paul was, and would be, contemptible.

The word used for "puffed up" in Greek is *phusioústhe.* It is a Pauline word found only in 1 Corinthians 4:6, 18, 19; 5:2; 8:1; 13:4, and Colossians 2:18. It is derived from *phusióō,* "to blow up, to puff up." It means figuratively to be proud or arrogant, or, in the passive voice, to become puffed up or conceited.

What Paul is telling the Corinthians here is that he who adds to the Scriptures is likely to be a proud and arrogant person, who looks down upon others because they lack his abilities. He is in the same class as the little girl who went to her priest and confessed her sin of vanity. "What makes you think that?" asked the priest. "Because every morning, when I look into the mirror," she replied, "I think how beautiful I am." "Never fear," said the priest, "that isn't sin; that's just a mistake." How true it is that those who are the proudest in their assumption of the right to think and act above what is written are the most mistaken.

They need to humbly accept what God says of them in His Word.

However, the refashioning that Paul did in his relationship to Apollos was not of this nature. It had a double purpose. The first was that the Corinthians might learn that nothing should be placed above the Scriptures. He wanted them to know that the agreement he and Apollos had reached as ministers of the mysteries of God could not stand over against those things already written in the divine revelation.

No apostle was to build anything that would overshadow what God had already revealed, and they did not. The New Testament stands on the Old; it cannot stand alone. Note how our Lord stressed that He was the fulfillment of God's promises through the prophets. The expression, "It is written," was continually on His lips. Nothing that any of us might add can supersede that which has already been written.

The second goal that springs from giving the written Word preeminence is that sectarian divisions may be avoided. "That no one of you be puffed up for one against another." The word translated "another" in Greek is *héteron,* meaning "another of a different kind." If anyone adds to God's written revelation, he feels superior because he has something more than another who has not added anything. Setting forth one's own tradition over the Scriptures tends to puff one up with the idea that his religion, his denomination or church, is superior and exclusive.

How true this is. Sects that have added or subtracted from the Scriptures stand aloof from those who accept only what is in God's written revelation. And the same is true of those who have their own private interpretation of a particular doctrine and constantly harp on it. These things are principal causes of divisions. Pride of possessing more knowledge than another is the basis of isolationism and sectarianism.

Oral Tradition Versus the Scriptures

Churches and individuals often split up and differ because they regard their oral traditions as being of equal importance and authority with the Scriptures. But, when God gave the Ten Commandments, He did not commit them orally to Moses but engraved them on two stone tablets with His hand. When we pursue this matter still further, we find that God's law and prophecies, and all the history of God's dealings with His people and the heathen nations were invariably committed to writing.

It is said of the king who might be appointed over the Israelites that he should "write . . . a copy of this law in a book" (Deut. 17:18). To Jeremiah God said, "Write thee all the words that I have spoken unto thee in a book" (Jer. 30:2). When the Israelites returned from captivity, Ezra began to teach them the law of God—not from memory or from what had been traditionally handed down among them, but he "read in the book in the law of God distinctly, and gave the sense, and caused them to understand the reading" (Neh. 8:8).

The Jews were extremely jealous for the Word of God as against anything except what was written. This attitude was confirmed afterward by the Lord Jesus as He frequently rebuked the Pharisees for violating this rule by their traditions, which had encumbered and vitiated what had been written.

Of course, the Christian religion began, as was natural, in the teaching of man to man by word of mouth. But the Holy Spirit soon moved the same apostles who had preached orally to concentrate and gather together all the great points of such oral preaching in the Scriptures.

Today, generally speaking, Christendom is divided into two main branches: the churches such as the Roman Catholic and Eastern Orthodox which place oral tradition on a par with the written Scriptures, and the Protestant churches, which accept the

Scriptures as their sole authority, and place nothing alongside them or above them.

The word "tradition" in Greek is *parádosis,* meaning "something that is handed down." That may be done orally or in writing. Thus, whenever we come across the word "tradition" in the New Testament, we need to understand whether it refers to oral or written tradition. For instance, in 1 Corinthians 15:3, Paul says, "I have delivered unto you." The word is *parédōka,* the verbal form of *parádosis.* Thus he is saying, "I have made a tradition to you . . . that Christ died for our sins."

And in 1 Corinthians 11:2 Paul says, "I will praise you . . . that ye . . . keep the ordinances, as I delivered them unto you." The word translated "ordinances" is *paradóseis,* "traditions." He praises them for keeping "the traditions which I have handed down to you." And in 2 Thessalonians 2:15 he says, "Stand fast, and hold the traditions [*parádosis*] which ye have been taught, whether by word, or our epistle." Here the word "traditions" refers to both oral and written teaching.

Unfortunately, however, the word "tradition" has taken on the ecclesiastical meaning of oral tradition only, in contradistinction to the written, which has assumed the name of "Scripture." Thus in actuality, Scripture is tradition, though it has lost the name, but "tradition" as understood and venerated today is not Scripture, because it lacks the essential addition of originally being set down in writing.

Before Scripture existed, there was oral tradition. Bennett explains how this tradition evolved into—not an independent corpus but—Scripture itself:

> Without tradition, there could have been no Scripture at all. . . . Our blessed Lord was crucified in the year 33. St. Matthew's Gospel was the first Scripture of the new covenant. Its date is not precisely agreed upon; some put it as late as 64, others as early as 38; then the other Scriptures, both Gospels and Epistles, were added from time to time, as

circumstances called for them, down to the close of the first century. . . . there must have been a period of *five* years (but this is most likely very short of truth: it was probably fifteen or twenty years) when there was no Scripture at all and then only one Gospel, circulated among a very scanty number of the Hebrew Christians. On what then during this period, throughout all those Gentile Churches already founded throughout the world, could Christianity depend? Only on that *oral* teaching, that *remembrance* of doctrines delivered by the preaching of the apostles, and handed about by word of mouth from one person to another. And this we call tradition.

It was not probable that that matter of such momentous importance as human salvation could be left to the uncertain and feeble authority of hearsay. Consider, my brethren, what your religion would be if it were to depend only on the sermons that you hear. . . . [words possibly] altered, either by subtraction or exaggeration.

And would it then be likely that God, who knows men and human hearts, would leave a matter of such vast importance as the salvation of the whole human race—a salvation which had to be made known over the face of the whole world, and among nations of endlessly different languages—a salvation which was to endure as the good tidings of the nations . . . to the changing humors of an oral communication? Surely not (William J. E. Bennett, *Lecture-Sermons: on the Distinctive Errors of Romanism*, 50–54).

No Other Gospel

In our study so far we have seen that in the Old Testament the Lord insisted on the safety of a written revelation of His Word. And in the New Testament the apostle Paul commanded that no one should think above what is written. The reason for this, of course, is that wrong behavior could be justified by unacceptable oral tradition. This may have been the case in the Corinthian church, to which Paul addressed this command. A church or an individual may seek to justify certain doctrines that are not grounded in the Scriptures by appealing to oral tradition. Bennett concludes his argument with the observation of "three important truths":

> I) First, we shall observe, that there could be no difference whatever between the Scriptures so written and the previously existing traditions. They were one and the same thing. The Scriptures could not contain one item more, and certainly not one item less, which was necessary to salvation, than had previously been circulated among the early Christians in the shape of creeds or summaries of faith, ceremonial observances, or forms of prayer.
>
> II) Secondly . . . these Scriptures . . . could not . . . contain anything which might have been done subsequent to their publication; therefore, if it should ever happen that we find a tradition asserted now by any Christians to be essential to salvation, which is not in Scripture also, we know that it must be a tradition invented subsequently to the apostolic age, but if we find a tradition which agrees with Scripture, or is contained in Scripture, or may be gathered out of Scripture, then we . . . embrace that tradition, but we do so now because Scripture confirms and establishes it, and not because it confirms and establishes Scripture.
>
> III) [T]he very fact of the traditions being committed to Scripture *at all* invalidates any supposition of traditional teaching being left among Christians as vital to their salvation. For it is obvious to ask, why should God . . . inspire holy men to record the words and actions of Christ in writing, if . . . some traditions, as previously existing, had been still necessary to be believed for their salvation? We might as well have been left even to this hour without any Scripture at all, for there would be no advantage in it, or benefit to be derived from it. Therefore traditions cease to be necessary to salvation by the mere fact of there being any Scripture at all.
>
> It is thus. Certain things were delivered by oral teaching during the life of Christ, by His apostles. It is impossible to suppose that Christ and His apostles could have taught an *imperfect* system of faith, or could have preached any gospel but what was sufficient for salvation. All that was required to be taught was taught: then, when the truth was in danger, by remoteness of time, or by transmission through the imperfect channels of human communication . . . to be changed, or mutilated, or added to, he vouchsafed to direct holy men, moved by His Holy Ghost, to write down all that had been said and done that was necessary for salvation. . . . (*Ibid.*, 57–59).

Note that not all that was said and done was recorded. Many sayings and miracles of Christ were left unwritten, as John himself testifies in the last verse of his Gospel: "And there are also many other things which Jesus did, the which, if they should be written every one, I suppose that even the world itself could not contain the books that should be written" (John 21:25).

This is what we should understand in the great controversy that exists between the churches that believe in the Scriptures only and those that believe the Scriptures must be complemented by oral tradition. "We allow beyond question that many things were said and done by Christ which are not in Scripture, but we cannot allow that any of those things *were necessary* to salvation" (*Ibid.,* 59, 60). What was the principle of selection? "But these are written, that ye might believe that Jesus is the Christ, the Son of God; and that believing ye might have life through his name" (John 20:31). The principle of selection was this: "that ye might believe that Jesus is the Christ." The selection gives you all that you require; it is needless to give you more. If there had been anything further that was required "that . . . ye might have life through his name," it would have been recorded.

We dare say that the apostle Paul even excludes his own teaching as something the Corinthians should accept if it should prove contrary to the teaching of the Lord Jesus Christ. He makes this plain in Galatians 1:8: "But though we, or an angel from heaven, preach any other gospel unto you than that which we have preached unto you, let him be accursed" (see also 1 Tim. 6:3, 4).

Against this sea-swept Rock
  Ten thousand storms their will
Of foam and rage have wildly spent;
  It lifts its calm face still.

It standeth and will stand,
  With neither change nor age,

The Word of majesty and light,
The Church's heritage.
—Horatius Bonar

Is the Written Word of God Sufficient for Salvation?

God is very explicit about the finality of His Word. In Deuteronomy 4:2 He says, "Ye shall not add unto the word which I command you, neither shall ye diminish ought from it, that ye may keep the commandments of the Lord your God which I command you." This is a command against two evils, that of adding to and that of subtracting from the Word of God—the Word that was first spoken and then written.

The Reverend T. C. Hammond anticipates the objection: "But," someone might say, "was anything ever added to these words?" (Rev. T. C. Hammond, *One Hundred Texts of the Society for Irish Church Missions*, 326). Of course there was, including the writings of the prophets, the Psalms, and other Old Testament books, and then the New Testament. Does that mean these are not valid? Of course not. What God prohibited was purely human additions to the divine Word. The Jews looked upon the rest of the Old Testament as God's expanded Pentateuch. Hammond anticipates further questions:

> What are we to understand by adding to God's Word? Bringing in heathen superstitions, or forms of worship different from those commanded. What is meant by diminishing from God's Word? Neglecting some duty, or leaving out some observance therein commanded.
>
> What is the object of keeping God's Word without addition or subtraction? That the people may fulfill all God's commandments as He commanded them. How would adding prevent this? It would put human commands on a level with God's and make confusion, and it would give wrong ideas a false authority. How would diminishing prevent this? It would conceal from the people important requirements of God. What does the last part of the text teach us as to our duty? That we are bound to carry out all that God requires of us. What temptation

> does our text guard us against? The temptation of taking part of God's Will for the whole (*Ibid.*, 326, 327).

Many students of the Bible are confused nowadays about a group of books included in some Bibles called the Apocrypha, which means "the hidden ones (or books)." These books were written by the Jews in the period between the Old and New Testaments. They are rejected by Protestantism as not part of the Canonical Scriptures. These books were not contained in the Bible of the Jews from whom we received the Old Testament. The Apocrypha was first included as part of Scripture at the Council of Trent in 1547.

Those who believe that the Scripture is incomplete without the unwritten oral tradition of the Church point to John 21:25, "And there are also many other things which Jesus did, the which, if they should be written every one, I suppose that even the world itself could not contain the books that should be written." So the contention, according to Hammond runs like this:

> [*M*]*ight* there not have been among these things . . . many important points of instruction, and many points of discipline which our Lord commended to the keeping of His Church?
>
> Of course, we cannot prove a negative; so, then, he would go on to say, "Not only *might* there have been, but when you consider other parts of Scripture, it is very probable, indeed, that there were. For instance, St. Paul to the Corinthians says, 'keep the traditions which I delivered' [1 Cor. 11:2]; and to Timothy 'Hold fast the form of sound words, which thou hast heard of me' [2 Tim. 1:13]. "Thus he would go on and conclude: 'Scripture, therefore, seems to say that the things which the evangelist and others left unwritten might be of equal authority with Scripture itself' " (*Ibid.*, 76).

Our answer to this would be that some traditions may indeed be valid. No one is denying the fact that the Lord Jesus Christ gave many instructions to His disciples that were not written. We do not have everything He said in the Scriptures. It is humanly impossible that this should be so, as John said. But what we are saying is that those things that were not written are not necessary for our salvation, and that what has been written is sufficient unto salvation. Otherwise God would have been doing something quite useless in inspiring holy men to produce a written record that was insufficient.

We are therefore prepared to concede many things unwritten, but nothing worthy to be believed as "necessary to salvation." We do not deny that tradition contains truths independent of and contrary to Scripture. All things necessary to salvation rest only on Scripture. It is interesting to note in this connection that many old so-called Gospels that claim to contain other words and deeds of Jesus are so at variance with the New Testament that their claims are patently false.

> We search the world for truth, we cull
> The good, the pure, the beautiful,
> From graven stone and written scroll,
> From all old flower-fields of the soul
> And, weary seekers of the best
> We come back laden from our quest,
> To find that all the sages said
> Is in the Book our mothers read.
>
> —Author Unknown

The Sin of Exalting Christian Leaders

Although we have seen that Paul's injunction to the Corinthian Church in 1 Corinthians 4:6 should properly read, "not to think of things above that which is written," instead of not to think of "men" in this way, it can properly be applied to men also, in a secondary sense. Paul was deeply concerned about the divisions and factions in the Corinthian Church, caused by their exalting of one leader over another. And he proceeds in masterly fashion to correct this.

But the Church is made up of individuals, and only as individuals are corrected can the Church as a corporate entity be made whole. So Paul sets out to deal with each individual.

In the middle of 1 Corinthians 4:6 we find the telic conjunction *hína,* "so that": "*So that ye* might learn in us not to think of men above that which is written; *so that* no one of you be puffed up for one against another." What does this signify? Paul is saying in effect, "I want to admonish each one of you as an individual, first of all not to go beyond what is written; stick to the Scriptures; for only thus can you be guided aright as an individual. And in the second place, don't let pride cause you to think that your leader is superior to someone else."

The principle Paul was stressing is that what each individual is, the local church is. The Corinthians approved of one apostle and disliked another. In thus setting themselves as judges, they were actually enhancing their individual self-importance.

Now, why does Paul connect the Scriptures with their opinions of men? Because the Scriptures do definitely teach what our relationship should be to those who minister the gospel. The Corinthians forgot that even an apostle was only a minister by whom the faith was propagated. In their minds they constituted him as their own party leader. They were the ones who attributed importance to him, not recognizing his true value as being that which God made him—a minister and steward of the mysteries of God. Their support of a man had the subtle philosophy of asserting, "Here is what we have made you; this is the position to which we have elevated you. If it were not for our support, you wouldn't be what you are or where you are."

By their elevation of one man over another, the Corinthians were actually proclaiming their own importance in the support they were giving him. We see this in their tendency to treat him like a political leader whose electorate says to him, "You are what you are because of us. Therefore look how important we are." As Judge Harold Medina observed: "Criticizing others is a dangerous thing, not so much because you may be making mistakes about them, but because you may be revealing the truths about yourself." And this holds true about praising men also.

A pastor, just before presenting a visiting minister to his congregation, prayed, "O Lord, blot him out so we can see only Jesus!" Wouldn't that be an appropriate prayer for each one of us? Esteem your minister as one who brings you closer to Christ and makes the Bible a book to be loved and obeyed. But don't puff up your minister, or yourself for belonging to him and what you consider "his party" in the church.

The apostle Paul seeks to counteract such a spirit by asking one probing question after another, the answers to which were self-evident. We shall examine these questions in detail a bit later. Paul uses the same method in 1 Corinthians 1:13: "Is Christ divided? was Paul crucified for you? or were ye baptized in the name of Paul?" Naturally such questions are meant to strip the Corinthians of their "puffery" in attributing more value to an individual than the Scriptures permit. They thought they had the right to introduce new situations that would make them innovators of unquestioned authority.

Christian, watch yourself, lest you begin to think you know better than anyone else what ought to be done in the church, so that everyone should listen to you and follow your advice. You may find yourself in the humiliating position of being rebuked by a Higher Authority, God Himself, as His Holy Spirit speaks to you through the Scriptures.

It is said that Billie Burke, the Hollywood actress, was enjoying a transatlantic ocean voyage when she noticed that a man at the next table was suffering from a bad cold.

"Uncomfortable?" she asked sympathetically.

The man nodded.

"I'll tell you what to do for it," she offered. "Go back to your stateroom and drink a lot of orange juice. Take five aspirin tablets. Cover yourself with all the blankets you can find. Sweat the cold out. I know what I'm talking about. I'm Billie Burke of Hollywood."

The man smiled warmly and said, "Thanks. I'm Dr. Mayo of the Mayo Clinic!"

Oh, these self-proclaimed experts who ride on an interpretative tangent and play a one-chord spiritual instrument! Lord, deliver us from believing that all the solutions rest in our own simplistic formulas, or in one man whom we believe to have all the answers. Deliver us from elevating anyone to such a degree that both Christ and His Word are obscured. Let us respect and honor Thy faithful ministers as we ought, but let us reserve our highest love, veneration, and loyalty for Thee.

Humility in Action

Admonitions to specific individuals and churches in Scripture, although they may be occasioned by a local situation, often have a wider application, for they address themselves to human nature. Thus, what the apostle Paul has to say to the church at Corinth may be applied to the churches today. Are we any better than the Corinthian Christians? Are we less or more divided than they? Are we, like them, introducing new attitudes or even doctrines above what is written in Scripture?

Many churches today, sad to say, seem very much imbued with the spirit of the Corinthian church One leader looks down upon another. And those who follow a particular leader sometimes refuse to have fellowship with those who follow another, as they consider them beneath them Pride is the cause of such divisions in the Church. But the saddest thing of all is the ease and cleverness with which we try to justify the pride of our factionalism.

Liddon observes that "[t]here are probably two leading objections . . . to cultivating the humility. . . ." (Liddon, "Humility and Truth," *Sermons Preached before the University of Oxford*, 22). In the first place, we don't want the humility that we think will compromise our sincerity and moral stature. We say in effect, "I believe something or in somebody, and therefore I must take a stand. If for the sake of humility I suppress my support, I am being insincere" (*Ibid.*, 22).

True enough, if that's what you think humility demands. But this is a false notion of humility. Those who entertain such a notion take humility to be something dramatic and unreal, a pretense put on for an occasion, instead of an attitude dictated by sincere feelings and conviction. This is not true humility, however. The humility we need is not a pretense, a winking at truth, but essentially the recognition of truth (*Ibid.*).

Just how does true humility manifest itself? It involves, Liddon says, the:

> . . . taking in act and word and thought, that low estimate of ourselves which is the true estimate. If we do not seriously think that such an estimate is the true one, it is only because we have never seen ourselves as we really are. We have yet to learn our real relationship to the Being to Whom we owe our existence, and the weakness which impairs our moral force, and the evil that clings to us within. In the meantime . . . it is better not to pretend that we have done so; while it is certain that such pretence, if we should be guilty of it, would not be rightly termed humility (*Ibid.*).

Christian humility, if it is genuine, is never exercised at the expense of truth, but as a result of the correct estimate of ourselves and the religious leader whom we may have elevated above what the Scriptures permit.

The second objection that may be advanced for failure to cultivate humility is the notion that it is something dramatic and fictitious, and therefore involves some loss of moral strength.

This is true only if the humility we refer to is false, Liddon continues, for:

> . . . moral force is lost by every form of untruthfulness; . . . but genuine humility is in its essence the planting of our foot upon the hard rock of truth and fact, often when it costs us a great deal to do so. To confess ignorance, to confess wrong, to admit incapacity, when it would be useful to be thought capable, to decline a reputation to which we have no right—these things and others of the same kind, are humility in action. If we are weak, sinful, corrupt, it is better to learn and to feel the true state of the case than to live in a fool's paradise.
>
> Every man is the stronger for knowing the worst he can know about himself, and for acting on this knowledge. And if religious men such as David and St. Paul use language about themselves which seems to any of us exaggerated in the excess of its self-depreciation [see, e.g., Ps. 51:1–3 and 1 Cor. 15:9], this is because they saw much more of the holiness of God . . . than we do: to them such language is only the sober representation of a plain fact. These great servants of God were not dazzled by any of the inherited or acquired status decorations which hide from so many of us our real selves, and which the apostle Paul in the text is so determined to strip off from us (*Ibid.*, 22, 23).

A government official in India who was engaged in irrigation work came to the owner of a field and offered to make it fruitful, to which the owner answered. "You needn't attempt to do anything with my field; it is barren and will produce nothing." The official replied, "I can make your field richly fruitful if only it lies low enough." He meant that a lowland would be much easier to irrigate than higher ground.

If you and I are willing to accept God's estimate of us as revealed in Scripture—as fallible, weak, and unfruitful apart from His enabling grace in Christ—He can fill us with the living water that will bring forth fruit.

One of the last messages of a great philanthropist was, "Tell my younger brethren that they may be too big for God to use them, but they cannot be too small."

LESSONS:

1. Paul refashioned (*metaschēmatísa*) himself, that is, changed his outward appearance or conduct—not his character as would be reflected in the verb, *metamorphóō*)—to be a good example to the Corinthians who were accustomed to bickering, dispute, and division.
2. His reference to Apollos has caused some to conjecture that he changed his approach to some of Apollos' teaching which may have been overleavened with Alexandrian philosophy.
3. Some have even suggested that the book of Hebrews is the content behind Paul's refashioning, possibly addressing all that bordered on heresy or contrariety to the established doctrine of the apostles in Apollos' teaching.
4. From this we learn that our approach to others, even heretics, should include a humble fashion (*schḗma*) or style without sacrificing the content or form (*morphḗ*) of truth.
5. Paul did this to model humility so that the divisive Corinthians would learn from his example.
6. We must reject, as Paul asserts here, all teachings that go beyond the Word of God. **True science** (*gnṓsis*, knowledge) always supports the Word of God. In his epistle to Timothy, he notes that there is a **false science**, one that is "so-called" (1 Tim. 6:20).
7. Those who subtract, add, or in any other way distort the Scriptures are proud—puffed up with air (*phusióō*).
8. Oral tradition, the "tradition" alluded to in Paul's writings, may be no more than verbally communicated truth prior to the full (plenary) incorporation of the New Testament canon. If not, there may be truths beyond—but not contradictory to—the Scriptures communicated by the apostles. None of these would be essential for salvation.
9. In addition to the truth that no truth is above or against the Scriptures, it is also true that Christian leaders should not be exalted beyond and above the realistic model of believers portrayed in the New Testament. Christian leaders are still sinners, subject to "like passions" (James 5:17).
10. True humility is taking in thought, word, and deed, the low estimate of ourselves that is the true one—the one revealed in Scripture. True humility never sacrifices truth.
11. True humility is moral strength, since moral force is lost by every form of untruthfulness. Humility includes a true estimate of strength.

1 Cor. 4:7 | *The Mystery of Life's Inequalities*

For who maketh thee to differ from another? and what hast thou that thou didst not receive? now if thou didst receive it, why dost thou glory as if thou hadst not received it?

Equality: A Utopian Dream?

The Declaration of Independence affirms: "We hold these truths to be self-evident, that all men are created equal, that they are endowed by their Creator with certain inalienable rights, that among these are Life, Liberty, and the Pursuit of Happiness."

Most men believe in equality. The Declaration of Independence proclaims this in no uncertain terms. The question, however, is what is meant by the term "equality." The equality of which the Declaration of Independence speaks is an equality of rights, not of personal endowments. The idealist, on the other hand, believes in an equality that would have created all men with equal abilities, opportunities, and material possessions. He frowns at the injustice of any form of inequality. He despises the employer who doesn't treat everyone equally. He even questions a God who disperses His gifts unequally.

And yet none of us can be so naive as not to realize we live in a world of inequalities. We have different innate intelligences.

Though we have all been created with pretty much the same physical equipment, the intensity of our strength differs. Our environments differ. We possess individual and differing abilities. And we can only conclude that God made us that way, whether we can understand it or not. It is one of those unfathomable mysteries that we must accept as a fact and come to terms with.

No two snowflakes, no two blades of grass, no two animals, no two human countenances, exactly correspond with each other. God could have made everything uniform within its kind, but He did not. His creation is characterized by variety.

What Paul suggests through his epistles is that the Author of differences between man and man is the infinitely wise and good God. Judging as sinful men, though we may not like it, and may even think we could have done better in God's place, we know there's nothing we can do to improve on the work of our Creator. It's a utopian dream to conclude that complete equality in all things would have been preferable. We just don't know. Nor will God permit our experimentation in such a situation in our present state of being and environment. Our nature is fallen and our environment is geared to such a fallen nature. Some day, with the complete redemption of our being and environment, this may become possible.

Paul wanted to correct the attitudes of the Corinthians in esteeming one servant of God more highly than another. Human esteem differs because people differ. We tend to appreciate and admire one whom we regard as a capable preacher. We become critical toward one whom we regard as an average or poor one. The fact that our appreciation of people varies is proof that people are different. But who is it that makes them different as far as their essential endowments are concerned? It is God.

In 1 Corinthians 4:7 Paul asks the question, "Who maketh thee to differ from another? and what hast thou that thou didst not receive?" "Who" and "what"? There is a giver behind every gift. Thus the two questions are practically one, for everything ultimately comes from God—including the differences that make human lives unequal. These differences are as much a part of His handiwork as anything else in the world of being. Therefore, to quarrel with them, or to make them the occasion of rivalry with and estrangement from others, is to declare war upon the wisdom and purpose of the Great Creator.

Variety and difference in our world are not the result of chance. They are not the fatal outcome of the inter-operation of self-existent matter and force molded by some self-existent system of complex laws It is God who has made us, and not we ourselves (see Ps. 100:3). And it is certainly not that indefinite abstraction that men call "nature."

What we are called upon to do is to note the differences that separate us as human beings, accept them as the framework within which we have to work, and examine how these refer to the will and power and wisdom of God. These differences can be classified first as external circumstances, second as personal endowments, and third as spiritual opportunities. We shall take these up in separate studies.

What we must do now is to allow God to be God in our thinking, and to acknowledge that He is all-wise, all-knowing, all-good.

John Greenleaf Whittier came to terms with this when he wrote:

> I have no answer, for myself or thee,
> Save that I learned beside my mother's knee:
> "All is of God that is, and is to be;
> And God is good." Let this suffice us still,
> Resting in childlike trust upon His will
> Who moves to His great ends unthwarted by the ill.

"Take comfort, and recollect however little you and I may know, God knows; He knows Himself and you and me and all things; and His mercy is over all His works."—Charles Kingsley.

Differences in Our External Circumstances: Can They Be Helped?

Human society is full of inequalities—often quite glaring. Some people are wealthy, some are starving; some have great influence, others are regarded as nobodies. There are inequalities of education, social position, and opportunities. And these often cause great dissatisfaction and unrest between the haves and have-nots.

We may blame the spirit of injustice among men, tradition, misgovernment, our social and economic systems, the selfishness of the rich, and the chronic inertia of the poor. But whatever or whomever we may blame for the inequalities of human circumstances, we are ultimately forced back on the conclusion that it is God Himself who makes one man to differ from another. He makes men differ originally in their productive powers, and this, in part, is responsible for the unequal distribution of wealth and the disparity in men's social position.

It follows from this that projects for reconstructing society on the basis of an equal distribution of property of whatever kind are in conflict with the original facts of human nature, that is to say, with what was ordained by the will of God. For instance, suppose you were to divide all the land equally among the inhabitants of a nation. You'd soon find out that a man capable of cultivating 1,000 acres was wasting his ability on the ten acres or so allotted to everybody, while a person given ten acres might be found incapable of handling even that little. No human theory or law can affect this original inequality of productive power in men, which is the main and permanent cause of differences in wealth and social position. Nature and fact would assert themselves against utopian theory.

Don't get me wrong. I'm not upholding privilege against right, wealth against poverty, the few against the many, or that which has been against that which ought to be. Nor am I trying to excuse wrong by making God responsible for it. This has been the contention of communism, causing it to reject God and religion. Since, it is maintained, God is responsible for these inequalities, we don't want anything to do with such a God.

The Christian points in reply to the future, in which whatever comes short of the requirements of justice here will be perfectly and forever redressed. Those who misunderstand this attitude accuse us of promising "pie in the sky" at the cost of neglecting efforts to improve man's present lot. Christianity never says, however, that inequalities which involve moral wrong are to be acquiesced in here because they will be corrected hereafter. Moral wrongs must be corrected here and now, whenever possible.

But not all the differences of position, education, and income in themselves involve moral wrong. The fact that you or I may occupy a so-called higher social position than someone else doesn't necessarily classify us as immoral, thus making us automatically responsible for the lower social position of another. Nor is the person who has remained on the lower rungs of the social or economic ladder necessarily to be held morally culpable for his nonadvancement.

It is sinful, however, for us as Christians to shut our eyes to the need of others. We are bound to do everything in our power to lessen the general inequalities of life. Our charities ought to throw bridges over the gulfs that separate classes. Christianity breeds a spirit of self-sacrifice that results in the voluntary abandonment of wealth and station for the sake of others, out of devotion to Jesus Christ, who, "though he was rich, yet for your sakes he became poor, that ye through his poverty might be rich" (2 Cor. 8:9).

But it is inevitably true that, when all that can be done in this direction has been done, great inequalities in men's outward circumstances will and must remain, because they are due to inherited differences of personal capacity. And this is so because in making us, our Creator has willed that one man should widely differ from another. Inequalities of circumstances are part and parcel of inequalities in personal endowments, and these are really beyond our control.

In 1 Corinthians 4:7 Paul says that those who have been more privileged have no reason to be proud, as though they were somehow responsible for their more fortunate lot. Scripture tells us that men are like clay in the potter's hands, God being the Potter, of course. Can a beautiful clay vase boast itself against a common pot, saying, "I am much finer than you and therefore worthy of praise"? As the vase contributed nothing toward its beauty, so man contributes nothing to his inherent individual make-up. True, he can develop himself, but only to the extent of "what he has been made to be in his real self."

In fact, those who have received more from God than others should not be proud, but acknowledge they are more in debt to Him for the bounty He has bestowed on them. Why should one man boast that he is deeper in debt than another? Let's regard our endowments as a trust to be used for the glory of God and the good of our fellow men.

How to Regard Inequalities Due to Differences in Personal Endowments

Men differ in the physical, mental, and other qualities with which God has sent them into the world. No two men are exactly equal even in the possession of a single faculty or talent. School teachers are keen observers of such inequalities.

What has heredity to do with all this? In our endeavor to understand present behavior we must analyze an individual's ancestry. But this poses another question: Why should a given individual have this particular ancestry, which has shaped him into the physical and mental person we now see? In fact, why should there be any antecedents at all, or any effects, anything to be transmitted, or any law of type to govern its transmission?

These are indeed difficult questions to answer. In their presence, science is wisely silent. We must turn to the Bible for authoritative answers to them. To those who believe in God the Creator, who made us all, and each one of us exactly what we are, there can be no question as to the true source of natural ability. Handel, the composer of "The Messiah," gave eloquent testimony to this. On one occasion when his oratorio was superbly rendered by an orchestra, chorus, and soloists, the audience broke out in thunderous applause, while all eyes turned toward Handel. He, however, turned their attention from himself to his Creator, as he stood up and silently pointed heavenward. How salutary and humbling to recognize that what basically distinguishes us from others is a gift from God.

Someone once had the temerity to say what many of us are tempted to think: "I am a self-made man." A friend replied, "That certainly relieves God of an embarrassing responsibility." Anyone who regards himself as a self-made man should stop and think that he must have had some material to begin with. Where did his mind come from? He didn't choose the circumstances of his birth. He could have been born with any of several handicaps. Even if he became a distinguished athlete, it was God who gave him his body. The voice, eyesight, and physical coordination, to mention just a few of our physical attributes, are all gifts we have received from God; and only because He gave them to us could we develop them.

We have made great advances in our study of heredity and how it works, including how traits are transmitted. It is truly gracious of the Supreme Artist to have allowed us to see further into

His workshop than our fathers did, and to discover some of the rules by which He conducts His work. But the work is none the less His because it is done by rules He allows us to observe. If every peculiarity of our minds and bodies could be accounted for by those of our ancestors, we would not be one bit less God's workmanship, each made to differ from others by a deliberate act of His will.

Now we come to the subject of inequalities in our spiritual advantages and opportunities. The words of the apostle Paul, "Who maketh thee to differ from another? and what hast thou that thou didst not receive?" were addressed to people who were proud of their spiritual leader and were boasting of him as well as their own spiritual superiority. Liddon remarks,

> The Corinthian of whom the apostle is thinking believed himself to differ from his fellow Christians, not in social standing or intellectual culture, but specifically in the possession of a truer religious faith.
>
> St. Paul, then, does not tell the Corinthian that the idea of his differing from another is of itself a presumptuous absurdity; he assumes the difference to exist, and even to be legitimate; he concentrates . . . upon the source of the difference (Liddon, "Humility and Truth," 32, 33).

If Apollos, for instance, had greater oratorical ability than Peter, that difference need not be concealed. Paul assumed that differences existed among preachers as well as followers. There was no reason to be proud of such differences, for the beginning of all spiritual life is the result of God's grace. Even the faith to receive the grace of God is a gift, as Paul points out so emphatically in Ephesians 2:8: "For by grace are ye saved through faith; and that not of yourselves: it is the gift of God."

However, you and I were born where we could hear the gospel and receive the offer of salvation. But millions on this earth were not. Inequality of opportunity to hear that wonderful gospel that changes men's eternal destiny raises many questions. Why should one person be born into a godly home, with all the opportunities of Christian example, and others not? If the differences of religious circumstances come from God, why? We just don't know. We can only be observers of such actions of God, not interpreters of them. We don't reject Him, however, because we can't fully understand Him, no more than a small child rejects his parents because their actions are often incomprehensible to him. Nor do we lament our lack of opportunities. God will judge us by what we do with the opportunities He gives us. And we to whom He has given the opportunity and privilege of receiving Christ must rush to share the knowledge of His grace with those who have not yet had the opportunity. For as Paul said, "I am debtor both to the Greeks, and to the Barbarians; both to the wise, and to the unwise" . . . and "Woe is unto me, if I preach not the gospel!" (Rom. 1:14, 1 Cor. 9:16).

Inequalities in Spiritual Endowments

If you will turn in your Bible to chapter 12 of First Corinthians, you will see that spiritual gifts and opportunities are unequally distributed. "Now there are diversities of gifts, but the same Spirit." But the inequality of gifts, even of spiritual gifts, doesn't imply that God loves those individuals less to whom He gives less. He gives according to our capacity to receive. He withholds, as He bestows, in love.

God often imposes drawbacks and difficulties, when He sees that these are needed for the training and discipline of the thoughts, emotions, and will; so that underlying the great differences of spiritual advantage there is a much truer equality than we may think. As in a well-ordered state all are basically equal before the law, so in the Church all are basically equal before their Maker and Redeemer.

To be specific, we are equals in that we must all face the solemn moment of death. We are equal in that we shall all be judged relative to the gifts and opportunities we have enjoyed. We are equal in that all of us can be saved only one way, through the blood of Jesus Christ shed on the cross. And we are equals in that we have all received a trust from God. Some of us may have been entrusted with five talents, some two, others one. Some may have received the abilities of Paul, others of Apollos. But the Church, after all, is like a great almshouse, in which everybody is a pensioner, and in which the difference between the greatest and the smallest pensions disappears before the fact that all are equally indebted to a bounty on which none have any real claim. All that God gives us is wrapped up in the word "grace." Liddon notes, ". . . we have nothing to do with winning it. We may cooperate with it, we may forfeit it if we neglect it; we may or may not have predispositions for receiving it. But in itself, it is, as its name implies, a free gift" (*Ibid.*, 34).

Is there anything that we have not received from God? Yes, there is. We all have it, but we can't blame God for giving it to us. It is the fatal product of our misused liberty. That is sin. God originally made man in His own image and likeness. But this meant that He created man with the original power of choice, even as He Himself had it. But God also had to set the consequences of the choices man would make. Man could choose whether to obey God or not, but he could not choose the consequences of his choice. Thus sin, and the will to sin, are not something we received from God, but simply a result of the choice to sin or not to sin.

Never blame God for your sin. You are right in ascribing to Him your freedom to choose, but when you stop to consider that privilege which distinguishes you from all the rest of creation, you will praise God for it rather than blame Him.

Dr. Pierce Harris, pastor of the First Methodist Church of Atlanta, Georgia, preached to some prisoners. One of the prisoners got up and introduced him to the others with these words:

"Several years ago, two boys lived in a town in north Georgia. They went to the same school, played together and attended the same Sunday school. One dropped out of Sunday school and said that it was 'sissy stuff.' The other boy kept on going. One rejected Christ; the other accepted Him. The boy who rejected Christ is making this introduction today. The boy who accepted Christ is the honored preacher who will speak to us today!" Choice made the difference.

What should our attitude be as we see others possessing gifts that we do not possess and that we cannot acquire? Jealousy, resentment, and disparagement of others are all too often evidenced by the less-gifted in the Church. A man came up to Moody once and criticized him for the way he went about winning souls. Moody listened courteously and then asked, "How would you do it?" The man, taken aback, mumbled that he didn't do it. "Well," said Moody, "I prefer the way I do it to the way you don't do it."

We should thank the Lord that others can serve God in ways that we cannot. After all, the important thing is not what you and I as individuals can do, but what can be done for the kingdom of God. Let's always look at the abilities of others as supplements to what little we can do, and praise God for the gifts He has given others. If no one cared who got the credit for services rendered to God, how much more might be accomplished for Him—and in the right spirit.

As we realize what God has given to us—the talents and abilities with which He has entrusted us—let's acquire a sense of urgent responsibility to use them for His glory. The more splendid the endowment the greater the possibility of its misuse. The higher the gift the more there is to be accounted for.

The realization that what men have was given by God ought to make us more sensitive toward the less-gifted instead of haughty and contemptuous. And, toward the more highly gifted than we, our feeling should be one of delight and gratitude that they can accomplish what we cannot.

LESSONS:

1. Equality is rarely, if ever, defined. The Declaration of Independence limits it to specific physical rights—not endowments. Secular and religious idealists question a God who dispenses natural talents and spiritual gifts unequally.
2. Yet according to the Bible, God is the One who makes us differ in intelligence, wealth, health, and spirituality—in general, created circumstances. Accordingly, worldly differences are not the products of chance but of a holy and wise God in agreement with His perfect plan.
3. Redistribution of these things on a non-biblical premise of equality will not usher in Utopia. The natural man never strives for equality anyway, but for dominance and status. No man is satisfied with equality.
4. Status or high rank is a lie according to Scripture (Ps. 62:9). Those who think they have it should no more congratulate themselves than non-achievers pity themselves. To whom more is given, more is expected (Luke 12:48). But in either case, we are not self-made.
5. Spiritual life is a gift of God's grace which generates even the faith to receive spiritual gifts for the edification of the church (Gal. 5:22; Eph. 2:8, 9; Phil. 1:29). Even birth in a country saturated with the gospel rather than heathen religions is ordained by God (Acts 17:26, 27).
6. The Lord gives us spiritual gifts according to our created or re-created capacities to receive. Trials are intended for discipline of our thoughts, emotions, and will.
7. Although the cause of all things, God is not accountable for sin. No creature is in the position to call Him into account. Only a higher God—and there are none—would have this authority. An infinite regress of higher-level Gods would imply that no single God has authority.
8. We must learn to appreciate the gifts God has bestowed on others, rather than resent or envy them. Spiritual qualities—for example love (the end), for which sake all the gifts (the means) are given in the first place—may be subject to godly jealousy, but not the gifts themselves. Our perspective should be the complimentarity God has ordained, as He fits the members of the church together into one living organism.

1 Cor. 4:8 | Material Progress Costs Spiritual Compromise

Now ye are full, now ye are rich, ye have reigned as kings without us: and I would to God ye did reign, that we also might reign with you.

Present Satisfaction Versus Future Joy

One of the most common pitfalls for a Christian is to be caught up in the spirit of the age, to live for the here and now. When a Christian believes that his full satisfaction is to be found in this world, he will tend to seek three things that man in his unregenerate state considers most important: physical satisfaction, the acquisition of wealth, and the power and prestige that enable him to rule over others. These are the cravings of the natural man, with which the Christian is all too often infected.

The Lord fully recognized this in the Beatitudes in Matthew 5:3–11 and Luke 6:20–24. But full satisfaction, riches, and rule over others are something He promises to the Christian in the world to come, not here. In this world, the Christian will often go without. "Blessed the hungering ones now: for they shall be filled" (Luke 6:21). Observe that the filling is future. "Blessed the sorrowing ones: for they shall be comforted" (Matt. 5:4). That's also in the future. "Blessed the meek: for they shall inherit the earth" (Matt. 5:5). That's future rulership over the earth.

The general tenor is that what the natural man craves and expects to enjoy fully here and now, the Christian either is deprived of because of the environment in which he lives, or voluntarily deprives himself of in order to serve God better.

"Already," Paul says to the carnal Corinthians, who were factional and critical even of apostolic authority, "you are filled to satiety." And in verse 11 Paul tells them: "Even unto this present hour we both hunger, and thirst, and are naked, and are buffeted, and have no certain dwellingplace." Paul draws contrast between the pleasure-seeking Corinthian Christians and the apostles who were voluntarily depriving themselves for the sake of proclaiming the gospel.

The Greek word *ḗdē* is very important. "Already" is a more correct translation than the "now" of the King James Version. It's repeated twice in verse 8: "Already" you are filled to satiety; "already" you grew rich. The apostle rebukes the Corinthians for seeking these things prematurely. You have sought and acquired that which you have been promised as children of the kingdom of the future, when the Lord returns in His rewarding glory.

Matthew 6 emphasizes seeking on earth what the Lord has promised us in heaven. He gives the example of three individuals doing something good, but with wrong motive. The first gave alms, not to help the needy but to be seen and praised of men. The second prayed in public, not to be heard of God, but to be heard and commended by men for his piety. And the third fasted, not to invoke God's attention, but man's pity. In all three the Lord says these people got what they sought— praise, attention, pity of men, but that's all they were to get. The Greek verb in Matthew 6:2, 5, and 16 is *apéchousin,* "they have their reward in full." They need not seek a reward in heaven; since they sought it here and now from men, they already have it.

In the Beatitudes in Luke 6:20–26, the Lord contrasts the self-sacrificing Christian (vv. 20–23) with the selfish Christian who seeks his satisfaction here and now, to the detriment of his effective witness (vv. 24–26). The whole section here is divided by the Greek word *plḗn,* "but," which contrasts the two classes of Christians—those who seek pleasure, wealth, and fame on earth, and those who sacrifice them here to find them in heaven.

It was so in Corinth. In Luke 6:24 we find the same word *apéchete* (*apéchō*) that is used in Matthew 6. "But woe unto you the rich! for you have in full your comfort." In Luke 6:21 the verb *apéchete* in the present tense, indicating "here and now, already," in contrast to the future of *chortasthḗsesthe* (you will be full), and *gelásete* (you will laugh), in the day that is coming. For the self-sacrificing Christian, the reward is future.

There is a story of an aged servant of the Lord who, on his death-bed, said, "It is true; it is all true." Someone asked, "Why do you keep saying that? What is all true?" The aged Christian said, "Well, although I have given up all my possessions to the poor, and although I have turned from the things of the world, yet I never could really believe those words, 'Whosoever giveth up father, or mother, or houses, or lands, for my name's sake shall . . . receive his full reward, and shall enter into life eternal,' but now that I am dying I have found it is true; it is all true."

When a friend once wrote to Dr. Livingstone about the sacrifices he was making in spending his days among the savages of Central Africa, he made the spirited reply: "Is that a sacrifice which brings its own best reward in healthful activity, in the consciousness of doing good, peace of mind, and the hope of a glorious destiny hereafter? Away with such a thought! I never made a sacrifice." May we, too, seek "first the kingdom of God, and his righteousness," rather than our own selfish satisfaction.

Suffering Here but Reigning Hereafter

What I am about to say may come as an unpalatable truth to those Christians who have been caught up in the spirit of the age, but I do not believe a Christian can possibly experience all the satisfaction, wealth, and fame this life can offer without some compromise of principle. The Bible tells us that the Christian's full pleasure, wealth, and fame is future. Though a Christian is free to seek these things, he cannot have his cake and eat it too. In that day of which the apostle Paul spoke so eloquently in the 3rd chapter of 1 Corinthians, when Christ comes to distribute His rewards, He will say to those who sought a full measure of pleasure, wealth, and fame on earth, "You have already had your reward in full."

The Greek word Paul uses to demonstrate "fullness to satiety" is *kekoresménoi*, from *korénnumi*. It is evident from the context that this implies physical food rather than spiritual, and by extension satisfaction that comes from physical things, that is, pleasure to the full. This same verb occurs in Acts 27:38, in the account of the shipwreck in which Paul and 276 others were involved. Paul encouraged them to eat. And then, "when they had eaten enough [*koresthéntes*], they lightened the ship, and cast out the wheat into the sea."

That Paul was referring to satiety with physical food, rather than the spiritual food lexicographers Arndt and Gingrich mistakenly assume this statement to mean, is proven by the verses that follow, which deal with the physical privations of the disciples: "Even unto this present hour we both hunger, and thirst, and are naked, and are buffeted and have no certain dwelling-place; and labour, working with our hands: being reviled, we bless; being persecuted, we suffer it" (1 Cor. 4:11, 12).

The riches referred to in the second clause of verse 8 must also refer to physical wealth in contrast to the apostolic plight described in verses 11 and 12: "We go hungry, we go thirsty, and we are naked." That's all physical. These Corinthians constituted the haughty Christians who were priding themselves on their physical possessions. Their seeking such material satisfactions was unwarranted in view of their spiritual riches in Christ of which Paul spoke to Corinthian Christians in general in 1 Corinthians 1:5: "That in every thing ye are enriched by him [or 'in him,' i.e., Christ, as the Greek has it], in all utterance, and in all knowledge." That's positional enrichment. We are rich spiritually by virtue of the fact that we are "in Christ." This kind of wealth never produces pride, for we realize that all we are and have is from Christ. To seek to become rich materially, at the expense of our spiritual wealth, is unwarranted and dangerous. It's possible, but it's a deplorable snare for a Christian to fall into.

The two verbs used in 1 Corinthians 1:5 and 4:8 are somewhat different. In the first instance, where Paul is referring to their positional spiritual enrichment in Christ, he says *eploutísthēte* (*ploutízō*), (1 aor. pass., 2d per. pl.) meaning, You were enriched by someone other than yourselves, and that, of course, is God. But in 1 Corinthians 4:8 the verb is *eploutḗsate*, (1 aor. ind., 2d per. pl.) of the verb *ploutéō*, which means "to become rich," on your own. Christ makes us spiritually rich, but we become materially rich on our own. Already, Paul says, you have become, or you grew, rich on your own. He implies that neither he nor any other apostle had helped them to achieve this material enrichment.

This disclaimer is further sustained by Paul's statement in verse 8: "Without us you reigned." "Without us" in Greek is *chōrís hēmṓn,* which means "without our participation." Paul uses the aorist tense in an ingressive form to indicate entering a condition: "You are still reigning," in other words, "You are full, you are rich, you are ruling." Actually the word "reign" (*basileúō*) is used to mean ruling over others, referring to fame. This contrasts with Christians' future role when they shall reign with Christ (see 2 Tim. 2:12). Again it implies seeking something in the physical world which the Lord has promised for the world to come.

Paul is quick to point out how deceived the Corinthians were to think they were really ruling in this world. "And would that you did rule," he says, "and continue to rule, so that we too might reign with you." The Greek verb *óphelon,* in the past tense, indicative mood, as here, expresses a wish that is, at the same time, impossible to attain (see Rev. 3:15). To rule over the world here and now is impossible, although we wish it were true, especially as we suffer so much for Christ's sake in this evil environment. Paul was writing to the Corinthians from Ephesus, where he was greatly persecuted. Read Acts 19 and see what he went through at the hands of devotees of the Ephesian goddess Diana. "I wish it were possible for you really to rule; and then there might be a chance for us to rule with your help," Paul says in effect. But that day will only come when we shall live and reign with Christ in His kingdom.

LESSONS:

1. Worldly satisfaction divides into three categories: health, wealth, and power over others. These are all cravings of the natural man.
2. The Beatitudes put the realization of these categories in the future world.
3. Pharisaism, something we should all steer clear of, is self-deprivation for the wrong motive, in all three instances given in the Sermon on the Mount—alms, prayers, fasts—to be seen by men.
4. It is unlikely that anyone, believers included, can fully satiate themselves in this world without compromising some ethical principle sooner or later. The kings of the earth, so it reads without restriction, commit fornication with the Whore of Babylon, the goddess of luxury (Rev. 18:3).
5. The norm for believers living godly in Christ Jesus is to suffer persecution, tribulation, and hatred from the world Christ has chosen them out of. Paul speaks of frequent deprivation of food and clothing among the apostles. Premature fame and self-glorification are forbidden. If we humble ourselves, the Lord will exalt us on the day of His choosing.
6. To exchange spiritual wealth for worldly possessions is spiritual suicide. The Corinthians Paul addressed had become materially prosperous "without" the apostles. He challenges them to exchange these possessions for spiritual blessings.

1 Cor. 4:9 — The Least among Men, the Greatest before God

For I think that God hath set forth us the apostles last, as it were appointed to death: for we are made a spectacle unto the world, and to angels, and to men.

Making the Higher Choice

What should be the attitude of the Christian toward seeking physical pleasure, material wealth, and worldly fame? In 1 Corinthians 4:8, the apostle Paul told the Corinthian Christians that they had enjoyed all these things, but that these were not the recompense that comes to faithful believers. They had sought that which earth bestows and had received it. That's the privilege of both unbeliever and believer. A believer, however, has the choice of forfeiting pleasure, wealth, and fame for that higher reward that will be his in heaven. The Corinthian Christians had made their decision—to eat their cake here on earth, so to speak—an attitude Paul wants to correct in them.

In verse 9, however, Paul proceeded to state the apostolic position, the choice which he and the other apostles had made. "For I think that God hath set forth us the apostles last. . . ." That is in contrast to you Corinthians, who have chosen to be first here on earth.

Not everyone is willing to accept this choice however. A young man who was trying to establish himself as a peach grower had worked hard, and invested all his money in a peach orchard. It blossomed wonderfully, but then came a killing frost. He didn't go to church the next Sunday, nor the next, nor the next. His minister went to see him to discover the reason. The young fellow exclaimed, "I'm not coming any more. Do you think I can worship a God who cares for me so little that He would let a frost kill all my peaches?"

The old minister looked at him a few moments in silence, then said kindly, "God loves you better than He does your peaches. He knows that while peaches do better without frosts, it is impossible to grow the best men without frosts. His object is to grow men, not peaches." We are sometimes so concerned about our material possessions that we fail to realize that setting our heart upon them can stunt our spiritual development. God often has to open our eyes to life's real values by taking from us its lesser ones.

Paul speaks here as a representative of the apostolic group. "For I think that God hath set forth *us*. . . ." He was speaking primarily of the apostles, but there is also a secondary reference to all the blessed whom God indwells and who have chosen a life of sacrifice instead of a life of abundance and luxury. Some Christians choose all they can get on earth, and others prefer to place their treasures where they can enjoy them not only for threescore years and ten but for eternity.

The implication here, however, is that, as an apostle or servant of Christ, you ought to belong to the group of sacrificing Christians—either that, or not profess to be an apostle or servant of Christ at all. If the minister, the missionary, the Christian worker, does not live as if heaven were his permanent home, he might as well not preach or teach others. It is a serious and awesome responsibility to be a servant of Jesus Christ.

You have to have the mind of Christ and be willing to live as He did, if you want others to listen to you and become Christlike.

A wealthy university graduate chose to live frugally in a single room, cooking his own meals. As a result he was able to give two million dollars to foreign missions. In explanation of his choice he wrote these words: "Gladly would I make the floor my bed, a box my chair, and another box my table, rather than that men should perish for want of knowledge of Christ." I am not suggesting that all Christians are called upon to forfeit the normal comforts of life; only that when God calls them to a life of sacrifice they be willing to leave all and follow Him.

Some missionaries were fleeing for their lives from pursuing bandits. They huddled together in an old abandoned building. It was filthy and vermin-ridden. Among the missionaries were Archibald Glover and his family. After a wretched night, little five-year-old Hendley Glover said, "Daddy, I think Jesus must have slept in a place like this when He had nowhere to go." "Yes, my boy, I think it very likely," answered Archibald.

"Then," said little Hendley, "we ought to be glad to be like Jesus, and suffer for Him."

There is a beautiful contrast between verses 8 and 9. All the verbs in verse 8 are in the aorist tense, indicating that the pleasure, wealth, and fame enjoyed by the Corinthians were their personal achievement. "You became full to satiety, you enriched yourselves, you became kings." This was all their own accomplishment. But in verse 9 the subject of the verb is God. "For I think that *God* hath set forth us the apostles last."

The verb *apédeixen*, "hath set forth," has God as its subject and the apostles as its object. The condition in which the apostles were found was not the result of any default on their part or the sheer fate of circumstances. It was the guiding hand of God. This verse is in full agreement with the truth the same apostle stresses in Romans 8:28: "And we know that all things work together for good to them that love God, to them who are the called according to his purpose."

"The Last Shall Be First"

Did you ever study plane geometry in school? If so, you know that, for every given theorem, you had to prove the truth of your postulate. And when you had proven it, you wrote QED at the end, meaning that you had demonstrated it, and it was so.

That's the significance of the Greek verb *apédeixen,* from *apodeíknumi,* "attest, set forth," in 1 Corinthians 4:9. It is akin to "he proved." The Lord had told His disciples that they would be persecuted and be considered the very offscouring of the earth. And now they were in the fray of the battle, in the situation predicted. Therefore in them God demonstrated what He set out to prove, that they would last through the predicted circumstances. On the forehead of the disciples could be written QED, *apódeixis,* "proof." They were proven by God, they lasted through.

If steel is to be used in a reliable manner, it must be tested and proven. So must the servant of Christ. Someone describes his visit to a steel mill as follows: "All around me were little partitions and compartments. Steel had been tested to the limit, and marked with figures that showed its breaking point. Some pieces had been twisted until they broke, and the strength of torsion was marked on them. Some had been stretched to the breaking point, and their tensile strength indicated. Some had been compressed to the crushing point and also marked. The supervisor of the steel mill knew just what these pieces of steel would stand under the strain. He knew just what they would bear if placed in a great ship, building, or bridge. He knew because the testing room revealed it."

It is often so with us as God's children. God doesn't want us to be like vases of glass or porcelain. He doesn't want us to be hothouse plants, but storm-beaten oaks; not sand dunes, driven with every gust of wind, but granite rocks withstanding the fiercest storms. To make us strong He must bring us into His testing room of suffering. Better the storm waters with Christ than the smooth waters without Him.

If you were to visit Paris, you could see the statues of two men, both named Louis. The first is of Louis XIV, France's absolute monarch, who is remembered today chiefly for his exclamation, "I am the State." He represents one of the supreme achievements of greatness through power. His philosophy of life was that the whole nation and the world, insofar as he could compel it, should serve him.

A few blocks away is a less pretentious statue. There is no uniform on this figure carved in stone, no badge of office, no sword, no crown. It is a memorial to Louis Pasteur, the servant of humanity and servant of God. His life of unselfish, devoted research conferred immeasurable benefits upon all humanity in all the years to come through overcoming disease and suffering.

The statue of the monarch is nothing more than a sculpture; the statue of Pasteur is a shrine, where pilgrims from all over the world pay grateful homage. It is the uncrowned servant of mankind who wears the real crown of men's love and honor. As you look back, would you rather be remembered as Louis XIV who became supreme ruler of France and now has just a statue to commemorate him, or Louis Pasteur who is now crowned as an apostle of mercy? God's Word enjoins us not to be affected by the glamor of the moment but rather by the judgment of eternity.

If you as a Christian have the capacity for occupying a much higher rung on the social, economic, or political ladder, but for the sake of Christ are occupying a lowly place, it may sometimes cause you a momentary pang of regret. However, there is no greater satisfaction than temporarily to occupy the last place for Christ's sake, out of love for Him who occupied the lowest place for you. He relinquished the glory of heaven to come down to earth as a helpless Babe, born in a stable, growing up as a carpenter by trade, being rejected and vilified by those whom He offered the gift of eternal life, and finally dying on a cross, the sinless One paying the penalty for the sins of mankind.

I can well imagine how Peter felt when he said to Jesus, "Behold, we have forsaken all, and followed thee; what shall we have therefore?" (Matt. 19:27). Study Jesus' answer carefully: "Verily I say unto you, That ye which have followed me, in the regeneration when the Son of man shall sit in the throne of his glory, ye also shall sit upon the twelve thrones, judging the twelve tribes of Israel. And everyone that hath forsaken houses, or brethren, or sisters, or father, or mother, or wife, or children, or lands, for my name's sake, shall receive a hundredfold, and inherit everlasting life. But many that are first shall be last, and the last shall be first" (vv. 28–30).

The last place is occupied only temporarily, while the first place will be occupied forever. It's worth sacrificing earth's honors and rewards for the joy that is set before us.

The Willingness to Risk Our Lives for Christ

In this world, we normally congratulate those who have achieved some degree of success and fame in their chosen field. But the Bible tells us that God sees not as man sees. His values are often far different from human values. The apostle Paul caught a vision of this when he enumerated what God had proved Christ's disciples to be, as they labored for Him.

1) They were at the bottom of the social ladder, last, *eschátous.* That's the Greek word from which we get "eschatology," the study of last things. This was in contrast to what the carnal or immature Christians in Corinth had been able to achieve: satiety, riches, and power or fame. While they were enjoying all this, God permitted the consecrated apostles to be at the bottom of the scale of pleasure, wealth, and fame. But to be where God places and

proves you is far better than any elevated position you yourself could achieve. If you are the last, you have nothing to pride yourself on except the One who put you there.

2) They were "sentenced to die." The Greek expression is *hōs epithanatíous,* as if you were condemned to die at any moment, or on the verge of death. This doesn't mean that any of the apostles to whom Paul refers had at that time been actually tried in court and were awaiting their execution date. It refers rather to the readiness of an apostle or servant of Christ to die at any time for His sake.

A small party of missionaries were invited to Tibet at a time when missionary activity was forbidden there. They were told their task was to help stem the tide of a plague that was raging out of control. When the plague was over, the government asked the missionaries to leave. But these servants of Christ felt a responsibility to minister to the souls of the Tibetans as well as to their bodies. The authorities threatened to kill them, but the fear of death did not deter them. They stayed on.

One night the Tibetans encircled their house with flaming torches. They began dancing around in a wide circle, ever diminishing in size seeking to achieve their aim of setting the place ablaze. The missionaries fell to their knees in prayer, and became so intent as the wild chanting came closer that they never realized it had ceased. When they arose, the mob had dispersed, and they were allowed to remain.

Years later, one of their converts told them that he had been in the circle, and that they had every intention of burning the missionaries to death with their house. However, as they approached the dwelling, there stood before the door a figure in white apparel holding a flaming sword. They fled in fright. And thus the door was opened for the gospel in Tibet, because God honored the faith of those who were willing to die at any time for their Lord.

Although many of the first-century apostles died a martyr's death, Paul did not intimate that all would. We must take into account the adverb *hōs* in our text; the Lord has proven us "as if" we were sentenced to die at any time. He has proved our readiness to die for Him, Paul says. It is our attitude toward life and death that the Lord wants to prove worthy of Him who gave His life as a ransom for us, when He could have saved it.

However, as servants of Christ we are not to precipitate danger or invite unnecessary persecution. We should not bring ourselves to the brink of death, but should be ready for such a situation if and when the Lord decided to bring it about. Let us not tempt God by irresponsible behavior, because self-incurred martyrdom does not bring the glory to God that He desires.

I would be yielded to Jesus,
Bearing His banner on high,
Ready to live for His glory,
Equally ready to die!

I would be yielded to Jesus—
Completely forever, His own!
Living my life for His glory,
Yielded to Jesus alone.
—Connie Calenburg

How Does Your Life Square with Your Profession of Faith?

In the last two sections, we have seen how the disciples of the Lord Jesus were made willing to accept a lowly place in life, and even to face death itself if necessary, for God's glory. It's interesting to note how the disciples and apostles are said to have found their death:

> Matthew suffered martyrdom by being slain with a sword at a distant city of Ethiopia.
>
> Mark expired at Alexandria, after being cruelly dragged through the streets of that city.

Luke was hanged upon an olive tree in Greece.

John was cast into a large kettle of boiling oil, but escaped death in a miraculous manner, and was afterward exiled to Patmos, where he died.

Peter was crucified head downward in Rome.

James the Greater was beheaded in Jerusalem.

James the Less was thrown from a lofty pinnacle of the Temple and then beaten to death with a blacksmith's club.

Bartholomew was flayed alive.

Andrew was bound to a cross from which he preached to his persecutors until he died.

Thomas was run through the body with a lance at Coromandel in the East Indies.

Jude was shot to death with arrows.

Matthias was first stoned and then beheaded.

Barnabas was stoned to death at Salonica.

Paul, after various tortures and persecutions, was at length beheaded at Rome by the Emperor Nero.

Such was the fate of these servants of Christ according to various traditional sources. As disciples and apostles their lives were constantly at stake. In certain sections of the world this is still true today of the missionaries of the cross. Death, physical death, may be around any corner. This is really not a detriment to anyone's life but a great blessing. To be ready to die at any moment, and to be sure that you are in the center of God's will, is cause for the greatest peace of heart anyone can enjoy in this life. You can live fully when you are ready to surrender life as if you had accomplished all that God meant for you to do till then. What would you do if this were to be the last day of your life? That's the attitude you should have now. If God were to put you to the test, would He prove you willing to die for Him?

Paul was willing to be made a spectacle before all. The word "spectacle" in the King James Version is actually "theater," *théatron* in Greek. The word is derived from the verb *theáomai*, which means to see or observe with our physical eyes. People go to the theater to watch other people engaged in some sort of drama. In the ancient world, everywhere you go you will find the ruins of a theater. It was actually a place of visual education and entertainment for the people.

When we say we are Christians, the world may not listen. But when we act like Christians, in all sincerity, of course, it becomes a living drama that commands attention.

Gustav Dore, the famous artist, once lost his passport while traveling in Europe. When he came to the boundary post between two countries and was asked for his passport, he fumbled about and finally announced, "I have lost it, but it is all right. I'm Dore, the artist. Please let me go in."

"Oh, no," said the officer. "We have plenty of people representing themselves as this or that great person! Here is a pencil and paper. Now, if you are Dore the artist, prove it by drawing me a picture."

Dore took the pencil and drew some pictures of scenes in the immediate area. "Now I am perfectly sure you are Dore. No one else could draw like that!" said the officer as he allowed Dore to enter the country.

So it is with us. People follow what we do on the stage of life. They look to see if our conduct squares with our profession. Are we drawing the picture of Christ, as it were, or of a different person? What the world wants to see is reality in our actions. It has been said that God has great and wonderful things to display if He finds suitable showcases. Are you a good showcase for Jesus Christ?

The world watches us, says Paul, just as people go to watch a theatrical performance. They follow our actions and our words. They evaluate us. They learn through what we do and what we say.

When Dr. Will H. Houghton was pastor of Calvary Baptist Church in New York City, a glib-tongued salesman came into his study and offered him some oil stocks that he said would make him a fortune. Dr. Houghton looked at the man and said in substance, "If this stock is as good as you say, why aren't you rich? You come in here in a shabby suit, with shoes run down at the heels, and expect me to believe you represent a going concern? I suggest you get into some line of work that produces representatives who inspire more confidence in their product."

By our actions, our love, our spirit of self-sacrifice, do we inspire confidence in the Lord whom we profess to serve, and whom we seek to lead others to accept as Saviour and Lord? In the lines of an oft-quoted poem, remember, "We are the only Bible the careless world will read. . . . What is the gospel according to you?"

The Drama of Your Life

"All the world's a stage," said Shakespeare, "and all the men and women merely players." But players presuppose an audience, and in writing to the Corinthian Christians Paul tells them that the audience watching the lives and actions of the apostles was both earthly and heavenly. "For we are made a spectacle . . . to angels, and to men."

The theater in ancient Corinth was large and open-roofed. Often there was a full house to see its variety entertainment. The officials came and so did the whole city. Paul is telling the Corinthians that God's theater is larger than that, and open-roofed under the vault of heaven. The people who play in a theater are often quite famous. In our day we call them stars. Popularity and theater performances are almost synonymous. But the apostles were not leading the lives of popular theatrical stars. Their lives were not filled with pleasure; they were not rich or famous. They were last on the social and economic ladder.

And yet they performed with an audience larger than those who were swimming in pleasure, wealth, and fame. They had a vertical audience as well as a horizontal one. Angels from above watched them, and men from every walk of life.

To be admired is one of man's deepest desires. It is inherent in our Adamic nature. The people of the world and carnal or immature Christians actively seek admiration. The worst affront you can give such people is not to pay any attention to them. But deeply committed or mature Christians don't speak or act for the purpose of being admired, or of drawing attention to themselves. Nevertheless that is inescapable. Though they don't seek it, yet heaven and earth cannot ignore them. "We became a theater to the world," declares Paul, "both angels and men."

Observe the verb "we became." In the King James Version it reads "we are made." In Greek it is *egenéthēmen,* from the verb *gínomai,* meaning "to become." Since the verb is in the aorist tense, passive voice, it should be translated, especially in this context, "we were made to become." It indicates that the apostles were not putting on a show, but that God Himself caused them to be observed by angels and men.

A theatrical presentation is a pretense. It's acting the part of someone else. It's making oneself temporarily be what one is not. But that's not what sincere and dedicated Christians do. They don't pretend to be what they are not. The Christian plays a role in this world, but he acts out what Christ has transformed him to be, and not what he merely makes a pretense of being.

The apostles became a spectacle to the world. It was not an occasional show of Christianity they put on, but their whole life was made by God to become a show of the Christ-life to the world. And so should our lives be, if we are really spiritual Christians. We are not to put on a mere show of piety, but let our lives be a day-by-day enactment of our life in Christ.

The Christian has a larger audience than any theatrical star because the show is continuous and to a large extent unconscious. He does not play on the stage from time to time for the purpose of calling attention to himself, but his whole life is a show that is being observed whether he realizes it or not. The spectators are also far more illustrious—not only men, but also angels.

In Hebrews 12:1 the apostle speaks of our being "compassed about with so great a cloud of witnesses," and in 1 Peter 1:12 we read of "things the angels desire to look into." Why do angels follow our actions on the stage of life? They watch with wonder the endurance with which we perform our God-assigned roles. Acting is an arduous task. Many actors collapse from the effort involved, often right on stage. The angels watch to see whether we are able to endure to the end of life's drama. They also strengthen and minister to us. "Are they not all ministering spirits, sent forth to minister for them who shall be heirs of salvation?" (Heb. 1:14).

Angels do follow our activities and they rejoice over our fruitful witnessing. In Luke 15:10 the Lord Jesus says, "there is joy in the presence of the angels of God over one sinner that repenteth." In order for them to rejoice, they must necessarily observe what is going on. We may be confident that angels do observe us and enable us to endure.

St. Francis said one day to one of the young monks, "Let us go down into the town and preach."

They passed through the streets and returned to the monastery without having said a word. "You have forgotten, father," said the young man, "that we went down to the town to preach."

"My son," Francis replied, "we have preached. We were preaching as we walked. We have been seen by many: our behavior has been noticed: it was thus that we preached. It is no use, my son, to walk anywhere to preach unless we preach everywhere as we walk."

Wherefore, seeing we are compassed about by so great a cloud of witnesses, let us play our part nobly, looking unto Jesus, the Author and Finisher of our faith.

Who's Watching You?

"When I get to heaven, Will I be an angel?" a little girl asked her Sunday school teacher. She was quite surprised when the teacher told her that this was a mistaken notion, and that the Bible did not teach this at all.

R. A. Torrey, in answer to the question, "Has every child a guardian angel?" quotes Matthew 18:10: "Take heed that ye despise not one of these little ones; for I say unto you, that in heaven their angels do always behold the face of my Father which is in heaven." He comments: "The angels of the children here spoken of are the angels who watch over the children. This seems to be the plain teaching of the text. Some explain the text in another way, that the angels of the children spoken of here are the departed spirits of the children in the glory, but there is not a hint in the Bible anywhere that the departed spirits of human beings are angels. The clearest distinction is kept all through the Bible between angels and men. The old hymn, 'I Want to Be an Angel,' has no warrant in Scripture."

Angels are spiritual creatures, created by God for the service of mankind. As John Calvin says, "The angels are the dispensers and administrators of the divine beneficence toward us; they regard our safety, undertake our defense, direct our ways, and exercise a constant solicitude that no evil befall us."

In the Bible we have many instances of angels exercising these functions.

In the book of Acts we read that Philip the evangelist was preaching in Samaria. Men followed what he was doing, but so did angels. One of the angels acted as God's messenger to him. "And the angel of the Lord spake unto Philip, saying, Arise, and go toward the south unto the way that goeth down from Jerusalem unto Gaza, which is desert" (Acts 8:26). The angel knew that Philip would meet an Ethiopian there to whom God wanted him to witness.

While John was on the island of Patmos, an exile for Christ's sake, angels ministered to him. It was there that the Lord revealed to John the unfolding panorama of the future, "by his angel" (Rev. 1:1).

In the 5th chapter of Daniel we find that an angel was following the ungodly actions of Belshazzar in Babylon. The king had invited a thousand of his followers to celebrate the greatness of his kingdom. They desecrated the sacred vessels they had taken from the Temple at Jerusalem. They worshiped before idols of wood and stone, silver and gold. The hand of an angel sent from God wrote on the palace wall, "Mene, mene, tekel, upharsin," which meant, "Your kingdom is finished. You have been weighed in the balances and found wanting" (see Dan. 5:25–27).

Later on, in Daniel 9:22, we read that it was an angel who informed him what was going to happen in the world ultimately.

In other instances we read of Jacob being ministered to by angels. It was an angel who announced the changing of his name to Israel at Peniel (Gen. 32:1, 24–30, Hos. 12:3–6).

Angels followed the lives of Moses and Abraham (Ex. 3; Num. 20:16). Isaiah, speaking of the children of Israel coming out of Egypt, says, "In all their affliction he was afflicted, and the angel of his presence saved them: in his love and in his pity he redeemed them; and he bare them, and carried them all the days of old" (Is. 63:9).

In the New Testament, we read that it was an angel who appeared to Zacharias the priest and announced that his wife would bear him a son, John the Baptist. It was the same angel Gabriel who announced to the virgin Mary that she was going to bring forth Jesus (Luke 1:35). And the same angel instructed

Joseph to take Mary as his wife, in spite of the fact that she was already expecting a child as a result of the energy of the Holy Spirit in her life (Matt. 1:20).

We who love and serve the Lord are being followed by angels. They follow our performance on life's stage and assist us when we are in danger of faltering. Their assistance is worth more than the reliance the natural men and carnal Christians place on their accumulated pleasures, resources, and people over whom they exercise power.

You may be at the bottom of the social, economic, and political ladder, Paul tells the Corinthians, but look who's watching your drama of endurance in the world—angels! That's more important than having all the armies of the world at your command. It's interesting to note that after the word "world" Paul mentions "angels" before "men." Angels are more important spectators for the Christian than men are.

The word for "world" in 1 Corinthians 4:9 is *kósmō* (dative of *kósmos*), which refers to the created material universe. Paul doesn't use the word *aiṓni*, "age," which would have implied time, but *kósmō,* the material universe as we know it. In our present state of existence as an immaterial spirit-soul and a material body, we are followed and influenced by the created material world around us and above us. But the material *kósmos* as we know it is also being linked with purely spiritual forces and personalities such as those of the angels.

This is especially true of those of us who are basically "spiritual" in our born-again personalities. Who can deny that metaphysical forces influence and inspect us in our physical world?

Our Angel Guardians

If an angel from heaven suddenly became visible to you as you were sitting alone, what would your reaction be? An ancient saint admonished Christians in these words: "In every apartment . . .

in every corner, pay a respect to your angel. Dare not do before him what you dare not do before others. Consider with how great respect, awe, and modesty we ought to behave in the sight of the angels, lest we offend their holy eyes, and render ourselves unfit for their company. Woe to us if they who could chase away our enemy be offended by our negligence, and deprive us of their visit."

We have a number of illustrations in Scripture that show angels observing the believers on earth and assisting them in times of need. The angels are the created but immaterial personalities of heaven who can take on temporary form and shape at will, so that they can at times actually be observed by the permanently material personalities of men who in their basic essence are spiritual beings. It is not a critical and chastening oversight that the angels exercise on behalf of dedicated apostles and lay Christians, but rather a helpful one.

One illustration concerns the life of the prophet Elisha. While he was at Dothan, the King of Syria sent his army against him. One of Elisha's assistants informed Elisha that the armies of the enemy had surrounded them. Elisha replied, "Fear not: for they that be with us are more than they that be with them" (2 Kgs. 6:16). Elisha then prayed that his assistant might see the invisible armies on which Elisha was counting. "And the Lord opened the eyes of the young man; and he saw: and, behold, the mountain was full of horses and chariots of fire round about Elisha" (v. 17). This was the angelic host sent by God to encourage and protect Elisha.

We also find an interesting account of an angelic visitation to Paul in Acts 27:23–25. And it may be that this event was vivid in his mind as he wrote to the Corinthians, "We became a theater to the world, both to angels and men." It seems that Paul was on his way to Rome in a ship carrying more than 200 persons. A great storm came up, and they were in danger of sinking.

Paul sought to encourage the crew, for they were terrified. His words are significant, for they reveal the role played by angels in the lives of believers in times of danger. "For there stood by me this night the angel of God, whose I am, and whom I serve, saying, Fear not, Paul; thou must be brought before Caesar: and, lo, God hath given thee all them that sail with thee" (vv. 23, 24).

And David in Psalm 91 says that God "shall give his angels charge over thee, to keep thee in all thy ways. They shall bear thee up in their hands, lest thou dash thy foot against a stone" (vv. 11, 12).

The story is told of a little boy who asked his mother if he could take his baby sister out to play. She had just begun to walk alone, and could not step over anything that lay in the way. His mother said, "Yes, if you'll be careful not to let her fall."

The man who tells the story says, "I found them at play, very happy, in the field. I said, 'You seem to be very happy, George. Is this your sister?'

" 'Yes, sir,' he replied.

" 'Can she walk alone?'

" 'Yes, sir, on smooth ground.'

" 'Then how did she walk over those big stones between here and the house?'

" 'Well, Mother told me to be careful she didn't fall, so I put my hands under her arms, and lifted her up when she came to a stone, so she wouldn't hit her foot against it.'

" 'That's right, George. You see now how to understand that text, "He shall give his angels charge over thee. . . . They shall bear thee up in their hands, lest thou dash thy foot against a stone." God charges His angels to lead and lift His people over difficulties, just as you have lifted little Anne over these stones. Do you understand it now?' "

As far as the Christian is concerned, he is better off being watched over and protected by angels than by mighty armies of men. "The angel of the Lord encampeth round about them that fear him, and delivereth them" (Ps. 34:7).

In Acts 12:1–11 we read how Herod the King had imprisoned Peter with the intention of putting him to death. But God intervened. As Peter was sleeping, an angel appeared and awoke him. "Arise up quickly," said the angel. "And [Peter's] chains fell off from his hands" (Acts 12:7). And Peter, following the angel, was liberated from prison, past locked doors and unseeing guards.

This, of course, doesn't imply that God always sends His angels to deliver us in time of trouble. God knows what is best in the furtherance of His over-all plans. If it is His will in His eternal wisdom and providence to deliver us, nothing can stop Him or the angels He sends to accomplish it. Peter and Paul, who were delivered on many occasions, were finally delivered by the hand of God to a cruel enemy, not because God could protect them in some instances and not in others, but because He knows and chooses when it is time for our earthly performance to end.

LESSONS:

1. The believer's higher choice is to forfeit the things of the world for the cause of Christ. This is preferable to indulgence, luxury, in short, the self-satisfaction of this age.
2. The Lord continuously strips us and others of worldly possessions to open our conscience and prompt our choice of the higher value of self-sacrifice, reflected in the mind of Christ, Who, being rich, became poor for our sakes (2 Cor. 8:9).
3. The apostles were the firstfruits of self-sacrifice (Christ Himself the firstborn of all things), God proving them to be the experiential—as well as doctrinal—cornerstone of the church. They were deprived by God Himself of worldly fame and made spectacles, "theatricalized" (*theáomai*), showcased to the world.
4. God does not ordain fragile Christians in the long-run. We will be weathered by storms for hard service ahead.

5. Since "the last shall be first," it is wise to seek low positions and status for the sake of Christ's kingdom.
6. As the firstfruits of self-sacrifice, the apostles were "sentenced to die." Of course, everyone is, since the "wages of sin is death," but this refers to an imminent martyrdom, the risk associated with serving Christ wholeheartedly. We should not invite disaster into our lives by tempting the Lord, but the least we should expect is persecution proportioned to godly living. The original apostles all died martyrs' deaths.
7. The showcasing of believers is "without commercials"—the "show" is continuous and to a large extent without our consciousness. The audience includes "clouds" of angels and past saints, probably demons if not Satan himself, and of course friends and enemies. We preach full-time in our words and actions, silences and inactions.
8. Both testaments teach the presence and guardian roles of angels who watch for, delight in, and probably report on, our perseverances. Sometimes they rescue us from very specific threats and circumstances.

1 Cor. 4:10 | Should a Christian Seek Man's or God's Favor?

We are fools for Christ's sake, but ye are wise in Christ; we are weak, but ye are strong; ye are honourable, but we are despised.

Wise Fools

No one wants to be thought a fool, a weakling, or beneath contempt. We all want to be considered wise and strong and worthwhile people. But a Christian is often placed in the position of having to choose between the favorable opinion of men or the approval of God. What a Christian, under the Spirit's guidance, chooses to be for Christ's sake may not be naturally pleasant, but if it is necessary then it can be greatly satisfying.

In 1 Corinthians 4:10 Paul presents three contrasts: foolishness versus wisdom, strength versus weakness, and honor versus disdain. He begins the verse with the personal pronoun "we." Who is meant by "we"? They are the apostles referred to in verse 9: "For I think that God hath set forth us the apostles last." He refers to himself and all others who have chosen to become Christ's disciples.

The word "apostles" here must not be taken in the strict and narrow sense of the Twelve Apostles in whose trust the gospel was placed for faithful transmission. In its wider sense it means all those who are "blessed," *makárioi,* for Christ's sake, as our Lord so eloquently spoke of them in Matthew 5:1–10 and Luke 6:20–24. The important phrase in the Beatitudes is "for my sake" in Matthew 5:11, and "for the Son of man's sake" in Luke 6:22.

The word "blessed" refers to those indwelt by God, who are characterized by *makariótēs,* "blessedness," a quality of deity. The Lord said to His disciples, "Blessed are ye . . . for my sake," because of what I am and have done for you. When we are indwelt by God we are fully satisfied.

The Beatitudes teach us that, if it is necessary for us to confess our spiritual helplessness (poverty of spirit), to be sorrowful because of sin, to be meek (not taking offense at personal insults, but being angry only at sin), to show that we have no righteousness of our own, to be merciful and pure in heart, to be peacemakers, to be willing to be persecuted, reviled, and maligned, all for Christ's sake, we will not be any less satisfied, but rather more.

And then, in the Beatitudes in Luke, Christ pronounces those "blessed" who voluntarily accept poverty, hunger, tears, the hatred and rejection of worldly people, and being reproached and slandered for the sake of the Son of man. The Christian who is "blessed" is willing to undergo all these privations of life in a spirit of acceptance and even joy.

Worldly people may think a Christian who embraces poverty for the sake of Christ is "crazy" for not keeping what he is able to earn for himself, to be spent for his own pleasure. According to the judgment of the natural man, that person is "crazy"—a moron—who gives away so much of what he has that he himself must do without. Sacrifice is foolishness in the eyes of the world.

Paul, with all his natural ability and intelligence, could undoubtedly have been a successful businessman. But he chose to use his mind and enterprising ability for the Lord. As far as the world was concerned, he was a fool, but as far as God was concerned he was wise.

The decisions Christians make often seem foolish to the world because the Christian seeks not his material advantage or comfort but God's glory. When you put God in the center of your life, you are considered wise by those who have done the same thing. But selfish people will consider you foolish.

"We are fools [or morons, as the Greek text has it] for Christ" or "for Christ's sake." We must differentiate between the two expressions, "for Christ" (*diá Christón*) and "in Christ" (*en Christṓ*). Notice that there are two prepositions used: "for," *diá,* and "in," *en.* We are considered fools for Christ's sake. Of course, we are not actually fools, but because our wisdom is different from the world's we are considered fools by the world, and we consider the worldly-minded who reject Christ for a life of sin and selfishness to be tragically foolish indeed. But we ourselves don't mind being considered fools as long as we have His approval, and know it is "for Christ's sake."

This reminds me of a street-corner evangelist who often went around wearing a sandwich board with the words, "I'm a fool for Christ's sake. Whose fool are you?"

The Wisdom of Men Versus the Wisdom of God

Why are Christians often regarded as fools? It's because they believe what seems foolish in the eyes of the world: God's Son born in a cattle stall; the Messiah working as a carpenter; the Saviour of the world crucified with criminals; the almighty God buried in a tomb; salvation without any deeds, merits, or virtue on our part; Christ dying for the ungodly; the pious, strict, right-living Pharisee condemned, and the wretched, sinful publican justified. "How unthinkable! How ridiculous!" cries the world. "Only a fool would believe in a religion like that!"

But Paul saw it with clearer vision: "The foolishness of God is wiser than men; and the weakness of God is stronger than men" (1 Cor. 1:25). The very thing that seems foolish to men is in fact eternal wisdom; and the very plan that appears to men as wholly wrong has actually been worked out in the councils of God, and so is divinely right. The way of salvation devised by God is so unique, so far superior to anything conceived by the mind of man, that its apparent foolishness is in reality the most profound and unsearchable wisdom. If we are fools for believing that, we are "fools for Christ's sake!"

The difficult expression in this verse is "But you are [the verb is not there but understood] wise *in* Christ." Who is "you"? The quarreling and proud Christians alluded to in verses 6 and 7, who sought their satisfaction in the things of the world (v. 8). The danger is that consecrated Christians will consider such selfish and proud Christians as still in the world, as not having been born again by the Spirit of God. Paul wants to correct any such misapprehension by saying that they are "in Christ." There have always been selfish Christians in the local churches and in the kingdom of God. Their selfishness ought not to lead to the hasty conclusion that they are unsaved. They are "in Christ" in spite of their natural abilities and achievements.

But the irony is that such selfish Christians consider themselves wise in their selfishness. And others of like mind applaud them as wise. Origen says that Paul was ironically advising the Corinthians to become wise in Christ. Yes, there are many believers who are "in Christ" but who are not disciples or learners in the sense that they are not wise toward God. With one hand they hold on to the Lord and with the other the world. They are fence-straddlers. Such half-hearted Christians can never enjoy Christ to the full extent that a whole-souled, unselfish Christian can.

Christian, since you are in Christ, don't seek to show off your worldly wisdom, either in the church or to your worldly associates. Preacher, ask yourself as you prepare your sermons, whether you are trying to show the wisdom that will commend you as wise in the eyes of the world, or the wisdom of God, which may lead the world to call you a fool.

In Corinth it was obvious that there were those who were preaching with an eye to acquiring a reputation for wisdom. It is quite possible that Apollos was one of that number. His background of Alexandrian philosophy was a great temptation. Paul had studied under Gamaliel, a prestigious accomplishment, but he was willing to be counted a fool for Christ. We preachers need to watch ourselves, lest we yield to the temptation of using our position to become celebrities, instead of exalting Christ as the Saviour of men. A man may become a famous preacher and not be a true disciple.

The first contrast of foolishness to wisdom here is more closely connected with teaching. But the second contrast concerns conduct: "We, weak, but ye, strong." The expressions "for Christ" and "in Christ" are understood in this antithesis also. "We [are] weak for Christ [or for Christ's sake], but you [are] strong in Christ." What kind of weakness and strength is Paul referring to?

The Greek words are *astheneís* (plural), "weak," referring to people without strength, and *ischuroí* (plural), "strong." *Asthenḗs* (singular) is made up of the privative *a* "without," and the noun *sthénos,* "strength," meaning "without strength." *Ischuroí* (*ischurós,* singular) is a word used for "strong men," referring to leaders who have seized power into their own hands, such as dictators. Those who are in Christ do not seize political or social strength to the detriment of principle. It is rare indeed to find social or political strength being seized without some compromise of spiritual principles. Somehow earthly strength tends to dim our spiritual eyesight. If it comes to a choice between the two, which would you choose?

Undoubtedly Paul is referring here to social weakness and strength. The Christian who wants to live for Christ rarely wields much strength in society, in the economic, educational, and social strata of life. If any such strength comes to him, it is not because he sought it, but because it comes as a result of God's intervention and bestowal. It is not that a Christian is unable to ascend the ladder of influence, but that, as a true disciple of Christ, he will not do it at the cost of compromise with worldly standards of behavior.

The Temptation of Compromise

After Christ's baptism, you remember that He was hurried into the wilderness to be tempted of the devil. And what was the nature of that temptation? It was the same kind that comes to us when somebody says of us, when we are proposing some high course of action, "Don't be a fool."

We read that the first thing Satan said to our Lord was, "If thou be the Son of God, command that these stones be made bread" (Matt. 4:3). In effect he was saying, "That's what the people like; give them that. There's no need for you to go by the way of Calvary. The world respects strength, not weakness. Let them see your miracles. They love miracles. They're a sign of power. Go ahead. Don't be a fool."

But Jesus' response was, "In My view of man, there are things that a man eventually recognizes his need for more than food." Let's imagine the rest of what might have taken place. "Oh, well," said the devil, "if You take that line, let's go up to the top of the temple. Now," he said, "those people down there are all praying for the Messiah to come from heaven. That's what they're there for. Providential, isn't it? Jump down into the midst of them. If You are what You say You are, You won't be hurt. And they will acclaim You as the Messiah descended before their eyes from heaven, and the whole thing will be done. They love that kind of thing."

Yes, Christ was tempted to usurp power at the cost of compromise with principle, just as we are. But He left us an example, "that ye should follow his steps" (1 Pet. 2:21). He chose the seemingly foolish way of the cross to conquer the hearts of men, rather than the way of worldly might and ostentatious miracle.

A Christian who is a faithful disciple often looks weak to a world which cannot understand someone who loves his enemies instead of hating them; who blesses those who persecute him; who prays for those who are spiteful toward him, and turns the other cheek to those who slap him. The world cannot appreciate the strength of character in a man who forgives those who wrong him; who denies himself and says "no" to the things that are tempting to the flesh; who travels a narrow path, and who, if necessary, is ready to forsake father and mother for Christ's sake. They suspect the sanity of a man who serves his neighbor and regards him more highly than himself; who renounces his pride and ambition for Christ's sake, and places no trust in himself, his own merits and works. " 'What a foolish way of life!' Ah, but 'God hath chosen the foolish things of the world to confound the wise; and God hath chosen the weak things of the world to confound the things which are mighty . . . that no flesh should glory in his presence' " [1 Cor. 1:27, 29] (Thomas Coates, *The Chapel Hour*, 53).

The third contrast presented by Paul is "Ye are honourable" in Christ, "but we are despised" for Christ's sake. Observe that the order is changed here. The "you [are] honourable" comes before the "we [are] despised." That is the estimate of the world in regard to how Christians live. The nondedicated ones are accepted and esteemed; the dedicated ones are held in contempt for renouncing the world's values.

The word "honourable" here is *éndoxoi,* "held in honor." It comes from the preposition *en,* "in," and the noun *dóxa,* which means "high repute or recognition," and consequently "glory," which means recognizing a person for who and what he is. The tragedy is that some Christians do not consider being "in Christ" sufficient honor for them, but they seek the honor of men, and in the process often dishonor Christ. There is no greater honor and glory for men and women than to be in Christ. To be recognized by God is far more important than to be recognized by the world.

The word "despised" in Greek is *átimoi,* which is made up of the privative a, "without," and the noun *timḗ,* which primarily means "value or honor." We are without value, in the opinion of the world, because we have sold out to Christ. At best they treat us with condescension; at worst with disdain. We would be fully acceptable to them only if we compromised our position in Christ.

Again let us recall Christ's example. After Satan realized that Jesus could not be tempted to show His strength prematurely, he tried the "honor" bid—to achieve glory among men. He took Jesus to an exceedingly high mountain and showed Him all the kingdoms of the world. Hutton paraphrases the devil's discourse with Christ:

> "Now young man," he said, "do not be a fool. Don't throw your life away. Take my word for it, men are not worth it. They don't want what you are proposing to give them; they know what they want, and it is not what you are proposing. Lower your terms and you can have them now. . . . play up to them, that is to say, play down to them—and you can have the whole thing" (John A. Hutton, "Fools for Christ's Sake," *The Christian World Pulpit*, vol. 105, 86).

Think of it—the kingdoms of the world in a moment of time! "All this power will I give thee, and the glory of them" (Luke 4:6).

That was Satan tempting Christ, and that's how Satan tempts those who are in Christ—to seek the honor and glory of Satan and the world, instead of honor through sacrifice. We can only resist that temptation as Christ did, by rebuking Satan with the Word of God and the standard He sets for our lives.

Was Christ a Fool?

When Jesus Christ resisted the temptations of Satan in the wilderness, His final word to him was, "Get thee behind me, Satan: for it is written, Thou shalt worship the Lord thy God, and him only shalt thou serve" (Luke 4:8). The devil must have gone away muttering under his breath, "Fool, fool! His life won't be worth a snap of the fingers! He's going to throw it away when He doesn't have to."

Has Satan ever tempted you like that, telling you to seek the honor of men, to use your time and talents and energy for your own glory and enrichment, instead of for the glory of God, in accordance with His standards of righteousness?

> Our Lord's own friends thought He was a fool; that must have been a hard thing to bear. His own mother, brothers and sisters, they thought He was beside Himself. The disciples . . . thought He was a fool . . . when Jesus said He was going into Bethany . . . His disciples Peter and John especially remonstrated with Him and asked Him why He proposed to go into Bethany where He had previously been stoned, and Jesus said . . . it is one of those things a man must do. . . . There is no man [who] appears to the world to be so foolish as the kind of man who uses the word "must" and cannot give a reason (see John 11:7–16).
>
> Judas particularly thought our Lord a fool for not asserting His power over His enemies. Some folk hold to the theory that Judas really was not a bad man, but he was a man who thought, and that Judas' ideas in betraying Jesus, were really not to betray, but to force His hand; that Judas believed that our Lord had some mysterious resources to call upon in an emergency.
>
> He planned to betray Him, believing that in the moment when the Roman soldiers were about to lay hands upon His shoulder, Jesus would

> assert Himself and call down the heavenly forces to destroy His enemies, and set up His kingdom in the world. And the night came, and the hour came, and the moment came, and Judas betrayed our Lord with a kiss. And the soldiers laid their hands upon Him, and He allowed Himself to be led away. And Judas thought He was a fool (*Ibid.,* 86, 87).

Pilate thought Jesus was a fool. He, like other Roman procurators, was scared that the Jews would revolt and his authority be lost. Actually we should not think of Jesus as standing before Pilate, but of Pilate standing before Jesus. In effect Pilate was asking Jesus, "What are you out for? What's your idea? What are you trying to accomplish?" And Jesus told him, "I am come to be a martyr to the truth." That's how the Greek reads. A martyr was basically a witness, according to the meaning of the Greek word (*Ibid.,* 87).

> "What is truth?" It was as though he had said, "My dear young man, take it from me, human beings are not worth the kind of thing You are proposing. You are wanting to show them pearls . . . but they are not looking for pearls. They will let You down. They will let You die. They will forget all about You. I know them. . . . Do not be foolish; You are young, only thirty-three" (*Ibid.*).

But was Christ a fool? He knew that it was only by the seeming foolishness of the cross that men could be saved. Wisdom—divine wisdom—led Him to Calvary. His was not a wasted life but a sacrificed life, for the redemption of mankind.

The life you give to Christ is not thrown away, wasted, lost. It is a life buried with Him and then raised again in glory, even as His was. "Whosoever shall lose his life for my sake and the gospel's, the same shall save it" (Mark 8:36).

An unknown author penned these revealings:

> Jesus and Alexander died at thirty-three;
> One lived and died for self; One died for you and me.
> The one died on a throne; the other on a cross;
> One's life a triumph seemed; the other but a loss.

One led vast armies forth; the other walked alone;
One shed a whole world's blood; the other gave His own.
One won the world in life and lost it all in death.
The other lost His life to win the whole world's faith.

Jesus and Alexander died at thirty-three;
One died in Babylon; and One on Calvary.
One gained all for self; and One Himself He gave;
One conquered every throne; the other every grave.

The one made himself God; The God made Himself less;
The one lived but to blast; the other but to bless!
When Alexander died, forever fell his throne of swords;
But Jesus died to live forever Lord of lords.

Jesus and Alexander died at thirty-three;
The one made all men slaves, but Christ made all men free.
One built a throne on blood; the other built on love;
The one was born of earth; the other from above.
One won all this earth, to lose all earth and heaven.
The other gave up all, that all to Him be given.
The one forever died, but Christ forever lives;
He loses all who gets, and wins all things who gives.

Adapted

LESSONS:

1. The Beatitudes teach us that satisfaction or blessedness comes with dependence on God, sorrow for sin, meekness in the face of insults, self-depreciation because of sin, mercy, purity in heart, peace-making, and a willingness to be deprived and persecuted for the sake of Christ.
2. The world's opinion of such a life is that it is for fools. This is the thinking of the natural man. The biblical view, however, is that foolishness for the sake of Christ is actually the eternal wisdom of God which is wiser and stronger than the wisdom of the world.
3. The wisdom of the world is not neutral towards the wisdom of God. It attacks with a great deal of hostility the doctrine, ethics, and ritual of the church—all accounted as worthless.

4. Paul commends "foolishness **for** Christ" as preferable to "wise [i.e., wisdom] **in** Christ," weakness to strength, and deprecation to honor. Even spiritual wisdom in Christ should not be shown off in the church. Of much greater impact is a life of sacrifice for the Lord.
5. Political, business, and/or social status' are rarely seized without compromising some ethical standard and/or spiritual principle sooner or later. Christians may ascend these ladders as a lower-level priority, but they must never do so at the cost of morality.
6. Christ victoriously resisted the devil's temptation to usurp power at the cost of ethical compromise. As our supreme example, we should follow in His footsteps against critics from among our relatives, friends, and enemies.
7. Ordained to suffer and die for the sins of the world, the Lord sinlessly resisted every temptation for quick glory and premature establishment of His kingdom.
8. Through the foolishness of the cross itself, the Lord purchased redemption for His people.

1 Cor. 4:11 — *The Joy of Sacrificing for Christ*

Even unto this present hour we both hunger, and thirst, and are naked, and are buffeted, and have no certain dwellingplace

No Exemptions for Christians

One of the ministries that has been my chief joy for many years has been inserting gospel messages as paid ads in newspapers and magazines all over the world. It has been very effective in reaching Hindus, Moslems, and other "unreachables" with the good news of salvation in Christ.

But in order to effect this in most countries, it is first necessary to find a qualified man of God who is willing to suffer the consequences of promoting the gospel so publicly. A man who is afraid to suffer for Christ will never be able to stand the pressures that will be brought upon him.

One of the most difficult non-Christian countries to reach is Muslim Pakistan. At a time when leaders from all over the Muslim world were gathered there to formulate plans to hinder the progress of the Christian faith, a Canadian missionary decided to stick his neck out and approach Muslim newspaper editors about publishing gospel messages. He succeeded in getting them into one newspaper called *Imroze.* The first message drew

1,373 responses from Muslims who wanted to learn about Jesus Christ through the gospel portion and Christian literature offered in the article.

This gave the missionary courage to take more audacious steps. In his letter he wrote: "I was in Lahore, which is about 250 miles from here. I visited the *Mashriq* newspaper office, a national newspaper here in Pakistan. *Mashriq* means 'East.' The men in the advertisement section of their big office were dumbfounded when they realized that a man from such a land of opportunity as Canada had chosen to live in a 'backward' area of the world in order to preach the gospel. It gave me a good opportunity to witness briefly and explain why I was willing to sacrifice and come to Pakistan happily for Christ's sake. They are all just dying to go to Canada.

"The great thing of the visit was that they agreed to take my ad for all the major cities where the *Mashriq is* published, namely, Lahore, Karachi, Peshawar, and Quetta. These cities cover the entire country of Pakistan, almost like the four corners. . . . The pile of mail still unanswered indicated that there could be a total of 2,000 requests for Christian literature from Muslims."

This is a good illustration of the attitude of the apostle Paul intimated in 1 Corinthians 4:11. "Even unto this present hour we both hunger, and thirst, and are naked, and are buffeted, and have no certain dwellingplace." The phrase "for Christ," or "for Christ's sake" (*diá Christón*) in verse 10 has to be understood as the motivation of the attitude of the Christian, and especially an apostle, to be willing to go without the physical necessities of life.

"Even unto the present hour." Why does Paul speak in this way? He closes verse 13 in a similar manner: "Being defamed, we intreat: we are made as the filth of the world, and are the offscouring of all things *unto this day.*" This is what he had found necessary to suffer for Christ's sake up to this point. But that did not mean it had to be like that forever. Paul could only look back over his experiences to see that his Christian life and ministry, to be what it was, had to include sacrifices for the sake of Christ.

The first lesson we learn from this verse is that life in Christ is not exempt from trouble, trial, and privation. Because we are Christians, we are not to suppose we are immune from the common distresses of life. Sickness and care, loss and pain, come to Christians as to others. In fact, sometimes it seems as if the godly had the larger share of life's misfortunes. David recognized this when he wrote, "Many are the afflictions of the righteous: but the Lord delivereth him out of them all" (Ps. 34:19).

We find an excellent illustration of this in the life of Elijah the prophet. God had used him to cause the drought to punish Ahab and the followers of Baal. But the Lord sent Elijah to the flowing waters of the brook Cherith. As he sat there enjoying God's special provision, he may have thought himself exempt from the common sufferings of humanity. But we read in 1 Kings 17:7, "And it came to pass after a while, that the brook dried up." Elijah was deprived, too. He suffered thirst. It was God's way of teaching him that even as God's prophet he was not exempt from the physical calamities of life. It was not punishment for disobeying God; it came in spite of his implicit and prompt obedience.

God is the Creator, possessor, preserver, and distributor of all things—physical and spiritual—but He does not necessarily enrich all believers materially. It's easy enough to say, "God's servant deserves the best." He may indeed deserve it, according to human estimate and expectation. But the fact of the matter is that our material abundance is not always proportionate to our commitment to Jesus Christ. In fact, it's often quite the opposite. If ever there was a person who was committed to Christ, it was Paul. And yet, as he looked back upon his entire life up to this point, he said, "Even unto this present hour we both hunger, and thirst, and are naked, and are buffeted, and have no certain dwellingplace." In other words, he says, in spite of his dedication to Christ he has not materially prospered.

The Formula for Happiness

Though the apostle Paul spoke of his great privations endured for the sake of Christ, he knew that the situation could change in the future. He would have welcomed it if it had pleased God to change it. He was just as human as we are in liking to eat, satisfy our thirst, and have a comfortable house to live in. But since privation was the state God permitted him to be in for the sake of the gospel, he did not complain.

Remember what he wrote to the Philippians? "Not that I speak in respect of want for I have learned, in whatsoever state I am, therewith to be content." And then he added, "I know both how to be abased, and I know how to abound: every where and in all things I am instructed both to be full and to be hungry, both to abound and to suffer need" (Phil. 4:11, 12).

There we have the formula for happiness. Of course, we are not to idolize privation and force ourselves to embrace it if there is no need. Certain people think it a virtue to go hungry and thirsty and live like nomads, because they feel there is an intrinsic value in poverty. That's not the point at all. If, for the sake of Christ, we have to go without certain necessities in serving Him, as Paul did, we should do so without complaint. But let's not confuse the goal with the means. Christ should be exalted and glorified, not we by calling attention to our privations. We must ask ourselves, "Who is at the center of my privation—self or Christ? Is it to show off my humility, or to advance the kingdom of Christ?" Others may be able to glorify Christ through their wealth put at His disposal, and still others by their poverty.

I believe that Paul indicated a chronological limit in describing his privations for Christ's sake because he knew that the future, especially when he laid down his mortal body, would be brighter than the present. "Until now . . . up to this hour . . . it has been physically rough," he seems to be saying, "but the future is as bright as the promises of God." Or as he puts it in Romans 8:18, 23, "For I reckon that the sufferings of this present time are not worthy to be compared with the glory that shall be revealed in us. . . . Even we ourselves groan within ourselves, waiting for the adoption, to wit, the redemption of our body."

This hope is what reduces the pangs of hunger, thirst, and exposure to the elements. If we are called upon to suffer for Christ's sake, let us do it with joy, knowing that a better day is coming.

Misjudged by a fellow missionary, David Livingstone gave up his house and garden at Mabotsa, with all the toil and money they had cost him, rather than have any scandal before the heathen. He began in a new place the labor of house and school building, and gathering the people around him. His colleague was so struck with his generosity that he said, had he known his intention, he never would have spoken a word against him. Parting with his garden cost Livingstone a great pang. "I like a garden," he wrote, "but paradise will make amends for all our privations here." Paul says, "I endure all things for the elect's sakes, that they may also obtain the salvation which is in Christ Jesus" (2 Tim. 2:10).

Paul mentions certain specific privations that he and other apostles had to suffer for the sake of Christ. These were physical necessities and constitute the highest degree of sacrifice. To give much out of our abundance, as the Corinthians were giving, as we deduce from 2 Corinthians 8:1–5, is not as great in the sight of God as to be willing as Paul was to go hungry, thirsty, be scantily clothed, beaten up, and homeless.

The translation of 1 Corinthians 4:11 leaves much to be desired. The King James Version begins the verse with "even"—

"Even unto this present hour" we suffer all these things. But the word "even" does not apply at all to the phrase "unto this present hour," but to the verb *peinṓmen,* "hunger." Actually it is the conjunction *kai,* meaning "and." In this usage it stands for emphasis and could be translated "even." The verse would then read, "To this present hour we even go hungry, we even go thirsty, we even go naked, we even are buffeted, we even have no dwelling place." Paul lists these privations as being the height of physical sacrifice. After all, what is more essential for our physical sustenance than food, water, clothing, protection from injury, and shelter? Without these we are exposed to death.

The poet, George Neumarck, knew that a right attitude in the midst of trials could change suffering to blessing. He wrote:

> Leave God to order all thy ways,
> And hope in Him, whate'er betide.
> Thou'lt find in Him, in evil days,
> Thy all-sufficient strength and guide.
> Who trusts in God's unchanging love
> Builds on the rock that naught can move.
>
> Sing, pray, and swerve not from His ways,
> But do thine own part faithfully;
> Trust His rich promises of grace,
> So shall they be fulfilled in thee.
> God never yet forsook at need
> The soul that trusted Him indeed.

Going Hungry for Christ's Sake

The specific privation the apostle Paul speaks of enduring in 1 Corinthians 4:11 is hunger. "We even are hungering, or go hungry." The Greek verb is *peinṓmen,* present active indicative first person plural. This does not mean that Paul was actually without food when he was penning these words, but that his attitude was one of readiness to go hungry whenever necessary for the sake of Christ. He was not to seek such an occasion but to accept it joyfully when God saw fit to allow it. This particular use of the present tense indicates that Paul and other apostles at intervals actually did go hungry, and this was a repeated occurrence, though they were not always hungry, thirsty, or otherwise in want.

The same is true of thirst. "We even go thirsty." If the traveling that the apostles engaged in to make Christ known necessitated their going without food and water for a time, they were willing to accept it. The Lord was not against the satisfaction of physical hunger and thirst. You remember that Satan tempted our Lord when He was in a state of hunger after fasting in the wilderness forty days. "And when they were ended, he afterward hungered" (Luke 4:2). That was a natural result of our Lord's humanity. To desire food is no sin; it is God's gift, to be received with thankfulness.

However, Satan knew how strong a desire for food we all have, including the Lord Jesus. That's why he tempted Him to command the stones to become bread. Could He have done it? Of course He could. But He didn't always do what He could, but only what would serve the higher purpose for which He came into the world.

Can the Lord miraculously feed us when we have to go hungry for His sake? Of course He can. He did it on a number of occasions, as in the case of the Israelites and Elijah. But God is selective in the performance of His miracles. As far as Paul was concerned, he was willing to go hungry for Christ's sake at any time. He felt that God would be equally good if He chose to feed him miraculously—something we have no indication He ever did—or if He allowed him to feel the pangs of hunger to the degree that He saw fit. Our attitude should never be one of presuming to impose on God the results we would like to have.

Let's be careful not to misunderstand Paul and go hungry without a purpose because we think there's some merit in it. Think of that time when the Lord and His disciples were going through Samaria. The Lord sat on Jacob's well while His disciples went to buy food, for it was midday and they must have been hungry. The Lord didn't hinder their doing that which was natural for the sustenance of their bodies. Nor did He make food out of nothing, though He could have done it. But when they brought Him the food, He refused it. Why? Not because He wasn't hungry or didn't need it, but because He was satisfying a higher urge, to bring the gospel to the Samaritan woman.

We, too, should be careful not to allow food to stand in the way of accomplishing the higher task of doing God's will. In this age, when we indulge in food so freely and thoughtlessly, each of us should pause to ask, "How much do my eating habits deprive me of opportunities to make Christ known?" Which comes first in our lives—Christ or the satisfaction of our creature comforts? "Master, eat. But he said unto them, I have meat to eat that ye know not of" (John 4:31, 32).

On one occasion Matthew invited his former colleagues to a meal at his house. Whom did he invite as the guest of honor? Jesus, the Master, Himself. Luke says he "made him a great feast in his own house: and there was a great company of publicans and of others that sat down with them" (Luke 5:29). The laxity of the new religious teacher in not adhering to Pharisaical laws of segregation moved the scribes and Pharisees to indignation. "How is it that he eateth and drinketh with publicans and sinners?" they asked in horrified surprise (see Mark 2:16).

When the Lord met Zacchaeus, He did not hesitate to go into his house, even though He knew that in such a well-to-do home He would be bountifully supplied with food. Jesus ate food as matter-of-factly as anyone to sustain His body. His enemies accused Him of being a glutton and a winebibber. "The Son of man came eating and drinking, and they say, Behold a man gluttonous and a winebibber, a friend of publicans and sinners" (Matt. 11:19, Luke 7:34).

Of course, their accusations were malicious and unjust. "A gluttonous man and a winebibber" is hardly consistent with Jesus' forty days' fast in the wilderness, or the statement that on one occasion He and His disciples "had no leisure so much as to eat" (Mark 6:31). And you remember His gentle rebuke to Martha for preparing too elaborate a meal (Luke 10:40–42).

We are quite sure Jesus was not "a gluttonous man and a winebibber." It does not harmonize with all we know of His character, with the supreme place that He accorded to the things of the Spirit. There was, however, a modicum of truth on which they based their charge, which might give it a superficial justification. Jesus did not make a great virtue of abstinence.

Willingness to Suffer for Christ

The Lord Jesus Christ did not regard fasting as an essential part of religion. In this He differed from the Pharisees, who fasted twice in the week as a religious duty (Luke 18:12). Neither did He resemble His forerunner, John the Baptist, who confined himself to such desert fare as locusts and wild honey (Mark 1:6). Jesus entered the homes of the people and accepted their hospitality without asking whether all the cooking and culinary operations had been carried out according to the strict rules of ceremonial cleanness. He was pleased to be the guest of Peter, Matthew, Zacchaeus, Martha and Mary, Simon the leper, and many others; and He doubtless paid His hosts and hostesses the compliment of enjoying the food set before Him. But when He deemed it necessary for a higher purpose to go without food, He did not hesitate. Such was Paul's attitude. Such should be ours.

The other verb in 1 Corinthians 4:11, "We even go thirsty," has the same meaning. Whenever Paul felt it necessary to sacrifice water for the sake of Christ, he gladly did so. Observe, however, that Paul uses the first person plural. He makes sure to include many other dedicated apostles and servants of Christ. He does not want to give the impression that he alone is willing to sacrifice by going hungry and thirsty.

Each of these experiences Paul describes was also the experience of our Lord on earth. He hungered and thirsted. On the cross He said, "I thirst" (John 19:28). He did not have to go to the cross or suffer thirst; He did it for our sakes. Thirst is a dreadful feeling, as it grows accumulatively worse. And for Him to cry out an agonizing "I thirst!" it must have been unbearable. How many times have we willingly suffered for Christ's sake, because of what He did for us?

In his enumeration of the necessities of life that we as Christians—and particularly as ministers of the mysteries of God—should be willing to forego if necessary for Christ's sake, he mentions food, water, and then clothing. "Even we shiver in the cold." The Greek verb is *gumniteúomen,* which comes from *gumnós,* meaning "naked, stripped, bare." It also means being without an outer garment, something no decent person would go without in public. It signifies being poorly dressed. Again, that doesn't mean we as Christians should go about shabbily or inadequately dressed. But we should be willing to spend less on clothes, or even graciously accept "hand-me-downs," for the sake of Christ.

The principle here is not to consider giving up luxuries a sacrifice, but giving up such essentials as food, drink, and clothing. We can be just as nicely and warmly dressed for less money, and have more money for the proclamation of the gospel. Again the question to ask is, "How wasteful am I in the matter of clothing? Am I dressing to show off?"

Paul may be referring to a willingness to give some of his clothing to others. I've been on both ends of this experience—the receiving and the giving. I remember when I first came to the United States from a warm climate. It was cold and I had no overcoat. How grateful I was to that servant of Christ, Melvin Wampler, who took off his coat and placed it on my shoulders. He went without so that I could be warm. In a similar manner I have often endeavored to do this for others. Believe me, however, there is more joy in giving and going without than in receiving and possessing.

A young man named John saw some ragged boys and invited them to Sunday school. One boy said he would go, but he had no coat. John gave him his coat and went in with him. Years afterward, a teacher of a Bible class told the story. A man in his class said, "I was that boy, and Dr. John G. Patton, one of the most famous missionaries of the ages, gave me his coat." Sometimes a servant of Christ is called upon to keep others warm by being cold himself.

The next verb in 1 Corinthians 4:11 is "we are buffeted." In Greek it is *kolaphizómetha,* which literally means "to be struck with the fist." This is what they did to our Lord when He was tried by the high priests. The same word is used in Matthew 26:67: "Then did they spit in his face, and buffeted him," or "beat him with their fists," as the New American Standard Version correctly renders it. If our Lord was roughly treated and beaten with men's fists, let's ask ourselves, "Would I be willing to undergo rough treatment for His sake?" Or are we going to deny Him in order to avoid being roughly treated, even as Peter denied Him in the hour of His trial? Paul was willing to be struck with the fist, to be roughly treated, for Christ's sake. Are we?

A memorable tribute is paid to the martyrs in the epistle to the Hebrews (11:35): "Others were tortured, not accepting deliverance." Too often we are tempted to accept deliverance, any kind of deliverance, on any pretext, as long as it excuses us from suffering. How much more Christlike it is to pray for grace to "endure unto the end."

As Paul said to those Christians who attempted to dissuade him from going to Jerusalem, "What mean ye to weep and to break mine heart? for I am ready not to be bound only, but also to die at Jerusalem for the name of the Lord Jesus" (Acts 21:13).

Facing Life's Trials with Courage

The last trial of which Paul speaks in 1 Corinthians 4:11 is expressed by the Greek verb *astatoúmen,* "Even we have no certain dwellingplace." This verb comes from *astatéō,* which means "to be unsettled, homeless, not to have a permanent place to live." Paul certainly knew by experience what this meant. He constantly traveled from place to place, with no permanent place to call home.

In this he was like his Lord, who said, "Foxes have holes, and birds of the air have nests, but the Son of man hath not where to lay his head" (Luke 9:58, Matt. 8:20). What was Jesus' permanent address on earth as He ministered to the multitudes? We know He lived in Capernaum, but He had no house of His own. He was a guest in various homes. He who created all things did not select one to make His own special dwelling place. What was Paul's permanent address? No one knows. He was constantly traveling to make Christ known.

How different we are, in our desire to put down roots and achieve a sense of security. When we find a place we like we say, "This is it. I'm not going to move from this place until they carry me out feet first. This is my home, and I intend to stay here for good." Maybe for your own good, but what about the Lord's and His kingdom?

"Too bad, son, that you don't have a home," said a sympathetic bystander to a little boy whose house had just burned to the ground. "Oh, but you're wrong, Mister," said the boy. "We have a home; we just don't have a house to put it in."

We may be sure of this: the servant of Christ may not have a permanent house, but he has a home no matter where he goes for the sake of Christ.

Let's ask ourselves this question: "Am I ashamed at what sacrifices I may be called upon to make in serving Christ?" Two young men were talking about this very thing. One of them said, "I cannot tell you all that the Lord Jesus is to me, or what He has done for me. I do wish you would enlist in His army." "I'm thinking about it," answered the other young man, "but it means giving up several things—in fact, I am counting the cost."

A Christian officer, just passing, heard the last remark, and laying his hand on the shoulder of the young soldier said, "Young man, you talk of counting the cost of following Christ, but have you ever counted the cost of not following Him?"

Paul was not in any way complaining as he counted his deprivations endured for Christ's sake. He considered them inevitable and actually rejoiced in them. Robert Hall, the great Baptist preacher, used to be subject to occasions of great physical pain in the course of which he would roll on the ground in sheer agony. But when the pain was over, the first words he used to say were, "I hope I didn't complain." How much more effective our witness for Christ would be if we didn't complain so much about our trials of faith.

Paul writes: "For Christ's sake up to this hour, we even go hungry, we even go thirsty, we are even dressed scantily, we are even treated roughly, we even have no permanent house to live in." But no word of complaint escaped his lips. He had learned to rejoice in tribulation. He sang his hymns of praise even at midnight when he lay in the inner dungeon at Philippi with his feet fast in the stocks. That was rough treatment. People couldn't help feeling there was something in the faith this man preached when they saw how it sustained him in the sea of troubles that surged over him.

Paul preached the gospel of the love of God. The good news he had to proclaim was that God loved men so well that He gave His only Son to die for them. Well, at any rate, Paul's own conduct confirmed the gospel he preached. For when it was blackest night with him he could sing, because he was so sure of the love of God. He commended himself as a true minister of God by the gallantry and joyful courage with which he faced life's trials and difficulties and calamities. How we face up to the inevitable difficulties and hardships which life brings is a pretty accurate test of the reality of our faith in God.

Chrysostom, the ancient church father, was a beautiful example of true Christian courage. When he stood before the Roman Emperor, he was threatened with banishment if he still remained a Christian. Chrysostom replied, "Thou canst not, for the world is my Father's house; thou canst not banish me."

"But I will slay thee," said the Emperor. "Nay, but thou canst not," said the noble champion of the faith again, "for my life is hid with Christ in God."

"I will take away thy treasures." "Nay, but thou canst not," was the retort; "for, in the first place, I have none that thou knowest of. My treasure is in heaven, and my heart is there."

"But I will drive thee away from man, and thou shalt have no friend left." "Nay, and that thou canst not," once more said the faithful witness; "for I have a Friend in heaven, from whom thou canst not separate me. I defy thee; there is nothing thou canst do to hurt me."

LESSONS:

1. As we learn from Paul, the Christian life is not exempt from troubles, trials, deprivation, sickness, family losses etc. Material blessing in this

life is not proportionate to our commitment to Christ; in fact, it is frequently the inverse; that is, the more committed we are, the less worldly possessions we enjoy. Paul's reference to the "present hour" shows that this was normal for the apostles at this period of time.

2. The formula for happiness is contentment in abundance **and** need. In both circumstances, our goal is to glorify Christ, nor parading either, as the Pharisees did.
3. The apostles apparently lacked food, water, clothing, and shelter at times in their travels and ministries. The Lord can miraculously provide these staples at any time, but when He does not, it is for higher purposes associated with the advancement of His kingdom and glory.
4. There is no intrinsic merit in self-deprivation. We do not impress God with such actions and they certainly do not merit eternal life. Public self-deprivation accompanied by private hoarding of gold or silver is particularly repugnant to God. All things public and private should be done for God's glory. The One who sees in secret rewards publicly, Jesus told us.
5. Neither Paul nor Jesus routinely fasted. But both did so on those occasions when such actions would promote the glory of the Father.
6. Paul and some of the other apostles also intermittently lacked adequate clothing. We should consider not competing in the world of fashion but dressing modestly.
7. Like Christ, the apostles experienced being beaten with fists (k*ola-phizómetha*). One of the greatest temptations is deliverance from physical pain at the cost of denying Christ. Peter apostasied in this manner, but He was "converted" afterward and bitterly repented.
8. Like Christ, Paul had no permanent address. He was always on the move, always changing his P.O. box, so to speak. What a marked contrast this is with our worldly tendency to pull out of the ocean, put into the cove, and drop so many security anchors! No wonder we are so unprepared for the appointed day of our final trip when, unpacked, we watch the Lord pull up the anchors to send us back into the ocean. To better prepare, we should spend much of each day living in the City of God, setting our minds on things above, familiarizing ourselves with the One who alone will carry us across the threshold between worlds.
9. Courage without complaint, witnessed in the lives of Jesus and the apostles, all whom were martyred, is part of our high calling in Christ.

1 Cor. 4:12 | Should a Preacher Work with His Hands?

And labour, working with our own hands: being reviled, we bless; being persecuted, we suffer it.

Manual Labor No Disgrace

King Antigonus, when he had not seen Cleanthes, the philosopher, for a long time, said to him, "Do you continue to grind (referring to the occupation by which he supported himself)?" "Yes, sir," replied the philosopher, "I still grind; and that I do to gain my living, and not to depart from philosophy."

Preaching is spiritual work, but no preacher should consider it beneath his dignity to engage in manual labor when necessary. Jesus Himself worked as a carpenter in Nazareth (Mark 6:3). To work with one's hands has the respect of most people. Paul didn't want people to get the idea that a preacher was an idler. Perhaps those whom he tried to win to Christ were of the opinion that to preach and pray were a lazy man's lot. That's why he chose to work with his own hands, despite the fact that all his life he had been a literary man.

When young, he was sent by his parents to Jerusalem to escape the heathen influence of Tarsus. In Jerusalem he may have had a sister, as reference is made in Acts 23:16 to a nephew. At any rate, while there he studied "at the feet of Gamaliel," although

Tarsus, his home city, was superior at that time in literary pursuits to Athens and Alexandria. It was the birthplace of many Stoic philosophies.

I believe it unlikely that Paul made his living by manual labor before his conversion. His parents must have been well off to be able to send him to Jerusalem to further his studies and become more involved in Judaic teaching. Yet we find Paul with a hand trade as an apostle. Did he learn it after he became a Christian, so that no one could accuse him of making preaching a gainful affair? It would seem so.

"We even labour, working with our own hands." The Greek verb translated "labor" is *kopiṓmen* (act. ind. 1 per. pl.of *kopiā́ō*), which means "to work hard, to become weary, tired, to toil." Although as an educated Jew he had not dirtied his hands with manual labor, he was not too proud to engage in it after he became a Christian. He repeatedly defends his philosophy of a working ministry.

In 1 Corinthians 9:1–15 he defends his right to have a wife, as the apostle Peter had, as well as his right of support from those to whom he ministered. Apparently Paul was a widower, since to be a member of the Sanhedrin he had to be married. He probably preferred to remain unmarried after his wife's death, so that he could have greater freedom to travel, preach, and establish churches. This was not because of a necessity laid upon him but by his own free choice.

The same was true with regard to his support. "Even so hath the Lord ordained that they which preach the gospel should live of the gospel" (1 Cor. 9:14). But he preferred to be self-supporting, so that no one could accuse him of preaching for the sake of money and an easy life.

No doubt some people looked upon his manual labor as demeaning to his office, but in his case at least he believed it was the proper thing to do for Christ's sake. In 2 Corinthians 11:7

he writes: "Have I committed an offense in abasing myself that ye might be exalted, because I have preached to you the gospel of God freely (i.e., without price)?" He didn't do it because the Corinthians were poor and unable to support a minister, but because he didn't want to bring offense on the gospel (see 2 Cor. 8:1–5). He forfeited an available right in order to promote the glory of Christ. If there were more Pauls in the Christian ministry, more of the world would have been exposed to the gospel. Paul gave up his right to be paid, not because there was no money in the treasury—for there was plenty—but because the reputation of Christ to the world and Paul's fellow believers was his overriding consideration.

How beautifully he reminds the Thessalonians of his conduct among them: "For ye remember, brethren, our labour (*kópon,* the noun form of the same word as in 1 Cor. 4:12) and travail: for labouring night and day, because we would not be chargeable unto any of you, we preached unto you the gospel of God" (1 Thess. 2:9). And then again in 2 Thessalonians 3:8 he wrote: "Neither did we eat any man's bread for nought, but wrought with labour (*kópō,* again the same word) and travail night and day, that we might not be chargeable to any of you." It was never because it was not right for a minister to be paid, but because he was willing to forfeit his rights for the sake of bearing a better testimony for Christ.

You Can Be a "Working Missionary"

When the apostle Paul went to Corinth to preach the gospel, he stayed in the home of Aquila, a tentmaker, and engaged in the same trade.

Had Paul expected to be paid everywhere he went to preach, it is doubtful whether he could have established any churches. We would not have had the Epistles to the Corinthians, or to the Ephesians, or to the Thessalonians, or any others from his pen.

How could he ask for pay, since he was the pioneering missionary? When he came to Corinth, was he sent there by a supporting church—the believers he had led to Christ in Philippi, Berea, Thessalonica, or Athens? No, he went as a tentmaker and used that trade to support himself, as we see in Acts 18:3: "And because he was of the same craft, he abode with them (i.e., Priscilla and Aquila), and wrought: for by their occupation they were tentmakers."

Someone reading these lines may be a businessman, as Aquila was in Corinth. Maybe there is no testimony for Christ in your area. Maybe you do not have a talent for teaching and preaching. Did you ever think of employing another Christian who can witness effectively for Christ? You will be served in your business and you will be used of God to provide another Paul-preacher-tentmaker for your spiritually needy community.

Or you may be a preacher who has some trade or profession in addition to being a preacher. If so, don't sit around waiting for some missionary society to send you out, or some church to call you. God has given you two hands with which to earn your living. The goal of a Christian's life should be to make Christ known. Making a living is only the means to the end. Why not discover where there is a need for Christian witness and seek employment there? Thousands of positions are open all over the world for Christians trained in the professions, trades, or services. Don't let them be filled by unbelievers where your testimony is so desperately needed. Would to God that every biblically trained person also had the ability to work at a job to earn his living. Don't seek the jobs that pay most, but the jobs that will take you where your witness for Christ will count the most. That was Paul's philosophy; let it be yours also, and you can help bring about a spiritual revolution in the place God sends you.

Just the other day I received a letter from a man whose company offered him an opening in Malaysia. It's very difficult for a professional missionary to gain admission there. This Christian businessman accepted the offer—which meant living in a strange land without many of the usual comforts. But his presence there has meant the opening of a Christian church in his home. We need missionaries like that, in addition to those who are dedicating all their time to the Lord's work.

And a word to those of you who are professional missionaries: If the Lord lays a burden on your heart for an unreached area, consider getting the training for a needed job and going there as a working man with a missionary's heart. Sometimes, as I have observed missionaries in many parts of the world, I have felt that, had they been also working with their hands as Paul was in Corinth, the effectiveness of the gospel outreach would be greater. Paul was a wise man to realize that such a course made the gospel more acceptable to the people of Corinth and Thessalonica. Let's examine our hearts and attitudes before we conclude that we have no opportunities or results because the Lord is not blessing us. Are we fulfilling God's conditions of blessing?

As a servant of Christ, never feel that it is degrading to labor with your own hands as Paul did. The Lord of glory Himself came down to earth and labored in a carpenter's shop. And "the servant is not greater than his Lord" (John 13:16).

When Bishop Patterson went among the South Sea Islanders, the natives were surprised to see that he was ready to put his hand to anything. He would do a piece of carpentry, wash up things after meals, and teach the little ones to wash and dress themselves. Other people who came to the islands tried to push all the manual labor on to the natives. So to express the difference, they called the bishop a "gentleman-gentleman," and the others "pig-gentlemen."

Jesus Christ when on earth was called "the Carpenter"; and if one of His chief apostles, Paul, worked with his hands as a tentmaker, manual labor ought never to be thought beneath the dignity of a Christian minister.

On a Friday morning an eager young man from Stanford University stood before Louis Janin seeking part-time employment. "All I need right now," said Janin, "is a typist." "I'll take the job," said the young man, "but I can't come back until next Tuesday." On Tuesday he reported for duty. "Why couldn't you come back before today?" Janin wanted to know. "Because I had to rent a typewriter and learn to use it," was the unexpected answer. That quickly prepared typist was Herbert Hoover.

Do you know of a place where there is almost no witness for Christ at all? Learn the job that will take you there. That's being as wise as Paul.

The only place in Scripture that gives us any indication Paul was a tentmaker is Acts 18:3. Priscilla and Aquila were tentmakers, and this verse says Paul "was of the same craft." When did Paul learn this trade? We don't know. Perhaps he learned it before going to Corinth, so he could find employment with Aquila. That's not really a farfetched assumption. You can do the same, with the exception that your employer need not be a Christian, as Priscilla and Aquila were. Your own hands, and the skill you acquire in using them, may help to fulfill your heart's desire to serve Christ where your life will count the most for Him.

When Is It Right to Speak Out?

The Greeks among whom the apostle Paul lived and ministered in Corinth and Thessalonica called the mechanics *banaúsous*, "vulgars." They applied this epithet to those handicraftsmen and artisans who led a sedentary life. Such people were despised among warlike and nomadic people. They considered Paul's manual labor *bánausos*—not hard enough. In modern parlance he was a "softy" in the eyes of these critical Greeks.

It is quite possible that this is one reason why Paul was reviled. Observe that "being reviled, we bless" comes immediately after his statement, "We even labor, working with our own hands." But tent-making was considered a *bánausos téchnē* a vulgar trade, which might very well have given rise to Paul's reviling by the proud Greeks who could always find something for which to criticize him.

The Greek word translated "reviled" is *loidoroúmenoi*, a common expression meaning "to reproach, to abuse verbally, to insult, to revile."

> In public life in Greece, insult and calumny played a considerable part, whether among the heroes . . . in political life in the democracies, in comedy, or in the great orators. Not to be susceptible was part of the art of living, though in fact a great deal of objective harm was done by this love of denigration (H. Hanse, "*Loidoréō*," *Theological Dictionary of the New Testament*, vol. IV, 293).

That's what Paul's enemies were trying to do by reviling him or remonstrating angrily with him.

In the New Testament we find the verb form of this word four times (John 9:28; Acts 23:4; 1 Cor. 4:12; 1 Pet. 2:23), the noun twice (1 Tim. 5:14; 1 Pet. 3:9), and the adjective twice (1 Cor. 5:11; 6:10).

To revile (*loidoreín*, infinitive) is an un-Christian act in those guilty of it. *Loídoros*, "a reviler," is twice mentioned in lists of vices. In 1 Corinthians 5:11 Paul says, "But now I have written unto you not to keep company, if any man that is called a brother be a fornicator, or covetous, or an idolater, or a railer (*loídoros*), or a drunkard, or an extortioner; with such a one no not to eat." And in 1 Corinthians 6:10 he mentions among those who will not inherit the kingdom of God, "nor thieves nor revilers (*loidoroí*), nor extortioners."

In the Old Testament, reviling superiors was particularly forbidden. This is brought out in Acts 23:1–5, where Paul was brought before the Sanhedrin to answer his accusers. Ananias, the high priest, took exception to something Paul said and ordered those who stood next to Paul to smite him on the mouth. Filled with righteous indignation, and not knowing who Ananias was, Paul burst out, "God shall smite thee, thou whited wall: for sittest thou to judge me after the law, and commandest me to be smitten contrary to the law?" This was taken as reviling by those who stood by, because they said to Paul, "Revilest thou God's high priest?" Paul was immediately apologetic and said, "I wist not, brethren that he was the high priest: for it is written, Thou shalt not speak evil of the ruler of thy people."

Was Paul's action in this incident contrary to the claim he made in 1 Corinthians 4:12 that "being reviled, we bless"? Did he just give lip service to such a course of conduct, without carrying through on it in actual practice? Not really. His enemies were stretching a point when they called this reviling; Paul himself considered it righteous indignation. It was rather in the category of sinless anger. He himself in writing to the Ephesians said, "Be ye angry, and sin not" (Eph. 4:26).

The Lord Jesus acted and spoke in the same way under similar circumstances, as we see in Matthew 23. In fact, the whole tenor of His denunciations against the Pharisees could be taken as reviling, especially the words that are almost identical with those of Paul. Compare what the Lord called the Pharisees with what Paul called Ananias: "Woe unto you, scribes and Pharisees, hypocrites! for ye are like unto whited sepulchers" (Matt. 23:27). Paul's term for Ananias was "thou whited wall" (Acts 23:3). The characterization "whited" here actually means "whitewashed for the purpose of hiding your real self." It is an alternate expression for "hypocrite." But nobody dared call such language reviling when it was spoken by the Lord Jesus. They did not indulge in scathing words for the sake of rabble-rousing, but to rebuke those who were using the letter of the law to cloak their failure to keep the spirit of the law. In the name of religion they were oppressing those who were seeking to serve God in spirit and in truth. To keep silence would have been cowardice.

James Russell Lowell had nothing but scorn for such people in the following lines:

> They are slaves who fear to speak
> For the fallen and the weak;
> They are slaves who will not choose
> Hatred, scoffing and abuse,
> Rather than in silence shrink
> From the truth they needs must think;
> They are slaves who dare not be
> In the right with two or three.

Our Lord spoke out in no uncertain terms against evil, regardless of the consequences; and the apostle Paul followed closely in his Master's footsteps. Do we?

How to React to Our Enemies

In the New Testament there are several passages dealing with the way the Christian is to react when he is the object of reviling (*loidoreín*) by others. In 1 Timothy 5:14 Paul advises, "Give none occasion to the adversary to speak reproachfully (*loidoreín*)." This means the Christian must avoid all occasion for calumny (*loidoría*).

The Lord warned believers that because of their association with Him they were subject to reproach. "Blessed are ye, when men shall revile (*oneidísōsin,* used here as a synonym) you" (Matt. 5:11). In the case of the blind man whom Jesus healed, as recorded in John 9:28, we read, "Then they reviled him (*eloidórēsan*), and said, Thou art his (Jesus') disciple, but we are Moses' disciples." Actually this was meant as a slur against Jesus.

We as Christians are to follow the example of our Lord, as recorded in 1 Peter 2:23, "Who, when he was reviled, reviled not again." Consider Him on the cross. When the scornful bystanders tried to make Him answer their reproach, He kept silence, as He had also done before Pilate (see Matt. 26:63; 27:29, 44; John 18:23). Note particularly the similarity of John 18:22, 23 to Paul's experience before the Sanhedrin. The Lord was smitten. "One of the officers which stood by struck Jesus with the palm of his hand, saying, Answerest thou the high priest so? Jesus answered him, If I have spoken evil, bear witness of the evil: but if well, why smitest thou me?" Here we see that the Lord Jesus objected to being smitten, even as Paul did. The Lord is not completely silent when reviled, but here He stresses the fact that His words were not wrongly spoken.

The principle that Christians are to follow is that they are not to revile those who revile them. As 1 Peter 3:9 says "Do not repay evil with evil, or insult (*loidorían*) with insult (*anti loidorías,* reviling against reviling), but with blessing, because to this you were called, so that you may inherit a blessing." But the Christian, as shown by the example of the Lord Jesus and the apostle Paul, need not remain wholly silent when he suffers abuse. He blesses not only by silence, but on occasion by indignant speech.

What does Paul mean by the expression "we bless," which he presents as the Christian reaction to the world's reviling? In Greek the word is *eulogoúmen,* which can be transliterated "eulogize" or "speak well of." It comes from *eú,* "well," and *légō,* "speak." Paul does not use the word *makarízomen*, from which the adjective *makários*, "blessed," is derived (the same word used in the Beatitudes). Only twice does the verb *makarízō* appear in Scripture: in Luke 1:48 in regard to the virgin Mary who was to bear God's Son: "From henceforth all generations shall call me blessed (*makarioúsin*)." This means by implication "indwelt by God," which in her case meant that the Lord Jesus, in whom dwelt "all the fulness of the Godhead bodily" (Col. 2:9) was conceived in her by the Holy Spirit. The generations to come would recognize that fact. The second use of this verb is in James 5:11, where James, speaking of the prophets, says, "Behold, we count them blessed (*makarízomen*), those who endured." The word is not "happy" here, as in the King James Version, but "blessed," as the New American Standard Version correctly renders it. Those prophets who endured persecution and privations we consider as being indwelt by God.

If Paul had used *makarizomen* for "bless" in 1 Corinthians 4:12—"being reviled, we bless"—it would have been completely nonsensical, for it would have meant "we consider them as being indwelt by God." They certainly would not have reviled the apostles if God was in them.

Instead, Paul used the word *eulogoúmen*, "we speak well of." The word "speak" here has the connotation of "wish." We are to wish well to someone who reviles us. But the "well" is not necessarily in accordance with what he does or wishes, for if he is a reviler that can only be the continuation of his evil ways. It is rather what we as Christians consider good for our enemies, and that is their salvation in and through Christ.

We don't love our enemies when we permit them to continue in their evil ways, but when we seek to bring about the necessary change in them for good. That change may be brought about by silence or by speech, by forgiveness or by punishment, depending on the person and the circumstances.

The poet Tasso was once told that he had an opportunity to take advantage of a bitter enemy. He replied, "I wish not to plunder him, but there are things I wish to take from him: not his honor, his wealth, or his life, but his malice and ill will."

Similarly the Christian aims, not at getting even with his enemy, but at winning him to Christ and in the process turning him from an enemy to a brother in the Lord.

Should Christians Expect Persecution?

So far we have seen that, when the apostles were persecuted, they accepted physical deprivation and psychological indignities as part of the price they were willing to pay for serving Christ in a hostile world. As the apostle Paul says, "Being persecuted, we suffer it."

What is the persecution he is referring to? The Greek verb is *diōkómenoi*, "being persecuted," in the present participial form, nominative case, plural number, passive voice of the verb *diṓkō*. It means to put to flight, to drive away. In this sense it is the people of the unbelieving world who try to drive Christians away from their presence. We are like flies in their ointment. Unbelievers are uncomfortable in the company of dedicated Christians and will do all they can to drive them away. The world very rarely tries to convert the Christian to its godless ways; it just wants to get rid of us so that it can pursue its own way unchecked by our presence.

Paul stated this as a principle in 2 Timothy 3:12: "All that will live godly in Christ Jesus shall suffer persecution." The same Greek verb is used here, *diōchthḗsontai*. Observe how all-inclusive Paul makes this observation—"all." No true Christian living in the world will have it easy. If he or she is truly in Christ, and not a compromiser, the world will make it plain their company is not desired. Persecution or an endeavor to minimize their influence in the world is the common lot of all outspoken godly persons.

Thus, when Paul said, "being persecuted, we suffer it," he was giving the negative statement of his previous positive assertion, "we live godly in Christ." The positive statement might have been interpreted as bragging; hence he chose to state the truth negatively. Those whose life is hid with Christ in God daily feed their souls on the invisible realities of another world.

Why, then, do so few Christians suffer persecution today? May it not be because so few live "godly in Christ Jesus"? The world has not changed its philosophy of antipathy toward the Christian, but in many cases the Christian has become worldly. The result is little or no persecution because our godliness has been greatly watered down. As Henry Ward Beecher said, "We preach cream and live only skim milk."

When our godliness begins to be felt, when we have the courage of our convictions, and practice what we preach, the world reacts. Lord Peterborough said concerning his contact with the French theologian Fenelon, "He is an energetic creature. I was forced to get away from him as fast as I possibly could, or else he would have made me pious."

A non-Christian lawyer attended a church service and listened incredulously to the testimonies of some who were known to him for their shady deals and failure to meet their honest obligations. "How did you like the testimonies?" a man asked him at the close of the service. He replied, "To a lawyer there is a vast difference between testimony and evidence." Words are cheap, and it is perilously easy to give a fine-sounding testimony for Christ, but quite another matter to demonstrate evidences of God's purifying power in our lives through Christ. "This people honoureth me with their lips, but their heart is far from me" (Mark 7:6).

Note that the Beatitudes in Matthew 5 give only one verse to each of the individual traits of being poor in spirit, mourning, meekness, hungering after righteousness, mercifulness, purity of heart, and peacemaking. But when it comes to suffering persecution, three verses are employed. In this way the Lord stresses how difficult it is for the world to believe that those who serve Him faithfully are blessed in spite of the world's persecution.

What happens when only one member of a family is converted to Christ? He is often isolated from the rest as a sore thumb. He interferes with their enjoyment of sinful pursuits. That is what the Lord meant when He said that He came to earth, not to bring peace but a sword, indicating that a man's foes would be those of his own household.

Persecution is a criterion of godliness when commitment and dedication to Christ are the cause of it. Why wasn't Judas persecuted? He was with Christ but not in Christ, and Christ was never in him. Look at Mark 10:30, in which Christ makes such extensive promises to those who have left all for Him. In His promise of blessing to them He inserts a word of caution concerning persecution. "But he shall receive a hundredfold now in this time, houses, and brethren, and sisters, and mothers, and children, and lands, with persecutions; and in the world to come eternal life." The word "persecutions" is in the plural number, including all kinds of persecutions, as Gillies summarizes:

> Our Lord was persecuted. Follow him from the manger to the cross. . . . How was he hated by wicked men! . . . called a blasphemer, a winebibber, a Samaritan, nay a devil, and, in one word, had all manner of evil spoken against Him falsely. . . . How did men separate from His company, and were ashamed to walk with Him openly! Again, how was he stoned, thrust out of the synagogues, as a deceiver of the people. . . . scourged, blindfolded, and at length condemned and nailed to an accursed tree! Thus was the Master persecuted . . . and the servant is not above his Master. . . . (John Gillies, *Memoirs of Rev. George Whitefield*, 332).

"If they have persecuted me, they will also persecute you," Jesus said to His disciples in John 15:20. Christian, if you want to be like your Lord, don't expect to escape suffering and persecution!

Overcoming Evil with Good

Why is it that godly Christians are persecuted? It is because of the incongruity of the natures of the believer and the unbeliever.

"Ever since the fall, there has been an irreconcilable enmity between the seed of the woman and the seed of the serpent" [Gen. 3:15] (*Ibid.,* 333). The woman was Mary, who was to bring forth the Son of Man, Jesus. The serpent is Satan.

> Wicked men hate God and therefore cannot but hate those who are like Him; they hate to be reformed, and therefore must hate those who . . . testify . . . that their deeds are evil. . . . If they commend them, they are afraid of being asked, "Why do you not follow them?" . . . [T]hough they may sometimes be even forced to approve their way, yet pride and envy make them turn persecutors. Hence . . . he that is born after the flesh, the natural man, does and will persecute him that is born after the Spirit, the regenerate man (*Ibid.*).

What should the Christian's reaction be? Paul expresses it by the Greek word *anechómetha,* "we suffer it or endure it." The verb is in the middle voice, present indicative. We are not forced to suffer persecution; we choose to do so out of love for Christ. It's up to us how we're to face it. We can resist it and counter-attack.

But Paul says the best policy for the Christian is to endure and restrain himself. In Modern Greek the word has come to mean "to tolerate." The English word "tolerance" is derived from the Latin *tolerare,* "to endure, to bear." But does this enduring mean that we cannot defend ourselves against those who try to harm us and others or the cause of Christ?

As Christians we are to love our enemies as ourselves. Therefore if our love for self is the pattern of our love for our enemies, it must be as good as that for our enemies—an extension of the love we have for ourselves. Therefore our attitude toward persecution does not infer careless abandonment of our lives or what belongs to us. If this were the case, then every effort to restrain the evildoer would be unscriptural. We can endure and at the same time do everything in our power to counteract the designs of the evildoers.

The substantive *anoché* (from the verb *anéchō*), "endurance" or "forbearance," is to be distinguished from two other Greek words: *makrothumía*, "longsuffering," and *hupomoné*, "patience."

> . . . *makrothumía* will be found to express patience in respect of persons, *hupomoné* in respect of things. . . . There may be a resistance to God in *men*, because He respects the wills which he has given them, even when those wills are fighting against Him. But there can be no resistance to God, nor burden upon Him, the Almighty, from *things*. . . . [W]hen God is called *theós tés hupomonés* (Rom. xv. 5), this does not mean, God whose own attribute is *hupomoné* but God who gives *hupomoné* to his servants and saints. . . . in the same way as *theós cháritos* (1 Pet. v. 10) is God who is the author of grace. . . (Trench, *Synonyms of the New Testament*, 198, 199).

Now *anoché*, used in its verb form in 1 Corinthians 4:12, is used of:

> . . . a truce or suspension of arms. . . . *anoché* is temporary, transient. . . . like our "truce," it asserts its own temporary, transient character; that after a certain lapse of time, and unless other conditions intervene, it will pass away. This is true of *makrothumía*, no less (R. C. Trench, *Synonyms of the New Testament*, 199).

Examine Romans 2:4, in which both *makrothumía* and *anoché* occur: "Or despisest thou the riches of his goodness and forbearance (*anoché*) and longsuffering (*makrothumía*); not knowing that the goodness of God leadeth thee to repentance?" God's forbearance and longsuffering have one aim, the repentance of the sinner. The same truth is seen in Romans 3:25, 26: "Through the forbearance (*anoché*) of God; to declare, I say, at this time his righteousness: that he might be just, and the justifier of him which believeth in Jesus." Again the forbearance (*anoché*) of God leads to belief in Jesus Christ.

This intricate meaning of the verb *anechómetha*, "we forbear or endure," throws light upon what Paul means when he says, "being persecuted, we forbear." We endure or tolerate the situation temporarily but not passively. We work with all that is at our disposal to change the persecutor, not reacting immediately in such a way that we lose the opportunity of long-range results. Striking back at our persecutors may be necessary to protect ourselves and others, but it is up to us to devise long-range plans to change our persecutors. And that's what it means to love our enemies, to be temporarily forbearing of them and work toward changing them to be friends. It is overcoming evil with good, not retaliating in kind, or merely passively enduring evil.

LESSONS:

1. Jesus the carpenter and Paul the tent-maker valued manual labor as a means of physical support to fuel the more important task of preaching the gospel. In Paul's self-supporting ministry, this preempted the criticism that preachers are indolent, which may well have been the expectation of Greek culture. This cuts across the grain of modern, missionary-dispensing churches.
2. Among the Corinthians and Thessalonians, Paul especially preferred to be debt free to cut off any occasion of slander that might hinder the spread of the gospel.
3. Aquila may have hired Paul in his tent-making business. If so, this is a good case for Christian employers to hire evangelical believers to plant churches in the local area as well as to enhance morale and work ethics within the business.
4. Carpentry and tent-making no doubt were not the highest paying professions. We can serve the Lord effectively along the entire salary spectrum. It is wrong to correlate directly the Lord's blessing with high pay and fat retirement accounts. Jesus had neither. His security was port-mortem. Only after and through death did He enter His glory.
5. To follow Paul's lead, we would take jobs where there is no or no adequate witness for Christ.
6. Since the philosophic Greeks customarily referred to manual laborers as *banaúsous*, "vulgars" (or "commoners"), it is highly probable that Paul received this reviling predication. But like the Lord Jesus, he blessed his revilers. Jesus Himself says that the believer is blessed when he is verbally abused for the kingdom of God's sake.

7. The Greek verb, *eulógoumen*, means "we speak well"—probably "to" not "of" someone or something. We cannot speak well **of** someone who reviles, unjustly or otherwise, but we can speak well **to** them.
8. The Greek passive verb, *dïṓkomenoi*, "being persecuted," means to be put to flight or chased away. Unbelievers cannot tolerate the presence of believers. They do not want to convert them but to put them out of their presence, to death—the ultimate banishment. Paul states that persecution is directly proportionate to godly living which refuses all compromise.
9. An implied correlate is that those who are not persecuted are not living godly. As Jesus said, if you are of the world, the world will love its own (John 15:19). The Lord came to bring a sword to divide His people from the rest of the world (Matt. 10:34).
10. Regenerated and unregenerated spirits are in natural conflict and have been at odds since the Fall. The wicked are not neutral toward God; they hate Him and His representatives.
11. The Christian will suffer but must endure under the beating of an alien, hostile world highly regulated and engineered by the devil, trusting the God behind the scenes. Endurance is not passive. Unlike floormats, we actively seek to change our persecutors over the long run.

1 Cor. 4:13 | *When Others Lie about You*

Being defamed, we intreat: we are made as the filth of the world, and are the offscouring of all things unto this day.

The Christian Reaction to Slander

One of the hardest things for a Christian to take is slander, especially when he's doing his best to serve the Lord and help others in need. That's one of the tools Satan uses to discourage God's servants. An evil person has no cause for complaint when others speak evil of him, for he has brought it on himself. But it hurts when what others speak of us is sheer falsehood.

In 1 Corinthians 4:11–13, the apostle Paul enumerates the sufferings that he and other apostles had to bear because of their witness for Christ. The first sufferings he mentions are physical: hunger, thirst, scant clothing, violent abuse, and uncertain shelter. And last in this list is the fact that, although they had so much spiritual work to do, they had to engage in manual labor to support themselves.

Then, in the middle of verse 12, he speaks of the sufferings they had to endure in the spiritual realm: being reviled and persecuted. Sometimes, of course, persecution may be altogether physical, but here we believe Paul is referring to spiritual persecution, since it occurs between the expressions "being reviled" and "being defamed or blasphemed."

It is this third form of spiritual suffering in the Christian's service and walk that we want to consider now. Verse 13 begins with the present passive participle, nominative masculine plural, of the verb *dusphēméō: dusphēmoúmenoi*, "being defamed." The Greek verb is a compound of the particle *dus*, conveying the notion of "untowardness, as hard, ill, unlucky, dangerous," like the English prefixes "un" or "mis." It is the opposite of *eu*, which has a good connotation. We have words prefixed by eu, such as euphemism (that which sounds good), and euphony (pleasing or sweet sound).

The other part of the compound verb from which *dusphēméō* is derived is *phēmí*, "to speak, to utter a sound." This involves our "fame," our good reputation, which is being distorted. The defamer is taking our good name and presenting it to third parties as bad. It is the misrepresentation and butchering of our character to others, behind our backs. This is what is known as slander. It is not a physical thing perpetrated by the hand, but a more subtle form of persecution through the tongue.

In the Beatitudes, our Lord mentions the three evils perpetrated against the Christian in exactly the same order. In Matthew 5:11 we read: "Blessed are ye, when men shall revile you [*oneidísōsin* is used here as a synonym for *loidoroúmenoi* in 1 Cor. 4:12], and persecute you, and shall say all manner of evil against you falsely, for my sake." That's defaming, more commonly known as slander.

We must be careful of two things when we hear that someone has said something derogatory about us:

First, is it true? If it is, then we must admit it and try by God's grace to correct our fault. Note that our Lord stated very clearly that it must be a *false* accusation, if it is to result in the furtherance of our blessedness: "And shall say all manner of evil against you *falsely.*"

Second, is it for Christ's sake that we are being defamed? Such defamation may result either from our own endeavors to elevate ourselves and show off, or from our earnest uplifting of Jesus Christ. We can be slandered for "self's" sake or for Christ's sake. If it is for self, our usual reaction is retaliation and countercharges. If it is for Christ's sake, we are to accept it with prayerful concern.

If we are innocent, and the accusations are false, our hearts should be free from fear. The world's unfavorable view of our character and conduct is like the fleeting clouds from which the brightest day is not free, or, to change the metaphor, the mud doesn't stick to the back of a smooth fish. In the same way, slander will not stick to us if we are innocent. In the long run, God will vindicate us. The poet was wise who said,

> Trust not to each accusing tongue,
> As most weak persons do;
> But still believe that story false
> Which ought not to be true.

In a sense, we are prisoners of the slanders leveled against us by those who speak evil of us for Christ's sake. But we can emulate the serenity of that man who stood in the courtroom who seemed to smile at the heavy charges leveled against him. A bystander asked him why he smiled. "Oh," he said, "it makes no difference what the evidence says, as long as the judge says nothing." It is no matter what the world says as long as God approves us.

There's no doubt that slander hurts. There's only a single letter's difference between "words" and "swords." Slanderers are like flies; they light only upon our sores, where they know they will hurt us most. Sir Francis Bacon expressed a profound truth when he said, "The worthiest persons are frequently attacked by slanderers, as we generally find that to be the best fruit which the birds have been pecking at."

When Slander Becomes Blasphemy

The Greek text of the New Testament sheds a great deal of light on the meaning of Scripture. For instance, in 1 Corinthians 4:13, when the apostle Paul says, "Being defamed, we intreat," some texts, instead of using the verb *dusphēmoúmenoi*, "being defamed," as we saw in our previous study, use the verb *blasphēmoúmenoi*, "being blasphemed," a far commoner New Testament word.

The noun *dusphēmía*, "slander, insult, evil report," is used only in 2 Corinthians 6:8 besides the verbal usage in 1 Corinthians 4:13. What is the difference? The verb *blasphēméō* is also a compound. It is made up of *blás,* which may be derived either from *bláx*, "stupid, sluggish, lazy" (still used in Modern Greek), or from *bláptō,* "to injure or hurt," and *phēmí*, "to speak." Interesting, isn't it? The one who blasphemes shows himself stupid in trying to injure someone else.

But the word "blaspheme" in the New Testament also took on the connotation of speech defamatory of the deity and the divine. A blasphemer is thus one who speaks contemptuously of God or of sacred things (as in Matt. 9:3; Mark 3:28; Rom. 2:24; 1 Tim. 1:20; and Rev. 13:6). The apostles and Christians in general represent God and that which is divine. Therefore when others speak against them it is as if they were speaking against God Himself and the sacred truths for which Christians stand.

What really angers the unbeliever is our claim to a special relationship with God. In a unique sense, this is what made the scribes call Jesus Christ a blasphemer—His claim of a special relationship with God the Father, which even Christian believers do not pretend to have, namely, equality in deity with God the Father. "But there were certain of the scribes sitting there, and reasoning in their hearts, Why doth this man thus speak blasphemies? who can forgive sins but God only?" (Mark 2:6, 7; Luke 5:20, 21; Matt. 9:2, 3). Their reasoning was clear: Christ presumed to forgive sins. Only God could do that. Therefore, by so doing, Christ claimed to be God, and that was blasphemy!

What Jesus had done was to give an explicit assertion of His special relationship to God the Father. He demonstrated that He had power to speak the authoritative word of forgiveness because of His perfect oneness with the Father, in mind and will and purpose. When was it that the people took up stones to throw at Him? When He said, "I and my Father are one" (John 10:30). The Greek word for "one" here is *hén,* in substance, in divinity, in essence; not one personality, as could have been expressed by the Greek *heis.*

The Lord asked them, "Many good works have I shewed you from my Father; for which of those works do you stone me? The Jews answered him, saying, For a good work we stone thee not, but for blasphemy; and because that thou, being a man, makest thyself God" (John 10:32, 33).

Even the Christian's claim to a special relationship to Christ as Saviour, and thus to God as Father, seems almost like blasphemy to the world. Our beliefs are repugnant to the natural mind. Therefore they call us fools, idiots, and worse. Paul wants us to be prepared for this by realizing that our defamation by the unbelieving world has its basis in our special relationship with God as His redeemed children.

What was Paul's reaction, and that of the other apostles, to this? "Being defamed, we intreat," he said. The rendering in the King James Version doesn't fully convey the thought here. The New American Standard Version says, "we try to conciliate," and the New International Version says, "we answer kindly." Let's see what the Greek verb *parakaloúmen* really means. It comes from *parakaléō,* a compound verb made up of the preposition *pará,* "near, to the side," and the verb *kaléō,* "to call." Hence it can mean to invite someone, to appeal to, urge, exhort, encourage, request, implore. It also means to comfort, to encourage, or to cheer up. It is in this latter sense that the word is used in the second Beatitude in Matthew 5:4, "Blessed the mourning ones, for they shall be comforted [*paraklēthḗsontai*]." He who mourns needs someone to stand by his side, to comfort him.

But in 1 Corinthians 4:13 the verb is used in the active voice, *parakaloúmen,* "we stand by, we beseech." To whom do we do this? It cannot be the one who has defamed or blasphemed us. It is doubtful that such a person would want us by his side, either to speak to us or have us speak to him. His work of ruining our reputation is usually done in our absence, to a third party. In this way we are left defenseless, as he poisons the minds of others against us.

The verb *parakaloúmen* in this instance has its own peculiar meaning. If we take its object to be God, then it can mean "We beseech or entreat God," in other words, "We pray, we stand by God." The word is used with the meaning of "pray" and is so translated in Matthew 26:53, where it is used in relation to the proclamation of salvation. What do we do, then, when we hear of someone slandering us because of our relationship to Jesus Christ? We beseech God for his salvation. That's the only way the slanderer may be stopped. We seek to be reconciled to him, not on the basis of sacrificing truth and principle, or even with a defense of our integrity, but on the basis of much entreaty, much prayer for his salvation.

"Love Your Enemies" . . . Pray for Them

When we think of slander, we usually associate it with the tongue. But do we ever stop to think we may be guilty of it simply by lending our ears?

Some young women were talking about one of their friends, when their pastor happened to enter the room. He overheard the epithets "odd," "singular," and other belittling words applied to the absent friend. The pastor asked about whom they were talking, and then commented, "Yes, she is an odd young lady, a very odd young lady; I consider her extremely singular." He then added very impressively, "She was never heard to speak ill of an absent friend." The rebuke struck home.

We must remember that we are guilty of assisting in the work of defamation when we allow someone to speak ill of an absent person to us. The slanderer wounds three at once: himself, the one he speaks of, and the one that hears. If we cannot stop his mouth, let us stop our ears. For as soon as we take pleasure in hearing slander we are ranked among the number of those who engage in slander. As Bishop Hall said, "There would not be so many open mouths if there were not so many open ears." And Leighton adds, "Calumny would soon starve and die of itself if nobody took it in and gave it lodging." Proverbs 26:20 puts it succinctly: "Where no wood is, there the fire goeth out: so where there is no talebearer, the strife ceaseth."

But what shall we do when slander becomes extremely personal? How can we stop those who are defaming us? Perhaps one way to get to our enemies is to say something good about them.

General Lee was once asked by military authorities about the merits and qualifications of an officer who had been particularly unkind to him, stooping even to slander and backbiting. The General, always a Christian and a gentleman, made an exceedingly favorable report. "What do you mean, General?" a friend asked him. "Don't you know how much harm that man has done you?" "I am well aware of this," was the dignified reply, "but you forget that I have been asked, not concerning what he thinks of me, but concerning what I think of him."

As Christians we must ever keep in mind what our Lord taught us in Matthew 5:44: "Love your enemies, bless them that curse you, do good to them that hate you, and pray for them which despitefully use you, and persecute you." Slander, defamation, and blasphemy is one kind of persecution. By telling us to love our enemies, the Lord doesn't mean we are to face them with honey-coated words that are the opposite of what we feel in our heart. That would be hypocrisy. We must rid our mind of all resentment and hatred toward them. Through acts of kindness we must try to meet their real needs. But what will really meet their need is prayer to God for their salvation. By prayer we acknowledge that words and deeds of kindness on our part are insufficient to change them. We need the intervention of the omnipotent God to bring salvation.

What do we as Christians see in the person who hates or defames us: an enemy only, or also a fellow human being for whom Christ died? If my enemy were a poisonous snake, it might be justifiable for me to hate and trample upon him. But am I justified in hating the seed of the woman as much as I do that of the serpent? God loves the most sinful members of the human race, so far as their being His creatures. Enmity does not obliterate humanity. Every man may see something of himself in his enemy, and must believe that an enemy is capable of being shamed and redeemed.

The scribes and Pharisees were defaming Jesus; they were His enemies. He didn't blind His eyes to them; He recognized them for what they were. That's what we must do if we are to help our enemies. The right diagnosis is the prerequisite to proper treatment. The Lord did not meekly avoid a confrontation with them, for this would have emboldened them to continue their evil attitudes and actions. He opposed them with all His strength. But at the same time He prayed for them. So ought we to pray that our enemies will see the error of their ways and repent.

Read the 23rd chapter of Matthew, and notice how the Lord first told the Pharisees what He thought of them. "Woe unto you, scribes and Pharisees, hypocrites! for ye shut up the kingdom of heaven against men: for ye neither go in yourselves, neither suffer ye them that are entering to go in. . . . ye devour widows' houses, and for a pretence make long prayer: therefore ye shall receive greater damnation" (vv. 13, 14; see also 23, 24).

He didn't hold anything back. This was exposure upon exposure, when exposure was necessary. He spoke the truth for the protection of others and to jolt them out of their self-righteous complacency. But He didn't stop with denunciation. In effect He prayed for them: "O Jerusalem, Jerusalem, thou that killest the prophets, and stonest them which are sent unto thee, how often would I have gathered thy children together, even as a hen gathereth her chickens under her wings, and ye would not! Behold, your house is left unto you desolate. For I say unto you, Ye shall not see me henceforth, till ye shall say, Blessed is he that cometh in the name of the Lord" (vv. 38, 39). This presupposes their repentance, of course.

Be Willing to Take It

Have you ever been deeply hurt because someone you loved and trusted turned against you? If so, you're in good company. Consider what Judas did to Jesus Christ. But before you begin thinking of your false friend as another Judas, and become bitter and revengeful, consider how Jesus acted.

Who defamed Jesus more than His traitorous disciple, Judas? Yet consider what the Lord did at the last supper. See Him kneeling at the traitor's feet, washing and wiping them with the same marks of love and tenderness He bestowed on the other disciples. When Judas follows Him to the garden of Gethsemane, what does the Lord do? He accepts his treacherous kiss and salutes him with the name of friend.

Now accompany the Saviour to the palaces of Annas and Caiaphas. In the one He receives a blow on the cheek; in the other His enemies buffet Him and spit in His face. He rebukes them but does not return blow for blow, or insult for insult.

On to Calvary. On the cross He neither heaps curses on His enemies nor calls down vengeance upon them. On the contrary, He lifts His eyes to heaven and prays for them to be forgiven. Dare we, as His servants, do otherwise?

The apostle Paul was of the same spirit as his Master. In concluding the list of sacrifices he and other apostles were making for Christ's sake, he says in the second part of 1 Corinthians 4:13, "We are made as the filth of the world, and are the offscouring of all things unto this day."

Up to now Paul has been using the present indicative or present participial forms of verbs. "We are hungry, we are thirsty, we are scantily dressed, we are mistreated, we are without an abiding house, we labor working with our own hands, being reviled, being persecuted, being defamed." But in the conclusion he changes the verbal form by using the aorist tense. Why?

Up to now he has been describing the continuous state of the apostles. It was one of privation and persecution. "We are constantly experiencing these things," he says in effect. "But now we have had it; that is what we became for Christ's sake." The verb here is *egenḗthēmen,* from *gínomai,* "to become." It's in the aorist tense, which means "we have been made." Made what? A heap of rubbish. By whom? Those who hate the gospel, as a result of the nature of the work we've been trying to accomplish. The apostles could have had a much easier life had they wanted to accomplish less for the Lord. Their accomplishments for God were proportionate to their willingness to sacrifice. It was not only the enmity of the world but also their love for the Saviour and the souls of men that made them so deprived.

"We are willing to take it," Paul intimates; although he elsewhere makes it clear that Christians should not allow Christ's servants to fall into abject poverty. That is to their shame. In writing to the Corinthians in 2 Corinthians 8:14, he rebukes them for having so much, yet giving so little. "Now," he writes, "your abundance may be a supply for their want, that their abundance also may be a supply for your want; that there may be equality."

If a Christian community can supply the needs of Christian workers, they should do so, in order that those who serve the Lord may not have to say, "We go hungry, thirsty, scantily clad," and so on. But no Christian worker should be unwilling to endure these privations for the sake of Christ. No Christian should shirk his responsibility in giving, and no Christian should give up working for God because he may have to suffer deprivation as a result. When Christians fail to support God's work, this does not give license to God's servants to give up their God-commissioned duty.

"We were made the filth of the world," says Paul. The genitive *toú kósmou,* "of the world," has by paraphrase the meaning "in the eyes of the world." The other genitive, *pántōn,* "of all," in the phrase, "the offscouring of all," should also be taken by paraphrase as "in the eyes of all people." Both expressions refer to unbelievers, who to a great extent cause of much of the suffering of God's servants. In their eyes, Paul declares, we are rubbish, offscouring, not worth anything. These are the most debasing terms he could apply to himself and other sacrificing apostles.

There is still a great deal of this sort of persecution going on in the world. In every city there are shops and offices and factories where anyone giving a consistent Christian witness by word and example is ridiculed and subjected to petty annoyances and harassment. And there are homes in which, under the safe cover of what ought to be the most loving relationships, the stabs of aversion and contempt are dealt to the one who faithfully proclaims allegiance to Christ.

Never shrink from wholehearted commitment to the Saviour because you fear its trials or its sacrifices. Remember that Paul in martyrdom was far happier than God's halfhearted servants.

God's Not Through with You Yet

The insults that Paul and other apostles had to bear for the sake of their faithful Christian testimony are seen to be even more debasing in the original Greek than in our English translations. The two words that appear in the King James Version as "filth" and "offscouring" are *perikathármata* and *perípsēma.* The uncompounded *kátharma* (singular) is more common. *Perí* as a prefix means "around." *Kátharma*, used even today in Modern Greek, is the worst name anybody could be called. Both words refer to the "sweepings" or "scrapings" scoured off in cleansing a vessel. Neither word occurs elsewhere in the New Testament.

Demosthenes addressed Aeshines as *hṓ kátharma* (vocative), a term of deepest insult. In another reference, he called some people *kathármata,* "scourings," *kai ptōchoí,* and "poor" (helpless ones) and not even men (*kai oudé ánthrōpoi*). The term denoted helpless creatures, less than human beings. *Perikathármata* is plural, denoting the sweepings that are gathered together from all around (*perí*).

The second term, *perípsēma,* is singular in number and means "offscouring," that which is removed by scouring or rubbing away (*psáō*) a filthy object. Both terms refer to that which is worthless. Paul is saying, "We have become the scum of the earth, the refuse of the world," as the NIV renders it in paraphrase. "We are not worth anything to the world up until now."

That phrase "until now" is very important. It refers to the whole paragraph from verses 11 through 13. All the sufferings that Paul and the other apostles were willing to undergo for the sake of Christ were temporary. A brighter day would dawn. The era in which we now live is the day of man, but the Lord's day will come, in which He will wipe away all tears. Revelation 7:17 says of the righteous ones, "And God shall wipe away all tears from their eyes." Isaiah 25:8 says, "He will swallow up death in victory; and the Lord God will wipe away tears from off all faces; and the rebuke of his people shall he take away from off all the earth: for the Lord hath spoken it." And again, in Isaiah 35:10 we read, "And the ransomed of the Lord shall return, and come to Zion with songs and everlasting joy upon their heads: they shall obtain joy and gladness, and sorrow and sighing shall flee away" (see also 51:11; 60:20).

"Till now," said Paul as he remembered God's promise in Psalm 30:5: "Weeping may endure for a night, but joy cometh in the morning." And the last book of the Bible gives an assurance that enables the believer to endure joyfully all kinds of suffering: "And God shall wipe away all tears from their eyes; and there shall be no more death, neither sorrow, nor crying, neither shall there be any more pain: for the former things are passed away" (Rev. 21:4).

The Lord is not through with us yet. He is still in the process of making and molding us through experiences of joy and suffering. Before the war destroyed it, in a certain town in France there was a curiously wrought crucifix. It gave the spectator two totally different impressions when seen from different angles of vision. Seen from one point of view, the Saviour's face was full of beauty; from another it was marred with cruel disfigurements. From one standpoint it was calm and peaceful, as though Christ were looking up into His Father's face and saying, "Father, into thy hands I commit my spirit." From another standpoint it wore a look of anguish, as though He were crying, "My God, my God, why hast thou forsaken me?" Standing in one place you would see the face of Jesus as one "rejoicing in spirit" (Luke 10:21); standing elsewhere you would see the same face as the index of a soul in deep sorrow: "Now is my soul troubled" (John 12:27).

In many ways the persecuted apostles mirrored this dual experience: "As sorrowful, yet alway rejoicing" (2 Cor. 6:10). God was not through with them yet, and this was all part of His making and molding process. And that explains much of the seemingly mysterious providences of His dealings with us.

A happily married woman with two children lost both of them. They were buried in the same grave, and she went into a deep emotional collapse. For some years she became as helpless as a little child. She had to be fed by members of her family, who ministered to her.

One day as her aunt, who was a joyful Christian, took her turn at feeding her, this woman who was unusually despondent that morning said, "Oh, Auntie, you say that God loves us. You say it, and you keep on saying it. I used to think that way, too, but if He loves us, why did He make me as I am?"

And the aunt, after kissing her gently, said with the wisdom of years, "He hasn't made you yet, child. He's making you now!"

> When through fiery trials thy pathway shall lie,
> My grace, all-sufficient, shall be thy supply;
> The flame shall not hurt thee, I only design
> Thy dross to consume and thy gold to refine.

LESSONS:

1 Defamation can be expected as part of the normal experience of those who live godly in Christ. The Greek word, *dusphēmeō*, "to speak ill of," carries the denotation of presenting a bad picture to a third party.

The present participle tells us that this is ongoing slander from a hostile world (reemphasized later by "until now").

2. Ordinarily, slander and libel are false accusations. We should always consider the claim directed against us. If true, we are responsible to repent. If false, Paul tells us to intreat, as those free from blame. No one, he says elsewhere, can condemn what God elects (Rom. 8:33).
3. Because the apostles and Christians in general represent God, unjust slander converts to blasphemy. Those who defame believers doing the work of God defame God's holy work of sanctification, and those who attack God's work attack God. Unbelievers run the risk of God's wrath.
4. Intreating, in this context, means to beseech, and the only valid object is God. We do not plead or beg the mercy of the slanderer. But we can intreat God to stop the slander one way or another, preferably by salvation.
5. Just as the media report bad things to satisfy the demand of subsidizing evil curiosity, so we should remind ourselves that our sinful natures enjoy—in plain language—slander. We are no more forced to read sensationalistic, junk newspapers and gossip columns than we are to listen to slander.
6. We should guard our souls against retaliation of like kind. We are commanded to return good for evil in order to heap coals of fire on our enemies (Rom. 12:20). And we should pray for their salvation.
7. At the same time, returning good for evil and praying are not opposed to speaking the truth in love.
8. Jesus and the apostles "took the beating" from friends and enemies, frequently abandoned by all but the Father Himself. Beaten and insulted, the apostles were made, literally, into a "trash heap of scraps" (*perikathármata*) by unbelievers.
9. In addition to "scraps," Paul uses the term *perípsēma* or "scourings"—that which is removed by scouring—to complete this vivid picture of filth. Both terms designate refuse, scum, worthless trash of one sort or another.

1 Cor. 4:14 | *Conduct Resulting from Conviction*

I write not these things to shame you, but as my beloved sons I warn you.

The Blessing of Sacrificing for Christ

The Corinthians were evidently wealthy Christians for the most part. They gave but they did not sacrifice. It was easy for them to compromise with the world around them, and thus escape scornful reproach. They had an easy time of it; persecution was not their lot. Unlike the apostles, they seldom if ever had to hunger and thirst for Christ's sake.

That was the choice they had made: the life of ease while still being in Christ. They were the rich who were not willing to become poor for Christ's sake. 1 Corinthians 4:8 shows us what an easy time they had of it: "Now ye are full, now ye are rich, ye have reigned as kings without us." Then Paul goes on to describe what he and the other apostles were enduring up till that time.

It was only natural that Paul's words should cause the Corinthians a sense of shame. "Look how good we have it, and what a hard time those poor preachers are having." But that was the last thing Paul wanted to inculcate in them. "I write not these things to shame you," he says in 1 Corinthians 4:14.

The Greek word *entrépōn,* translated "shame" here is the present participle of *entrépō,* a compound verb made up of *en,* the preposition meaning "in," and *trépō,* "to turn." Three Greek words are translated "shame" in English, one of which is the noun *aischúnē,* which expresses that feeling that leads one to shun what is unworthy for fear of incurring dishonor. It is as though we realize our imperfections and are grieved, but our grief is not because of our shortcomings but because of what other people will think who take notice of them.

As a noun, this word is used in Luke 14:9, 2 Corinthians 4:2 (translated "dishonesty"), Philippians 3:19, Hebrews 12:2, Jude 13, and Revelation 3:18. As a verb it is used in Luke 16:3, 2 Corinthians 10:8, Philippians 1:20, 1 Peter 4:26, and 1 John 2:28. With the preposition *epí,* "on," as *epaischúnomai* it is used in Mark 8:38, Luke 9:26, Romans 1:16; 6:21, 2 Timothy 1:8, 12, 16, and Hebrews 2:11; 11:16.

Take the well-known verse of Romans 1:16: "For I am not ashamed of the gospel of Christ." It means "I do not realize a sense of shame when others recognize that I am a Christian." This shame is coupled with what others will think of us when they learn of a certain thing we do or believe.

The second Greek word translated "shame" is *aídōs,* used only in 1 Timothy 2:9. It means the shame that finds its motive in itself, that is, modesty, propriety. No honor and reputation are attached to this sense of shame. We are not ashamed because of what others think of us, but because of the regard we have for our own self or for goodness and God. Thus it could be said that *aischúnē* would sometimes restrain a bad person, while *aídōs* would always restrain a good person from an unworthy act.

Entropḗ is used in 1 Corinthians 4:14 in its verbal participial form: "I write these things not shaming you [*entrépōn*]." As a verb it occurs in Matthew 21:37 and Mark 12:6, where it means "respect or regard," Luke 18:2, 4; 20:13, where it also means "respect or regard," and in 1 Corinthians 4:14, 2 Thessalonians 3:14, and Titus 2:8, where it means "shame." As a noun it occurs only twice: in 1 Corinthians 6:5 and 15:34.

Entropḗ is rendered "shame" as is *aischúnē* and *aídōs*, but it has something in it that neither of these words has. It slightly suggests a change of conduct. It means "a return upon oneself"; it involves a change in conduct as one turns upon himself. That was what Paul was hoping would happen as he wrote to the Corinthians about their material riches and ease and his own privations and sufferings for Christ. His aim was not to produce a sense of shame in them as a result of what he and the other apostles thought of them, nor by what they thought of themselves, but to cause them to turn upon themselves for to change their conduct (see R. C. Trench, *Synonyms of the New Testament*, 66–69).

Entropḗ in Classical Greek may mean "respect or reverence for one," as well as "shame or reproach"; the context determines which. The verb *entrépō* in the passive form may mean "to respect, to regard, to reverence, to pay deference to (anyone)."

We should never shame others for their conduct that we find unbecoming to the principles we have set for ourselves. If we really believe that our conduct is exemplary, we should endeavor to show others the superiority of our way with the motive of changing their conduct. That was Paul's purpose as he spells it out in 1 Corinthians 4:16 by saying, "Wherefore I beseech you, be ye followers of me." He knew the blessing of sacrificing for Christ's sake and didn't want them to miss such a blessing.

A fable tells of a piece of wood that once complained bitterly because its owner kept whittling away at it, cutting it and filling it with holes. But the one who was cutting it so remorselessly paid no attention to its complaining. He was making a flute out of that piece of ebony, and he was too wise to give up because the wood moaned so piteously. His actions seemed to say, "Little piece of wood, without these holes and all this cutting, you would be a black stick forever—just a useless piece of ebony. What I am doing now may make you think that I am destroying you, when actually I am changing you into a flute, whose sweet music will comfort sorrowing hearts. My cutting you is the making of you, for only thus can you be a blessing to the world."

Right Motives for a Change of Conduct

When the apostle Paul wrote to the Corinthian Christians of the deprivations he and the other apostles were suffering for the cause of Christ, while the Corinthians were living at ease, he did it because he saw they needed correction, a change of conduct. But there was really nothing he himself could do to bring this about. Sharp words and criticism bring shame, but they do not necessarily cause a change in conduct and attitude. They may make a person "turn in" (*entrépō*) on himself, resulting in some change, but such a change is accompanied by resentment. It is not a joyful change resulting from conviction.

We can change our conduct if we have to, in order to survive in a world in which people are prone to shame and ridicule us for behavior of which they disapprove. Our attitude may change only because we want to avoid being treated with contempt. This is a hypocritical change of attitude, not of character. We act differently from the way we wish we could if we were not afraid of incurring the displeasure of others.

That was not the kind of change Paul wanted to bring about in the Corinthians' conduct. Take generosity as an example. Paul touches upon this in 2 Corinthians 8:1–5. He contrasts the giving of the Corinthians with the sacrificial giving of the Macedonians. The Corinthians gave, not because they wanted to, but because the sacrificial giving of the Macedonians, although insignificant in quantity, made them ashamed. Paul didn't want them to change on that account, but out of conviction that giving carried in itself a blessing, as our Lord taught when He said that it was more blessed to give than to receive. Thus we can be givers out of shame or out of conviction. Which kind are you?

That's why Paul writes to the Corinthians, "I do not write these things in order to shame you," that is, to make you "turn your eyes inside you" (*entrépōn*) for the purpose of bringing about a superficial and hypocritical change in your attitude. The principle verb here is *gráphō*, "*I* write," and the verb "shame" is in the present active participial form (*entrépōn*). Paul reveals the underlying purpose of his writing—not just to let off steam but to accomplish something. Far too many people write or speak in order to cause others to do as they do, without any personal conviction or real change of character. Do we try to shame people into a position they do not believe in? That was never the purpose of apostolic preaching, writing, or teaching, and it should not be ours. It disregards entirely the work of the Holy Spirit, and puts us in the position of "playing God."

From the negative Paul moves on to the positive. "I do not write in order to shame you, but as my children [who are] beloved I admonish you." The word "admonish" here is *noutheteō* in Greek. It is derived from the noun *noús*, "mind," and the verb *títhēmi*, "to place." If we were to translate the verb literally, we could render Paul's statement, "I place your mind in its proper place"; in other words, I make you think rightly; and only as a result of this can I expect the hoped-for change in your conduct. I want you to be like me, a sacrificial Christian, but only as a result of self-examination and conviction. Your action must be the result of your thought—not to avoid shame in relation to others, but for the purpose of satisfying God who has set your thought process aright. I am doing this because I consider you my children who are beloved to me. I am your spiritual father.

Is not this how a loving father acts? Does he want his children to be puppets, merely acting good before others in order to avoid bringing shame upon themselves and him? No, he wants his counsel to affect their minds so they can think for themselves to determine what is right and wrong, and then to be able to choose between what is merely right and what is excellent.

Translated, that could be called "nouthetic" counseling, that which rectifies the thinking processes, rather than merely causes action to avoid shame as a form of punishment. The latter is avoiding the consequences of evil, while the former is avoiding the evil itself simply because it is evil, and not just for fear of the consequences. When we reach that elevated position of thinking (*nouthesía,* the noun form of the verb *noutheteín*), we have really arrived at the stature of Christ. If we love our children, our aim will be not simply to make them follow our example, but to cause them to think that we are worthy of being followed. They will not do what we do simply because that's the way we expect them to act, but because that's the way they themselves think and consequently believe to be proper behavior.

As Kenneth W. Sollitt says in the last three lines of his poem, "God Must Be Like That":

> For something in [Christ's] godliness
> Has gripped the soul of me—
> And I would be like that.

Christian Maturity a Matter of Growth

An easy mistake for Christian parents to fall into is to seek to make their children carbon copies of themselves. But, if we really love our children, we will want them to learn to think things through for themselves, and be able to act out of conviction rather than merely parroting our convictions.

The apostle Paul truly loved the Corinthian Christians. He does not merely refer to the fact that they were his children in the Lord, but that they were "beloved" children. The word for "children" in 1 Corinthians 4:14 is *tékna,* from the verb *tíktō*, "to give birth to." Paul indeed gave birth to these Christians, in the sense that it was through his preaching that they were born into the family of God through faith in Christ.

But one can give birth to a child without necessarily exercising love toward him. That was not Paul's way. He not only gave spiritual birth to the Corinthians, but he also loved them. That is why he words his counsel to them in a way that will lead them to think aright, and in so doing to act as their spiritual father.

The adjective Paul uses to express his love is one of apposition. He says, "but as my children, beloved ones [*agapētá*]." He could have used another Greek word, such as *pephilēména*, from *philéō,* which denotes the love of equals having common interests. But he doesn't; he uses the adjective derived from *agapáō,* which may express the love of the superior for the inferior, not for the sake of taking advantage of the person who is the object of love, but for the sake of helping him.

This is a beautiful example of Christian grace. The Corinthians could very easily have misunderstood what Paul meant when he wrote to them about a life of sacrifice and privation. They might have concluded that he was trying to get them to help him financially. He wanted to avoid giving that impression, for it was the farthest thing from his mind. He was not admonishing them for his own sake or benefit, but for their sakes, so that they might realize that there is inherent blessing in living a life of sacrifice and privation for the sake of Jesus Christ.

God Himself does not love us for His own personal gain. He doesn't want us to give so that He can have more, but so that we may experience a joy that we couldn't have in any other way. A truly loving father doesn't admonish his children so that he may be served and lack nothing, but so that they will grow up to think right and act right. A loving father does what he does for his children, and counsels them, primarily because he wants to help them to become mature, wise adults. Children can easily see through a person whose counseling has a selfish motive and will comply only as long as they are forced to. Then, when the bonds of necessity cease to exist, the bonds of filial obedience will be terminated.

What Paul wrote to the Corinthian Christians was to make them think right about the blessing of a sacrificial life of faith for the sake of Jesus Christ. To be motivated to such sacrifice, Christians must be convicted and inspired from above, not merely shamed into it for the sake of avoiding embarrassment.

Paul didn't want the Corinthians to think of him as a teacher who was merely doing his duty in instructing them about what was right. "I am not a mere teacher in my relationship with you," he says in effect; "I am a father who loves you. One can have many teachers, but only a single father." He wanted that singular relationship to be realized by the Corinthians. He knew it in his own heart. He loved them; therefore he wanted them to learn to think right in their attitude toward the material things of this world. Hence his words in 1 Corinthians 4:15: "For if you have ten thousand teachers in Christ, yet have you not many fathers."

He refers to spiritual teachers, for he uses his favorite expression, "in Christ." He recognizes that the Christian life is one of growth, and not of instant maturity. Upon being born again, we are "babes in Christ." Just as in our natural life we must first learn how to speak, then how to write, then how to reason, and each age has its proper teachers, something similar takes place in our spiritual life. Just as we would not attempt to teach integral and differential calculus to a child of seven, we should not expect the babe in Christ to grasp all that is implied in Christian doctrine and its outworking in daily life all at once. If we could only realize this principle in our experience and the lives of others, we would not have so many frustrated pupils. Frustration can come in two ways: through teaching a baby what he cannot understand or learn, and teaching an adult what is suitable for an infant.

One of the greatest misfortunes in the Christian Church today is the lack of growth evidenced in its members. As one pastor put it in a letter to me, "In most of our churches the Christians are constantly fed pabulum, baby food, instead of food for grown-ups."

As someone else has truly observed, "You are only young once, but you can stay immature indefinitely."

LESSONS:

1. Shame is not a good end in itself. More often accompanied by evil motives, shame tends to paralyze action, to cause people to turn inward (*entrépō*). Paul tells his Corinthian brothers this is not his purpose which is, rather, to admonish, as he would a child.
2. Admonishment occurs when the Holy Spirit impresses upon us a good role model. Accordingly, Paul appealed to his own life: "Be ye followers of me as (i.e., to the extent) I am of Christ" (1 Cor. 11:1). Shame requires little more than an arrogant self-righteous attitude.
3. The Greek work translated admonish, *noutheteō*, means to put the mind in its proper place, that is, to think correctly. Paul wanted His Corinthian readers to have the right perspective on wealth and the true wealth of the knowledge of the power of Christ's resurrection. This is "nouthetic" counsel, counsel which changes thinking.
4. Internal shame is more a reaction to the consequences of evil than to the evil itself. Only right thinking about evil is genuine repentance.
5. Paul could speak of the Corinthians as His *tékna*, children, in the same sense that we can of any who are born again on the occasion of our bringing them the gospel. He even contrasts this superior filial or parental role with that of a teacher in 1 Corinthians 4:15.
6. Christian maturity is an advancement from childhood to adulthood. We do best to abide under the tutelage of a spiritual father like Paul. Advanced topics should be learned **only** after foundational courses have been mastered through personal, victorious application.

1 Cor. 4:15 | Are You a Mere Teacher or a Spiritual Parent?

For though ye have ten thousand instructors in Christ, yet have ye not many fathers: for in Christ Jesus I have begotten you through the gospel.

The Function of Christian Teachers and Fathers

In referring to "ten thousand instructors in Christ," the apostle Paul was indicating the great multiplicity of teachers in the Christian Church. The number is hypothetical, of course, for effect. But we do need a great many teachers for the various stages of spiritual schooling and growth. No one teacher is fully qualified to teach all the classes in the school of Christ. It is better to divide up our pupils according to their capacity and our ability to teach.

Some teachers in the Christian Church cannot go beyond the ABC's. They are fine for teaching children, or babes in Christ, but cannot reach those on the college level, spiritually speaking. Teacher, find out what spiritual grade you can teach and stick to it. Let those qualified to teach other stages do it.

In this connection, a word of warning. Let's not presume that because some Christians are in the first grade, so to speak, they are not "in Christ." Observe what Paul says: "For if you have ten thousand teachers in Christ." "In Christ" there are all kinds of pupils, from kindergarten to graduate students. We need discernment to recognize the grade to which each belongs. The temptation may be to consider the weak, carnal, baby Christians as not really "in Christ" at all, and so miss the privilege of helping them grow. Let us heed Paul's admonition in Romans 15:1: "We then that are strong ought to bear the infirmities of the weak, and not to please ourselves." A realistic way of looking at this matter is to recognize that there is always someone who knows less than you do, and you can teach him; and that there is always someone who knows more than you do, who can teach you. We have pupils in all grades in the school of Christ and teachers for all grades. Know yourself and then start teaching and learning.

The word used for teachers ("instructors" in the King James Version) is *paidagōgoús,* from the noun *país,* meaning "child," and the verb *ágō,* "to lead." From this Greek word we derive the English words pedagogue and pedagogy. Teachers are leaders of children for the most part. Paul refuses to classify himself merely as a teacher of children, a pedagogue, in his relationship to the Corinthian Christians. Perhaps by using this term, however, he was implying that the Corinthians were still babes, children in their Christian walk and understanding. In fact, he has already told them so in 1 Corinthians 3:1–3: "And I, brethren, could not speak unto you as unto spiritual, but as unto babes in Christ. I have fed you with milk, and not with meat: for hitherto ye were not able to bear it, neither yet now are ye able. For ye are yet carnal. . . ."

A teacher is usually a stranger to those whom he teaches. He is appointed by the state or the community or the parents to teach the children. There is no blood relationship that would insure affection between. teacher and students, as there is between father and child. The relationship is one of duty on the part of the teacher, and of need on the part of the child. Paul felt that he was more than a teacher and, though he was actually one of the teachers, he was their only spiritual father.

In our lifetime we need many teachers, but we have only one father who cares for all the phases of our life. He is qualified for this distinct and unique relationship, not because he will always know more than his child does, but simply because at one time he begot him. "But you don't have many fathers," Paul says. He may have been implying that Apollos, for instance, who followed him as a minister in Corinth, would be classified as one of their myriad teachers, but in spite of his brilliance he could not qualify as a spiritual father because he did not beget them. "For in Christ Jesus through the gospel I gave birth to you," Paul says in effect. "I introduced you to the gospel first. That and my consistent love for you as my children in Christ qualified me as your spiritual father."

The verb "I gave birth to you" is *egénnēsa* in Greek. It is in the aorist tense, which refers to a particular time in the past. Paul claims his spiritual fatherhood on the ground of his having been the first one effectively to bring the gospel to them. No matter how many taught these Corinthian Christians afterwards, they were never to forget what Paul had done for them, and the special relationship that resulted.

Of course, this does not mean that he was responsible for their salvation, but simply that he was used as God's instrument in the mystery of bringing forth a new spiritual life. A man can be said to beget or father a child, and a woman to give birth, but in reality all that the parents do is to follow the God-prescribed method of procreation. The method and the results have been pre-set and predetermined by God, the Author of all life. Birth is a mystery in the physical world and an even greater mystery in the spiritual world. As Eugenia Price expressed it, "I found I was not only converted, but I was invaded." And that invasion is the very life of Christ in the soul.

Christian Character Dependent upon the New Birth

When the apostle Paul writes to the Corinthian Christians, "I gave birth to you through the gospel," he is setting forth God's prescribed method. This was not something he did by the force of his own personality; it was his proclamation of the gospel, energized by the Holy Spirit, that resulted in spiritual children being born in Corinth. Without the gospel, the good news that Jesus died for sinners and that we are saved by faith in His atoning sacrifice, there would have been no spiritual children brought to birth in Corinth. Let us be faithful in preaching the gospel; it's "the power of God unto salvation" (Rom. 1:16).

However, when we've brought spiritual children into the world, we are not merely to act as teachers to them, but as fathers. This is not to minimize the efforts of dedicated teachers, but the relationship of fathers is so much closer and dearer. No one could and should have the same affectionate interest in them as we who first brought the gospel to them. A parent sustains the relationship of affection, mutual help, and caring, in spite of the fact that he may no longer be able to teach the child.

That child, grown to manhood or womanhood, may be a graduate student or a professor in theology, yet he should never cease to look up to his spiritual father. He may know more than he does, but the example and experience of the father are something he may never equal. In addition, there is a great debt of gratitude owed to that person who first led us to the Lord.

A teacher has comparatively few rights over his pupils, but a father has many rights and expectations. So do the children, for that matter. The relationship of teacher-pupil usually ends with the termination of the lesson or the course of study, but the relationship of father-child is an everlasting one, in time and for eternity. I am speaking, of course, of born-again fathers and children. However, even on the purely human level, the father expects respect from his children, and the children expect concern on the part of their father, which may not characterize the teacher-pupil relationship.

There is an innate similarity in the make-up of the children because of the father, which may not hold true in the pupil-teacher relationship. Paul speaks of himself as "father" more often than teacher because he wants his character to be mirrored in the Corinthians; he specifically tells them to follow his example, to be followers of him "as I also am of Christ" (1 Cor. 11:1; see also 4:16, and Phil. 3:17).

At this stage of their spiritual development, however, the Corinthians were far from mirroring the character of Paul. He was so sacrificing in his manner of life, they so careless, selfish, and extravagant. "You are full, you have already become rich, you are like kings . . . but we are at the bottom of the ladder, ready to die; we are ridiculed, we are considered insane for the sacrifices we are making; we are sick and weak, but you are strong and famous. We are without fame; hungry, thirsty, ill-clad, buffeted, and have no place we can call home." That, in effect, is the contrast Paul presents to the Corinthians in verses 8–13.

And yet, in verse 15, he declares, "I am your father; I gave birth to you. I am not one of ten thousand teachers. Usually, as fathers and children, we should be characterized by the same qualitics, but we are not. Usually it is not the father who imitates the children, but the other way around." All this and more is what Paul implies in verse 15. He gives them to understand that though they were his spiritual children, they didn't evidence it in their every-day conduct. They were compromising for the sake of an easy life, while he was suffering for the sake of Christ.

The unlikeness of character between him as a father and them as his spiritual children must have greatly hurt and embarrassed him. Look at your own spiritual father (and here I am speaking in a general sense, for there are Christian mothers who are worthy to be respected and emulated also). How like him are you? In Galatians 4:19 Paul expresses the grief of a father's heart at the slowness of heart of those who failed to grasp the most elemental facts of law versus grace in the Christian life. "My little children, of whom I travail in birth again until Christ be formed in you," he laments over them. He is not speaking of a mere matter of teaching them to be like Christ, but of giving birth to them. "I gave birth to you through the gospel," he tells the Corinthians.

The character of Christ is only formed in us when Christ Himself is born in us. No one can learn to be like Christ; he has to be born again, and then Christ enters into him. It is a blood relationship, when, through the efficacy of Christ's blood shed for us, we are cleansed from our sins, and by faith in Him as the Son of God are adopted as sons and daughters into the family of God. The gospel alone is the power of God that can regenerate in man a truly Christlike character.

What Kind of Example Are You Setting?

Although Scripture expressly states that it is the gospel that is "the power of God unto salvation" (Rom. 1:16), God employs human instrumentalities also in the regeneration of human souls. The apostle Paul was not being egotistical when he told the Corinthian Christians, "I gave birth to you." In fact, he uses the personal pronoun *egṓ,* from which we derive the English word egotism. The "I" of the verb could have been implied merely by adding the suffix *sa,* that is, *egénnēsa.* But Paul added the personal pronoun *egṓ,* "I."

Why did Paul stress the personal element here? Certainly not to show off, but to intimate that, if he had not come to them at the end of his difficult second missionary journey, the Corinthians would probably not have heard the gospel and might never have become born-again children of God. Paul felt a sense of satisfaction and gratitude to God that his labor of love had not gone in vain.

I certainly believe in the sovereignty of God, but at the same time I believe that He has laid on me the responsibility to preach the gospel to every creature I possibly can. God can effect His purposes alone, and He still does, but while I am around He expects me to preach the gospel.

A Christian girl fell in love with a missionary. Before he left for India, he wrote and asked her to become his wife. "If I do not hear from you, I'll know you have other plans," he wrote. She immediately sat down and wrote an acceptance of his proposal. She gave the letter to her brother to mail, but it was never mailed, and she never heard from the missionary again. Years later she found her letter in the lining of her brother's coat, yellow and crumpled. It had slipped there through a hole in the pocket lining, and the brother had forgotten all about it.

Have we done something similar with the gospel of the Lord Jesus Christ? Have we just hidden it in our hearts without externalizing it by sharing it with others? Of how many people can we say, "I gave birth to you through the gospel"?

The apostle Paul had nothing to reproach himself with on that score. At all times, and in all places, he proclaimed the gospel in the power of the Holy Spirit; and almost everywhere he went on his missionary journeys he left a nucleus of born-again believers who banded together to form growing Christian communities as local churches.

But, as the spiritual father of the Corinthian Christians, Paul felt an obligation to set before them a good example to follow. Having spoken of his own sacrificial way of living, he doesn't hesitate to ask them to imitate him. He could possibly have been a good teacher without setting a good example. But as their spiritual father he dedicated himself to this life of sacrifice for their sakes, out of love for the Saviour. He could conceivably have lived a so-called Christian life that sought to enjoy all the material amenities of life, in disregard of what that would have meant to God's kingdom, God's people, and the unbelieving world that he was witnessing to.

But Paul evidently asked himself two questions whenever he had to choose between the permissible and the commendable: First, will it glorify God by advancing the gospel? Second, will those who are my spiritual children be encouraged by my example to seek self-satisfaction and self-advancement, or will they be willing to sacrifice for Christ's sake? He knew that what he did never affected only himself but also had an influence on others; that what he did and how he lived spoke louder than what he taught.

The question every servant of God must ask himself is, Can I sincerely and honestly ask the people I led to the Lord through the gospel to do as I teach and preach, because I'm living up to what I tell them to do? Can I say to my spiritual family, Come to my home and see how I behave Monday through Saturday, or would I prefer that they keep completely out of my private life because of the spiritual inconsistencies with which it is riddled? Though Ecclesiastes 12:11 tells us "the words of the wise are as . . . nails," we would do well to remember that their examples are the hammers that drive them home.

A good example rings louder than any bell to toll people to church. An African prince, after interpreting the missionary's message, said, "I can't read this Book myself," referring to the Bible, "but I believe the words of it because I have watched the missionaries for two years, and they have told me no lies about anything else; so when they tell me this Book is God's Word, I believe it, and I believe that Jesus died for me, and I am going to follow this Jesus."

How many of us could say what Paul did in 1 Corinthians 4:16: "Wherefore I beseech you, be ye followers of me"? That "wherefore" is important. It is the Greek word *gár*, which could render the meaning here, "This is why I ask you to imitate me." Had Paul not lived the way he did, as described in the previous verses, he could hardly say "therefore follow my example." How do our attitudes in life and service for Christ compare with Paul's? Can we say to newborn babes in Christ, "Therefore imitate me"? Think about it.

LESSONS:

1. We all need "many instructors in Christ," since no one person is fully qualified to teach all the courses.
2. There is a broad bandwidth of maturity "in Christ." Some are infants, others in elementary, junior high, or high school; still others in college and graduate school. We need spiritual discernment to know any one person's maturity level. Carnal or baby Christians are legitimately "in Christ." Paul's reference to *paidagōgoús*, literally "child-leaders," here and to "babes in Christ" elsewhere (3:1) implies that he thought of the Corinthians as in very early stages of development.
3. Filial rights and responsibilities come when we beget others through the gospel. It is expected that we mature those we bear (Gal. 4:19). This relationship is much closer than that of a teacher. The spiritual father-child relationship is eternal and includes the replication of character as well as content. The child is expected to copy his spiritual father's actions and lifestyle.
4. The new birth is the presupposition and antecedent cause of Christian character. Without it, a person advances or matures only in new layers of Pharisaism, hypocrisy, legal self-righteousness and spiritual death.
5. In His sovereignty, God ordains his elect to preach the gospel so that the full number of His people will be saved. By doing this, we become part of His church, that great structure of spiritual generations of fathers and sons, headed up by Christ, the cornerstone.

1 Cor. 4:16 | *Are You an Example for Others?*

Wherefore I beseech you, be ye followers of me.

The Life That Wins

A minister was called to the bedside of a dying girl, who had lived for the sinful pleasures of a Christ-rejecting world. The faithful minister did his best to lead her to the Saviour, pleading, praying, and quoting Scripture. Seemingly he could make no impression on her. As a final effort, he called in her mother, who with heartbreaking sorrow also pled with the girl to receive Christ as her Saviour. The girl listened stonily, then said, "Mother, you can't talk to me now. You haven't lived the life before me!"

What a terrible indictment to hear! Those who profess Christ must realize that others are looking to them to be examples worth following. Christ's servant must realize that his spiritual children are ever ready to copy him. When they see him preaching one way and living another, they will be tempted to think, "If he, a supposedly spiritual man, does it, why shouldn't I?" Children often emulate the behavior of their father. A smoker is likely to beget a smoker; a drinker, a drinker; a liar, a liar.

The apostle Paul realized that those to whom he had given spiritual birth were weaker and less knowledgeable than he, and were therefore ready to copy him. "I have shewed you all things," he wrote to the elders at Ephesus, "how that so labouring ye ought to support the weak" (Acts 20:35). He must always have checked up on himself by asking, Is my weak child in the faith going to become weaker or stronger by observing what I do?

A Salvation Army captain was preaching in Hyde Park in London when a man in the crowd interrupted him. "We haven't anything against Jesus of Nazareth," he said, "but we have something against you Christians because you ain't up to sample." Living examples of Christ is what the world wants to see in Christians.

Primarily what Paul meant by saying, "Therefore be ye followers of me," is that they should follow his example of voluntary suffering for the sake of Jesus Christ. Was there any intrinsic value in such suffering? Not really. But as we look at Romans 8:18 we see how Paul brings out the relationship between the future glory of the believer and the suffering he is willing to undergo for the sake of his Lord. "For I reckon that the sufferings of this present time are not worthy to be compared with the glory which shall be revealed in us," he says. The glory to come will be proportionate to our willingness to endure necessary suffering for Christ here and now. Again, let me stress that suffering in itself, or that we bring upon ourselves, is without merit. It is suffering that comes to us as a result of serving Christ that, willingly accepted, is praiseworthy in His sight.

Paul was a gentleman by education and position. For him to take up with a small sect of ignorant fanatics, as the Jewish world held the primitive Christians to be, was the extreme of foolishness so far as material advantages were concerned. Again and again this faithful servant of Christ alludes to this, and so did others. "Paul, thou art beside thyself," said the Roman magistrate; "much learning doth make thee mad" (Acts 26:24). This is what his whole circle of acquaintances outside the Christian community must have thought.

And what a life it was he chose! He says, "What things were gain to me, those I counted loss for Christ. . . . for whom I have suffered the loss of all things, and do count them but refuse, that I may win Christ, and be found in him" (Phil. 3:7–9). Paul longed for every believer to partake of as much of the glory yet to be revealed as possible. But he also knew that this would be in proportion to their sufferings undergone for Christ's sake. That is why he was emboldened to write out of his own experience, "Be ye followers of me."

Paul knew that such a life is really unpopular. Therefore he was careful to attract the Corinthians to it, not by command, but by request. He does not say, "I command you to be followers of me," but "I beseech you." The Greek word translated "beseech" is *parakalṓ*, (or *parakaléō*, as it appears in the lexicons), which literally means "to stand near one and call on him." It is the same word used today in Modern Greek to say "please." It's a polite request, not an order.

What preacher could order his congregation to embrace a life of sacrifice and tears for Christ's sake? One by one his spiritual children would abandon him. He has to set the example first. Even then, the preacher can't force anyone to do as he does and live as he lives. Christ gives the prerogative of choosing a life of suffering over a life of compromise. No one loses his salvation by giving only five percent of his income to the Lord, for instance. But he does lose the joy of obedience to Christ's example. But even if you were so sacrificial as to give fifty percent, you would get nowhere by ordering those around you to follow your example. To win followers to a life of sacrifice, you have to be persuasive and beseeching. Christ Himself proved by His life and death that love is more powerful to win followers than any array of mere physical force or psychological coercion.

Should Christians Imitate Others?

Every dedicated minister of the gospel knows the heartache and frustration of preaching his heart out to a congregation that listens politely to what he says on Sunday, and then goes about "business as usual" the rest of the week. Sometimes he may be tempted to thunder at them in tones of ringing denunciation in order to awaken them to their responsibilities as Christians. But, if he yields to this impulse, he will only arouse resentment.

If the children of God are to be persuaded to sacrifice for Christ, they must not be coerced but convicted by the Holy Spirit and impelled by Him whose name is the Paraclete, *Parákl̄etos* in Greek "the Comforter, the Beseecher," whose name is derived from this same word Paul uses for "beseech," *parakal̄ō.* Let us not become angry with those who do not do as we do, but let us beseech them through the Holy Spirit. It's no use living in a hut for Christ's sake and complaining all the time that others aren't following our example. When people see how cheerful and undemanding we are in the state we have chosen to live for Christ's sake, they are more likely to see the advantages of such a life. Let's never say, "Do as I do, or you are no good!" Rather let us say with Paul, "I beseech you" to find out how joyful it is to be fully surrendered to Christ. The joy of personal surrender is the greatest destroyer of the spirit of compromise. Be loving as you call upon others to follow your example. And of course, be very sure that your example is worth following.

How should you express Christianity? In the home, by love and unselfishness. In business, by honesty and diligence. In society, by purity, courtesy, and humility. Toward the unfortunate, by sympathy and mercy. Toward the weak, by helpfulness and patience. Toward the wicked, by overcoming evil without compromise. Toward the strong, by trust and cooperation with good. Toward non-Christians, by witnessing to Christ and His gospel.

Toward the penitent, by forgiveness and restoration. Toward the fortunate, by rejoicing with them without envy. Toward God, by reverence, love, and obedience.

A veteran minister in an address to a group of newly ordained ministers said, "Young men, believe me, you will make more people Christians by being Christians yourselves than you will by all the sermons you will ever preach."

Henry M. Stanley found Livingstone in Africa and lived with him for some time. Here is his testimony: "I went to Africa as prejudiced as the biggest atheist in London. But there came for me a long time for reflection. I saw this solitary old man there and asked myself, 'How on earth does he stop here—is he cracked, or what? What is it that inspires him?' "

"For months after we met, I found myself wondering at the old man carrying out all that was said in the Bible—'Leave all things and follow Me.' But little by little his sympathy for others became contagious. My sympathy was aroused, seeing his piety, his gentleness, his zeal, his earnestness, and how he went about his business. I was converted by him, although he had not tried to do it."

Actually, the apostle Paul was not asking the Corinthian Christians to be his "followers," as the King James Version has it in 1 Corinthians 4:16, but his "imitators." The Greek word is *mímētai*, which is similar to the Greek word from which we get the English word "mimic." A mimic is one who copies another person's actions. But should even the most consecrated Christian set himself up as a model for others to copy? What about the individuality God means each of us to have? Am I supposed to be what someone else is? Are you? Or am I to expect others to be what I am? Isn't that being somewhat presumptuous and egotistical on the part of the one who says it, and a little unintelligent on the part of those who unthinkingly follow such a course? Who does anyone think he is to suggest that everyone follow him? Why shouldn't people be allowed to express their own individuality? Why encourage them to be mimics? As Louis Albert Banks says, "To be a mere copyist of other people is the most dreary and monotonous outlook that can be presented to any human soul. Nothing cramps and fetters and cripples progress more than that."

One thing Paul did not mean by asking the Corinthians to imitate him was that they should mechanically copy all his actions. As a literal imitation of Christ in all the circumstances of His life (such as being a carpenter, riding a donkey into Jerusalem, chasing the money-changers out of the temple, etc.) was out as far as Paul was concerned, so was his idea of a literal imitation of himself by others.

For instance, Paul chose to remain single, either never having been married, or, as seems more probable, having become a widower. That does not mean that all Christians should remain single. A mechanical imitation of anyone does not demonstrate intelligent appreciation of the spirit but a stupid and slavish conformity to outward appearances. Even if such an imitation were possible, it would be like the mechanical actions of a robot.

No word of Paul's is more penetrating than this: "The letter killeth, but the spirit giveth life" (2 Cor. 3:6).

How Can We Imitate God?

In the last section we concluded that slavish imitation of even the best Christians is not what is meant by following their example. When the apostle Paul wrote to the Corinthian Christians, "Wherefore I beseech you, be ye followers of me," he didn't want to set himself up as some sort of moral or spiritual hero on whom everyone should mechanically pattern his actions. Nor did he consider Christ in that light. To him, Christ was not merely the Jesus of history to be copied, but the heavenly Visitor who becomes the possessor of our spirits. Only as God the Son indwells us, can we do the acts that He performed when He was here on earth. To live as Christ lived, we must have Christ in us. And, if we are to be imitators of Paul, the Spirit of Christ that prompted him to live as he did must live in us also.

Could I be called a Christian
  If everybody knew
My secret thoughts and feelings
  And everything I do?
Oh, could they see the likeness
  Of Christ in me each day?
Oh, could they hear Him speaking
  In every word I say?

Paul's request for the Corinthians to imitate him was based on the assumption that they knew that he was an imitator of Christ. In fact, in 1 Corinthians 11:1 he states this very clearly, "Be ye followers of me, even as I also am of Christ." If he were not, he would be inexcusably presumptuous in asking others to imitate him. If we are not faithfully following Christ, we have no right to ask others to follow our example.

The fundamental truth, then, is that it is possible for a redeemed human being like Paul to be what Christ is, not merely by mimicking the human Jesus as He lived on earth, but by imitating God. Paul tells us the way to do this in Ephesians 5:1, when he says, "Be ye therefore followers of God, as dear children." That's the only way it can be done. We can only be imitators of God when He is our Father through the new birth, and we are His children. No unregenerated person can imitate God.

This is the only place in Scripture where "imitation" is applied to man's relation to God. Imitation is natural to a child. So it is to the child of God. This indicates that by His indwelling Spirit we have the capacity to act as God acts, to show forth to the world what God is. Of course, we do not acquire full maturity immediately on being born of God. As the child imitates the father at various stages of growth, so we imitate God more faithfully as we grow in our spiritual lives.

God made us for no other end than to be like Him. He didn't make us in the image of any of the heavenly host. Genesis 1:26 tells us, "God said, Let us make man in our image, after our likeness." We lost that image and likeness through sin, which is why Christ had to come to die to redeem us. Through Him God's image and likeness are restored in us, when we receive Him as Saviour and Lord.

Just as a cat cannot imitate a human being, so an unregenerate human being cannot imitate God. It takes a basic correspondence of nature before there can be the possibility of sincere imitation.

But how can we imitate God? In Christ, we have the Father represented to us in the infinite Son incarnated in finite human form. Looking at Him, we behold as in a mirror the glories of the invisible God reflected in the person of Jesus Christ; and contemplating these glories we "are changed into the same image from glory to glory even as by the Spirit of God" (2 Cor. 3:18).

One of the causes of defective holiness among us is the neglect of the careful study of God's character, as revealed in Christ. We accept the doctrine of justification in the Epistles, but then forget to seek to be like Christ, the perfect Man in the Gospels. No wonder we are so little like Him, if we do not even spend time contemplating His perfections.

It was as their spiritual father that Paul besought the Corinthians to imitate him. Without the filial relationship, imitation of God is impossible. If we are truly His children, there have been implanted in us certain instincts, desires, qualities, and attributes which are in their nature divine; and these will have a tendency to assert themselves in our life and conduct. To yield to those tendencies is to become imitators of God; to check such tendencies—and they may easily be checked—is to neutralize the privileges of our new birth, and to lose the special spiritual benefits that belong to us as children of the heavenly Father.

How important it is, then, that in our personal experience we should watch over all within us that seems to come from God. These holy aspirations and purer instincts of which we are conscious have been introduced to our nature by divine grace; they come not of earth; they have their home in the very heart of God Himself.

How to Follow Paul's Example

Someone has observed that the acid test of anyone's dedication to a cause is his pocketbook. It reminds me of the Quaker who met an acquaintance on the street. In the course of conversation, the name of a poor family came up. "I really feel for them," said the second man. "How does thee feel for them, friend?" asked the Quaker. "With thy pocket?"

It's often difficult for those who are well off to understand how anyone would voluntarily accept a life of poverty. Probably the Corinthian Christians in their affluent state felt a bit contemptuous of the apostle Paul for choosing a life of privation. By telling them they ought to imitate him, even as he had imitated Christ—since they were his spiritual children—he was telling them they needed to strengthen their filial instincts and develop them into habits of life.

Children ought to want to be like their father. A little child naturally thinks his father the greatest man in the world—that is, if he is worthy of the name father. That's the attitude the Corinthians should have entertained for Paul, who had labored so lovingly and untiringly among them to exemplify Christ, and to lead them to experience the new birth. As natural sonship prompts an admiration that leads the child to attempt an imitation of what the father does, however feebly, so the Corinthians should have felt that way toward Paul, whose spiritual children they were. A true imitation begins within, in the condition of the spirit, rather than outwardly, in conduct; though the lessons that the inner spirit learns will surely express themselves in outward actions.

What Paul meant by saying "Be ye imitators of me" was not that the Corinthians should slavishly follow everything he did in minutest detail. The application to ourselves, therefore, is not that we should thoughtlessly do what Paul did, with careless disregard of the circumstances and the needs of the times, as well as the cultural and family setting in which each of us is found.

I have spoken previously of Paul's choice to remain single, either as a widower or as never having been married. Although we have no clear indication of his marital status, it seems likely that he was a widower, since he was a member of the Sanhedrin before he became a Christian, and all members of this Jewish high court had to be married.

Paul preferred to stay unmarried, but he did not insist that others should imitate him in this. "If thou marry, thou hast not sinned," he said in 1 Corinthians 7:28, "and if a virgin marry, she hath not sinned." In fact, he wrote of marriage in general, "I will therefore that the younger women marry, bear children, guide the house, give none occasion to the adversary to speak reproachfully" (1 Tim. 5:14). And again, in 1 Timothy 3:12, he said, "Let the deacons be the husbands of one wife, ruling their children and their own houses well."

What did Paul mean, then, when he requested us to follow his example? Not necessarily to stay single simply because he chose to. That was his own choice as a means to accomplish an end that he believed God had set in his life—to make Christ known to the far corners of the then-known world.

It is attitudes that count in our Christian lives. Staying single or getting married is not significant in itself and has no merit either way. The question to ask when making such a decision is, In view of what God has called me to accomplish in life, how can I best accomplish it—by being married or staying single?

And there are other considerations to take into account. What impression will I leave on others? Will my staying single encourage others blindly to follow me, to the detriment of their own lives and the cause of Christ? When we have considered all things, then we should decide on the merits of the case as they affect God's work, others, and last of all our personal comfort, pleasure, and idiosyncrasies.

Take another instance of Paul's attitudes in his service for Christ, that of being paid for his ministry. He preferred not to be paid for preaching and pastoring, but to support himself by his trade of tent-making. When he desired to go to Corinth from Athens, he didn't have to wait until he "raised" enough support, as so many missionaries do. Instead he was able to go there fully depending upon his profitable trade. That was also the case with his co-workers and hosts in Corinth, Priscilla and Aquila; they, too, were self-supporting (Acts 18:3).

Had Paul been other than self-supporting, he might never have traveled to Corinth to bring the gospel to some half-million people who lived in heathen darkness. I wonder whether Paul would have refused an offering had it been forthcoming. I doubt it. The main purpose of his life at that time was to carry the gospel to Corinth by all means—whether by tent-making and thus preaching only part time, or by receiving support from God's people and giving his full time to the ministry. The goal is the important thing, not the means—either of which would have been legitimate in this case.

Should Preachers Demand Their Rights?

The apostle Paul was very careful not to bring the gospel into disrepute by any action or attitude of his. That's why he labored with his own hands to support himself in the ministry. With what satisfaction he must have said to the Ephesians, "Yea, ye yourselves know, that these hands have ministered unto my necessities, and to them that were with me. I have shewed you all things, how that so labouring ye ought to support the weak, and to remember the words of the Lord Jesus, how he said, It is more blessed to give than to receive" (Acts 20:34, 35).

Did Paul demand a free parsonage? No. In Rome, when he was taken there as a prisoner, he hired his own house. That was toward the end of his life. Couldn't all the people he had evangelized, and especially the well-to-do Corinthian Christians, have contributed to the rent of that house? It is to their shame that they didn't. But Paul may have preferred to pay the rent himself.

In Acts 28:30 we read, "And Paul dwelt two whole years in his own hired house, and received all that came in unto him." I can imagine how he must have felt as he wrote to the Corinthian Christians. "Now ye are full, now ye are rich, ye have reigned as kings without us." And then he contrasts the fate of the apostles: "appointed to death: for we are made a spectacle unto the world. . . . Even unto this present hour we both hunger, and thirst, and are naked, and are buffeted, and have no certain dwellingplace" (1 Cor. 4:8–11).

Think of Paul, that self-sacrificing servant of God who had evangelized thousands, at the very end of his life waiting to die in Rome at the hands of his persecutors, having to pay his own rent! Pastor, teacher, parent, do you sometimes feel neglected by those to whom you ministered in the past, or are still ministering? Think of Paul in his hired house in Rome paying his own rent from the proceeds of his past tent-making. And then listen to him say, "Be ye imitators of me." I'm sure he would have accepted a rental allowance or a prison parsonage had it been offered to him, but apparently it had not. Nevertheless, he did not give up the goal set before him, to preach the gospel in Rome also.

What is the example we are to follow, in the light of Paul's words and actions? Not necessarily that we must have a secular job or pay our own rent if we are ministers of the gospel. But if those we minister to as a pastor or missionary refuse to support us, and do not provide a rent-free home, we do not give up preaching and making God's grace known. Paul didn't want us to follow the less excellent way of giving God only part of our time, but, if it had to be that way, he felt that part-time ministry was better than none.

Paul was very sensitive about possible criticism of his actions that could adversely affect the gospel. He took the times, the people, and the circumstances into account when making his decisions. Decisions ought not to be made in a vacuum. We must ask ourselves not only about the rightness or wrongness of our acts, but also about how they will affect God's work, our fellow believers, and those whom we are seeking to win to Christ.

What Paul did in certain circumstances may not be what God wants you and me to do in our own particular circumstances. Our situations may vary widely from Paul's but we must learn to surrender our rights for the gospel's sake. This does not mean we must concede that they are not our rights; we simply relinquish them freely out of a desire to serve Christ whatever the cost. God pity anyone who gives up ministering simply because his rights cannot be satisfied.

Listen to Paul speak about the rights of ministers: "Even so hath the Lord ordained that they which preach the gospel should live of the gospel. But I have used none of these things: neither have I written these things, that it should be so done unto me: for it were better for me to die, than that any man should make my glorying void. For though I preach the gospel, I have nothing to glory of: for necessity is laid upon me; yea, woe is unto me, if I preach not the gospel! For if I do this thing willingly, I have a reward: but if against my will, a dispensation of the gospel is committed unto me. What is my reward then? Verily that, when I preach the gospel, I may make the gospel of Christ without charge, that I abuse not my power in the gospel" (1 Cor. 9:14, 18).

Thus, in saying "Be ye imitators of me," Paul doesn't necessarily mean his actions but his attitudes and philosophy of life—always taking into consideration the circumstances and culture of the time and the need of the hour. Never allow the attitudes of others to hinder you from doing what you believe to be your God-appointed task.

Let us follow Paul's example in that, while we do our task—and others are not doing their duty toward us—we do not become bitter toward them. Consider with what sweetness Paul wrote to the Thessalonians, "For ye remember, brethren, our labour and travail: for labouring night and day, because we would not be chargeable unto any of you, we preached unto you the gospel of God" (1 Thess. 2:9).

No Instant Perfection

We have seen in our study of the life of the apostle Paul that he voluntarily accepted a life of hardship, even to the extent of earning his living by tent-making, so that he could preach the gospel without charge. Does that mean that Paul refused help from those he ministered to? No, for we are told that at Melita he was showered with many gifts. In Acts 28:10 we read that the people of Melita "also honoured us with many honours; and when we departed, they laded us with such things as were necessary." Also the Philippians must have contributed to Paul's needs, as he expressed his gratitude to them in Philippians 4:10: "But I rejoiced in the Lord greatly, that now at the last your care of me hath flourished again; wherein ye were also careful, but ye lacked opportunity."

And then, in verses 15–18 he adds: "Now ye Philippians know also, that in the beginning of the gospel, when I departed from Macedonia, no church communicated with me as concerning giving and receiving, but ye only. For even in Thessalonica ye sent once and again unto my necessity. Not because I desire a gift: but I desire fruit that may abound to your account. But I have all, and abound: I am full, having received from Epaphroditus the things which were sent from you, an odour of a sweet smell, a sacrifice acceptable, well-pleasing to God."

The verb Paul uses in the clause "be ye followers of me" in 1 Corinthians 4:16 is *gínesthe*, which is the present imperative of *gínomai*, meaning "to become." Paul is not calling Christians to a state of being they can attain by a single act. He is not beseeching the Corinthians to do something that will instantly make his choices theirs. Their imitation of Paul was to be gradual. They were to grow into the measure of his stature in Christ.

This was a little different from the imitating he spoke of in 1 Thessalonians 1:6 and 2:14. In these verses he used the aorist tense of the verb *gínomai* to express their instantaneous and once-and-for-all following of his example in accepting the word of truth unto salvation. "And ye became [*egenḗthēte*] our imitators, and of the Lord, having received [*dexámenoi*, the aorist participle] the word in much affliction, with joy of the Holy Spirit." As Paul had received the word of salvation once and for all and instantly, so did they. That is regeneration, our entrance into the kingdom of God.

But then comes the constant imitating of Paul's life. We need to examine his attitudes and philosophy with an eye to the principle involved. His own comfort and worldly glory never came first; it was always what was best for God's work, even if it meant suffering and privation. As we decide to go without one thing, we will find it easier to go without another. We do not generally reach a life that is fully satisfied by the indwelling presence of Christ in an instant. It is a gradual process. As we face the circumstances of life one by one as Paul would have, as Christ would have, we discover that we gradually are conforming to the characters of these personalities.

There are stages of life in each of which we can show our perfection in Christ. Take a six-month-old baby; we don't expect him to act as a six-year-old should. But we would be disturbed if after five years he still acted like a six-month-old. Growth is necessary; and that was Paul's burden for the Corinthians. They were saved but they were not growing spiritually. "Therefore be ye imitators of me" meant "Keep growing in grace. Keep getting more and more mature. Don't attempt to reach the height of God's expectation for you by a boisterous and instant act."

So many of us are like that gourd that wound itself around a lofty palm tree, and in a few weeks climbed to the very top. "How old are you?" asked the newcomer. "About one hundred years," said the palm. "About one hundred years, and no taller?!! Only look, I have grown as tall as you in fewer days than you count years." "I know that well," replied the palm. "Every summer of my life a gourd has climbed up around me as proud as you are, and as short-lived as you will be."

Paul didn't want the Corinthians to be like spiritual gourds whose climb was fast but short-lived. The moment we reach the conclusion that we have attained our full growth as Christians, that is the moment we need to re-evaluate our lives to see where we really are. We need to go over Paul's experiences for Christ's sake, enumerated in 1 Corinthians 4:9–13, and ask ourselves whether in each of them we have become his imitators. We may not have had to make the same choices he did, but if it came right down to it, would we be willing to? It's a soul-searching question.

Compromise or Sacrifice—the Acid Test of Faith

If the apostle Paul were writing to your church or mine today, I wonder if he could say what he wrote to the Thessalonian church in his day. "For ye, brethren, became [*egenḗthēte,* in the aorist tense] followers [imitators] of the churches of God which in Judea are in Christ Jesus: for ye also have suffered [*epáthete,* aorist] like things of your own countrymen, even as they have of the Jews" (1 Thess. 2:14).

Paul wrote these words to a church that in a particular instance imitated another church that suffered for the sake of Christ. Just as one gets used to compromise and is no longer deeply distressed by it, so it is with suffering as a consequence of faithfulness; it becomes second nature. The important question is, are we moving toward the pull of our carnal nature in compromising with the world, or toward conformity to Christ and Paul in resisting evil and suffering privation so that Christ may be glorified?

So many of us think of compromise only in theological matters and the common practices of the world in which Christians might feel tempted to participate. But Paul here intimates a compromise that few of us like to think about. It is keeping up with the Jones'! It is spending our time and money acquiring things we don't really need but which would enhance our social status and fame.

The converse of this is choosing to live modestly or even sacrificially when we could live it up for the glory of self. When we quit the Lord's work just for the sake of an easier life, that's compromise. The apostolic way may not be as easy, or provide us with all the comforts of the world, but it's the Christlike, the Paul-like way.

Moses, in his day, had to make such a choice. We read in Hebrews 11:24, 25: "By faith Moses, when he was come to years, refused to become the son of Pharaoh's daughter; choosing rather to suffer affliction with the people of God, than to enjoy the pleasures of sin for a season." Moses' choice represents one of the most extraordinary and deliberate acts of renunciation of worldly advantage in favor of spiritual values that the world has ever known.

And why did he do it? Why did he give up the palace, with all its luxuries, pleasures, and privileges, and identify himself with the downtrodden children of Israel? What was his reward for incurring Pharaoh's displeasure and enmity? Hebrews 11:26 goes on to tell us his motive: "Esteeming the reproach of Christ greater riches than the treasures in Egypt: for he had respect unto the recompence of the reward." He was influenced in his choice by the promise God had given to Israel of a coming Messiah.

His reward by worldly standards was hardly one to be envied. His life was fraught with peril as he braved the wrath of Pharaoh in pronouncing God's plagues on Egypt. It was no easy task he had organizing the Israelites into a faith-filled and cooperative marching band as they fled toward the Red Sea. And his forty-year endurance contest in the wilderness, leading an often discouraged and rebellious people, would surely seem a poor exchange for the pleasures of Egypt. What was his secret? Hebrews 11:27 tells us, "He endured, as seeing him who is invisible."

Moses and the apostle Paul were cast in the same self-sacrificing mold, for the sake of Christ. And we who strive to follow in their footsteps must be willing to make the same hard choices when the cause of Christ requires them of us. John Newton knew something of this when he wrote:

I asked the Lord that I might grow
In faith and love and every grace;
Might more of His salvation know
And seek more earnestly His face.

'Twas He who taught me thus to pray,
  And He, I know, has answered prayer;
But it has been in such a way
  As almost drove me to despair.

I hoped that in some favored hour
  At once He'd answer my request,
And by His love's constraining power
  Subdue my sins, and give me rest.

Instead of this, He made me feel
  The hidden evils of my heart,
And let the angry powers of hell
  Assault my soul in every part.

Yea! more; with His own hand He seemed
  Intent to aggravate my woe;
Crossed all the fair designs I schemed,
  Blasted my gourds, and laid me low.

"Lord, why is this?" I trembling cried.
  "Wilt Thou pursue Thy worm to death?"
" 'Tis in this way," the Lord replied,
  "I answer prayer for grace and faith.

"These inward trials I employ
  From self and pride to set Thee free,
And break thy schemes of earthly joy,
  That thou mayest seek thy All in Me."

LESSONS:

1. Paul's primary exhortation to the Corinthians was that they follow him in voluntary suffering for the sake of Christ. That meant sacrifice and deprivation, things to which they were not accustomed. According to Romans 8:18, future glory will be proportioned to—not self-imposed or every kind of suffering but—suffering endured for Christ.
2. Worldly things that are gains for us are actually losses for Christ (Phil. 3:7). Paul parted with all such things so that he might win

Christ and be found in Him. This is as unpopular a message today as it was then.

3. Believers should copy or mimic (*mímētai*) what they find of Christ in their spiritual fathers (1 Cor. 11:1)—not just the external actions but the compassionate and pure heart.
4. It is impossible to mimic Christ unless Christ, the power, wisdom, and righteousness of God, is in us. The new birth is absolutely essential, God's divine nature giving us the power for godliness. No unregenerate person can imitate Christ.
5. The ultimate criterion in the imitation of godly character is that which contributes the most to the glory of God through Jesus Christ, how we may best accomplish what God has called us to.
6. Paul characteristically made no economic demands of his spiritual children, however right it would have been for them to minister these commodities to him. We should not give up freely ministering the gospel just because others are not financially committed to our ministries. No actions on the part of others—right or wrong—should ever hinder our faithfulness.
7. The purity of Paul's motives is seen especially in his desire that others would obediently sacrifice to the work of Christ for their own sake—"fruit that may abound to **your** own account" (Phil. 4:17).
8. Becoming Christ-like imitators is not a one-time decision; it is a lifelong, arduous struggle against the flesh—our natural will and mindset for the things of this world. There is a one-shot (aorist) imitation of our spiritual father's conversion (1 Thess. 1:6; 2:14) that corresponds perhaps with the Spirit descending upon Christ, but from then on, it's a faith-to-faith process.
9. Sacrifice and indulgence are antithetical habits. They are in opposition and we get used to one or the other. The ideal is for sacrifice to become our dominant habit, a second, overpowering nature. We must survey our lives diligently, always asking whether in this or that our regenerate nature is getting a permanent handle or hold on the old man. Modest, sacrificial living for the sake of Christ makes our calling and election assured, as we begin to prefer, like Moses, the invisible for the visible (Heb. 11:25–27).

1 Tim. 4:17 | *Timothy's Role as Paul's Delegate to Corinth*

For this cause have I sent unto you Timotheus, who is my beloved son, and faithful in the Lord, who shall bring you into remembrance of my ways which be in Christ, as I teach every where in every church.

Don't Be a "Feudamentalist"

Before Paul sent his First Epistle to the Corinthians, he prepared the way for it by sending Timothy to Corinth. 1 Corinthians 4:17 is made clearer to us by paraphrasing what he had said as follows: "Not only am I writing to you to tell you of my conduct as an apostle, but I have also sent you my spiritual son, Timothy, to tell you all about it." According to 1 Corinthians 16:10, Timothy must have arrived in Corinth after Paul's letter (1 Cor.) got there. So first they were told of Paul's attitudes through this letter, then by the mouth of Timothy, and then Paul intended to follow up Timothy's visit with one of his own, which may or may not have taken place.

Thus Timothy left Ephesus for Corinth to convey Paul's message in person. He wanted Timothy to bring them an explanation of his attitudes in general, to prepare them more or less for the receipt of his letter to follow with more explicit information concerning his apostolic ways. Why did he choose Timothy for this particular mission? Who was Timothy?

His name meant "to honor God," and was derived from the Greek verb *timáō,* "to honor," and *Theós,* "God." He was the son of a mixed marriage. His mother was a Jewess and his father was a Greek (Acts 16:1). It was his mother Eunice and his maternal grandmother Lois who taught him the Scriptures from an early age (2 Tim. 1:5). He was a native of Lystra, in Asia Minor. The fact that Paul calls him his child in the Lord in 1 Corinthians 4:17 suggests that he was actually converted to Christ through Paul's ministry in Lystra. In spite of the fact of his godly upbringing by his mother and grandmother, he needed to come to the point of personal acceptance of Jesus Christ.

When Paul wrote his first letter to Timothy as a pastor, he called him "my own son in the faith" (1 Tim. 1:2). He took an affectionately paternal attitude toward him. And he maintains the same attitude toward the Corinthian Christians as he had maintained all along toward Timothy—that of a spiritual father. That is the sweetest attitude one could have toward anybody. Thus Paul sent one spiritual child of his to encourage and admonish his fellow children in Corinth.

The sense of brotherhood in the Christian Church is one of the greatest cohesive powers in the world. Paul wanted Timothy to go, not as a teacher with an attitude of superiority, an air of "Do as I tell you or else," but as a fellow child of Paul and a brother in Christ. The bond of having Paul in common as their spiritual father was an important consideration in making Timothy Paul's corrective emissary. The apostle felt that the Corinthians ought to listen to Timothy if for no other reason, at least, than that he was his son in the Lord, just as they were his spiritual sons, as he pointed out to them in 1 Corinthians 1:16.

Another reason Paul may have chosen Timothy to go to Corinth was that his father was a Greek and presumably a pagan. He was the product of a mixed marriage, a common thing in Corinth, as we see from the 7th chapter of this epistle. It was therefore easier for him to understand the problems of homes with mixed marriages, where the children were perplexed by the duties they owed to the Lord and those they owed to their parents.

As the son of a Greek father, Timothy would also have been well acquainted with the tendency of the Greek mind to make *a priori* philosophical judgments, such as the biological impossibility of the resurrection of the body. If you read 1 Corinthians 15, and study my exposition, *Conquering the Fear of Death*, you will see how methodically and pragmatically Paul proves that facts—such as the historically authenticated resurrection of the body of Jesus—negate any such philosophical speculations. His thesis is, here are the proofs; it happened; Christ arose. Therefore the resurrection of the human body is not only possible, but it will most certainly occur.

Furthermore, Timothy was a living demonstration of Paul's attitude toward certain matters he deemed not essential to the Christian faith, such as circumcision. As the child of a Jewess and a Greek, Timothy had not been circumcised as the Jewish law prescribed. Apparently this aroused opposition to Timothy and Paul among Christians of Jewish background as well as among unbelieving Jews.

Although Paul stood for the principle of not subjecting Gentile Christians to the Jewish ceremonial laws, he decided to circumcise Timothy so that the ministry among the Jews might not be hindered. "Paul . . . took and circumcised him because of the Jews which were in those quarters: for they knew all that his father was a Greek" (Acts 16:3).

This was not compromise but an example of how a Christian should act in similar circumstances. This philosophy is predominant in all Paul's teaching, as seen also in Romans 14, where he says that, if by eating or not eating certain foods he might offend others, he would accommodate himself to their customs. Timothy was a living example of Paul's attitude. He could say to the feuding Corinthians, We must learn to respect the culture of others if that does not entail the abandonment of fundamental principles. The failure to distinguish between what is fundamental and what is trivial makes "feudamentalists."

Trying to Remedy a Bad Situation in the Church

In the previous section we were talking about Timothy, Paul's son in the faith, whom he sent to the Corinthians to share with them the things that were on Paul's heart concerning their spiritual welfare.

In Acts 16:3 we read that Paul, Silas, and Timothy traveled westward toward the Aegean Coast of Asia Minor. Nothing more is recorded of Timothy in the Acts until they reached Berea (Acts 17:14). There they agreed that Paul would go on to Athens, leaving Silas and Timothy behind. From Athens, Paul went on to Corinth, where Silas and Timothy later joined him (Acts 18:5). This was not the visit referred to by Paul in 1 Corinthians 4:17. It was a later visit. Thus we see that Timothy was no stranger to the Corinthians, as he had been there with Paul and Silas (2 Cor. 1:19).

When we next hear of Timothy, he is in Ephesus with Paul, and was sent from there to Macedonia, along with Erastus (Acts 19:22). It was from there that he proceeded to Corinth on the occasion referred to by Paul in 1 Corinthians 4:17.

Apparently Timothy was of a retiring nature, for Paul urges the Corinthians to set him at ease and not to despise him. "Now if Timotheus come, see that he may be with you without fear: for he worketh the work of the Lord, as I also do. Let no man therefore despise him: but conduct him forth in peace, that he may come unto me: for I look for him with the brethren" (1 Cor. 16:10, 11).

From the situation that developed in Corinth, it is evident that Timothy's mission was not successful, and it is significant that though Timothy's name is associated with Paul's in the greeting in 2 Corinthians 1:1, it is Titus and not Timothy who has become the apostolic delegate (see 2 Cor. 7:6, 13, 14; 8:6, 16, 23; 12:18).

Between the time Paul sent Timothy to Corinth to make his ways known to them and the time he wrote his first epistle to them, he had received news about their situation from Chloe's people, who came from Corinth to see him at Ephesus. Thus in 1 Corinthians 1:11 we read, "For it hath been declared unto me of you, my brethren, by them which are of the house of Chloe, that there are contentions among you."

News also came to Paul about conditions in Corinth from Stephanas, Fortunatus, and Achaicus, as we see in 1 Corinthians 16:17. These three had apparently gone from Ephesus to Corinth, and back to Ephesus, to bring the news to Paul. And in the meantime Paul must have received a letter from the Corinthians asking his advice on several perplexing problems. It was probably in answer to this information from individuals and their letter that Paul wrote to them about certain specific matters.

Thus in 1 Corinthians 7:1 he wrote, "Now concerning the things whereof ye wrote unto me. . . ." And he goes on to give answers to their questions. This letter must have arrived in Corinth before Timothy got there. Paul wanted it to prepare the Corinthians to give Timothy a good reception. That's why he said in 1 Corinthians 16:10, "Now if Timotheus come, see that he may be with you without fear: for he worketh the work of the Lord, as I also do."

Paul fully intended to follow up Timothy's visit to Corinth by his personal presence, as we see in Acts 19:21, 22: "After these things were ended [in Ephesus, from which he wrote the Corinthian epistles], Paul purposed in the spirit, when he had passed through Macedonia and Achaia [of which Corinth was the principal city], saying, After I have been there, I must also see Rome. So he sent into Macedonia two of them that ministered unto him, Timotheus and Erastus, but he himself stayed in Asia [that's Ephesus and its environment] for a season."

Whether Paul was able to pay a second visit to Corinth, as he expressed a desire to in 1 Corinthians 4:19, is not clearly stated in the record. "But I will come to you shortly, if the Lord will. . . ." However, since he speaks of coming to the Corinthians for the third time, in 2 Corinthians 12:14 and 13:1, 2, we can safely assume that the second visit spoken of in Acts 19:21 and 1 Corinthians 4:19 must have taken place. Unfortunately, we only have the record of Paul's first visit to Corinth, and that briefly, in Acts 18:1–17. Of the second and third visits we have no record as to his teaching and ministry among them. Corinth from Ephesus was about two or three days by boat. Both were important port cities joined by ships.

Despite Paul's first letter to the Corinthians in answer to theirs, and the sending of Timotheus, followed by his second and third visits among them, apparently the troubled situation in the church of Corinth did not get any better. Paul consequently had to write a very stern letter to them, which we shall take up in our next study.

Situational Ethics Versus Moral Absolutes

As a parent, what do you do when kindness and reasoning fail to bring about a change of conduct in a rebellious child? You adopt sterner measures, right? And that's what the apostle Paul had to do when his first epistle to the Corinthians, and the sending of his spiritual son Timothy, failed to correct the disturbing situation in their church.

In 2 Corinthians 2:4 we read, "For out of much affliction and anguish of heart I wrote unto you with many tears; not that ye should be grieved, but that ye might know the love which I have more abundantly unto you." And then in chapter 7, verse 8, he wrote, "For though I made you sorry with a letter, I do not repent, though I did repent [i.e., changed my mind]: for I perceive that the same epistle has made you sorry, though it were but for a season."

The letter referred to here apparently was so severe that Paul was sorry he had ever sent it. Where is this letter? Most probably it is what we have in 2 Corinthians 10 to 13. These four chapters, then, should actually precede chapters 1 to 9 of 2 Corinthians. This sternly worded letter contained in chapters 10 to 13 was sent by Titus (see 2 Cor. 2:13 and 7:13). Apparently this letter, and Titus, were more successful in setting things in order in Corinth.

After learning of the improved situation, Paul wrote what may be considered as the Third Epistle to the Corinthians, actually contained in 2 Corinthians 1 through 9. He wrote of Titus' visit among them in 2 Corinthians 7:13, "Therefore we were comforted in your comfort: yea, and exceedingly the more joyed we for the joy of Titus, because his spirit was refreshed by you all." Then, after Titus' visit and the wonderful results of his second epistle, he wrote his letter of reconciliation contained in 2 Corinthians 1—9. Read chapters 10—13 first, and then chapters 1—9, and you will see that the sequence makes sense.

One more question, and that is, where do we find the letter that apparently preceded 1 Corinthians? In 1 Corinthians 5:9 Paul says, "I wrote unto you in an epistle not to company with fornicators." Where is this epistle? It may have been lost. However, some scholars believe that it's what we have in 2 Corinthians

6:14—7:1. Its contents fit the subject mentioned in 1 Corinthians 5:9. As you come to 2 Corinthians 6:13, skip to 2 Corinthians 7:2 and see how naturally they connect.

Let us not forget that the words of Scripture are inspired, but the divisions into chapters are the work of men in the 13th century and the divisions into verses in the 16th century.

Here, then, is the probable order in which the Corinthian epistles should be read:

1) 2 Corinthians 6:14—7:1
2) 1 Corinthians
3) 2 Corinthians 10—13
4) 2 Corinthians 1:1—6:13; 7:2—9:15

As we study 1 Corinthians 4:17, we see Paul's method of dealing with the immediate problems of a local Christian congregation. He sends a letter to them after having received personal information about their problems through informants and their own letter. He sends Timothy as his emissary, who arrives after the letter. He would have liked to go himself, but he couldn't. He knew that if he were to accomplish his task he would have to use others to help him.

In all these things, he is an example for us to follow. When we cannot attend to a thing personally, we should use associates who are beloved and faithful. Never mind if they cannot do all that we can. Never mind if those to whom we send them do not welcome them as they would us. We must put first things first, and establish right priorities as far as the apportionment of our time is concerned.

Paul was not in any way abdicating his responsibilities to the Corinthians. He was still dealing with them. He sent Timothy because he had no time to go himself. Observe, however, why he sent him: To "bring you into remembrance of my ways which be in Christ." This implies that they were already aware of Paul's way, but Timothy was sent to remind them of Paul's attitudes and add his own testimony that there was no change. It was not Timothy's responsibility to introduce his own personal opinions among them. He was willing to play a subservient role out of loving obedience to and respect for his spiritual father.

Paul reminded the Corinthians that what he said to them was what he taught in all the churches. He didn't want them to feel they were being treated differently, but he firmly believed that truth should not be accommodated to individual preferences. He was no advocate of situational ethics where absolute moral principles were concerned, but believed truth should be absolute for all. The Corinthians wanted him to sanction a different kind of Christianity among them, one that allowed worldly and immoral practices. Aren't there Christians like that today? Paul wanted them—and us—to know that Christian principles cannot be compromised at will.

LESSONS:

1. Failure to differentiate the fundamental from the trivial produces "feudamentalists," like the Corinthians. Paul addressed these feuding schisms in his first letter, and sent Timothy, a half-Greek, to these spiritual offspring who, unfortunately, were children in the bad sense as well. Timothy was probably familiar with Greek philosophy and remained uncircumcised, revealing a thorough understanding of the gospel of grace.
2. That these problems in the Corinthian church were not easily remedied is evidenced by their original letter to Paul, Paul's response (1 Cor.), Timothy's delegation, Paul's second and third visits, then finally Paul's very stern second epistle. Apparently, Paul felt a very high level of spiritual, parental authority and responsibility to the Corinthians.
3. When we cannot attend to particular ministries, we should entrust them to delegates or emissaries whom God has proven faithful to and knowledgeable of the truth.
4. Paul carefully restricts Timothy's mnemonic (memory) mission to "[Paul's] ways in Christ." There is no good reason for believers to

recall bad things about us. Our virtue lies in the extent to which we model Christ's perfect life. This is worth remembering.

5. The "ways [that are] in Christ" are universally right. Accordingly, Paul taught such things, as he says, "in all the churches."

1 Cor. 4:18, 19 | *How to Know God's Will and Do It*

Now some are puffed up, as though I would not come to you. But I will come lo you shortly, if the Lord will, and will know, not the speech of them which are puffed up, but the power.

Man's Will Versus God's Will

Arrogance is an unbecoming trait in anyone, but especially so in Christians. In writing to the Corinthian church, Paul foresaw what their reaction would be to his sending Timothy to deal with their problems, instead of coming himself. "Now some of you are puffed up, as though I would not come to you" (1 Cor. 4:18). Paul knew their pride would be hurt because of their sense of self-importance, which led them to feel they deserved his personal presence among them. "We deserve the number one man, not the second-in-command" was their attitude .

How many churches are like that! They will not even consider calling a pastor who is not nationally known. There may be a true saint of God available, whose message and ability are Christlike and Spirit filled, but he may lack the fame to satisfy the pride of the Pulpit Committee. They may not want to consider anyone unless he has a Ph.D. and a national reputation.

There was a church once whose choice lay between two seemingly acceptable candidates for the pulpit. But one had a scar on his face, and the other was smooth-cheeked and handsome. They chose the latter; and when his ministry proved weak and ineffectual, a wise old deacon said, "Well, they got what they wanted; a pretty minister, but 'the Lord taketh not pleasure in the legs of a man' " (Ps. 147: 10).

Pride was the fundamental sin of the Corinthians. They believed that they ranked first among all Christians and therefore deserved to be ministered to by no one less than Paul himself. They remind me of that sophisticated lady in the Orient who attended a dinner given by a high-ranking British official. The general's assistant seated her at the left of her host rather than at his right. She fumed inwardly until she could no longer bear it. Haughtily she said, "I suppose you have great difficulty getting your aide-de-camp to seat your guests properly." "Not really," said the general. "Those who matter don't mind, and those who mind don't matter."

Some of the Corinthians misunderstood Paul's not coming to Corinth at the time they thought he should. They thought to themselves, "You see, he didn't have the courage to face us himself, so he sent us a letter and then this inexperienced young fellow Timothy, who is not even an apostle. I guess we've won our case. If he were right and we were wrong, he wouldn't have hesitated to come running. Evidently what's happening among us isn't very serious, then." Such reasoning led them to become puffed up, arrogant, proud.

"As though I would not come to you"—that's how the verse begins in Greek. And that forms the basis of their reaction, expressed in the verb *ephusiṓthēsan*, "puffed up." Paul's thought could be paraphrased as "Some, not all, were puffed up on the presumption that I was not coming to you at all." The verb *phusióō,* which is a later substitute for *phusáō, is* largely limited to

Christian literature, and means "to blow up, to puff up." Observe that it was not all who felt that way; not all believed that Paul's failure to come was a sign of weakness.

For the sake of those few who became proud because he didn't visit Corinth, he decided to go, and he tells them so in verse 19: "But I will come to you shortly, if the Lord will, and will know, not the speech of them which are puffed up, but the power." Paul first expressed his determination to go to them quickly; that was the expression of his own will. But he is immediately arrested by a consideration of that greater will, the will of the Lord in his life. And so he adds, "if the Lord will."

There was also a third "will" involved here, the will of the Corinthians. Look at verse 21: "What will ye?" His will, God's will, the wills of the Corinthians. . . . Stop and think. Those are the determinant factors of life.

Although Paul appeared to be putting his will first, "I will come to you shortly," he really placed God's will first. He knew that his will to go was completely subject to God's directive will. The Lord could have made it impossible for him to go in any number of ways. God's will, therefore, must be the Christian's first consideration. The spirit and its will as well as thoughts are the center of man's being. My will is the expression of my character. So God's will is really the expression of God Himself—what God chooses, what God prefers, what God eternally purposes. All man's relationships to God are determined by the relation of God's will to man's will.

Paul's first question when confronted by Christ on the road to Damascus was, "Who art thou?" As soon as he learned it was the Lord, his next question was, "What wilt thou?"—and that was the question he asked for the rest of his life. From that moment he surrendered himself to the mastership of Jesus Christ, and henceforth he knew no other master. He could sing with the hymn-writer: "I own no other Master; my heart shall be

Thy throne. My life I give henceforth to live, O Christ, for Thee alone."

The Joy of a Yielded Will

Suppose you were to go into an automotive factory and stand before some great piece of machinery. As you stood there, a small wheel, no bigger than a quarter, came loose and fell into the midst of the machinery. That great mechanism moving round and round would grind that little wheel into fragments.

The universe is one great machine, so to speak, and God is its power; and when because of sin a soul drops out of its place in this great machine and falls among the great wheels of God's purpose, it is ground into powder, unless the grace of God puts that wheel back in its place in the machinery.

The moment you find out what the will of God is for you, and drop into your place, all the universe moves with you, and all the universe moves for you. The whole Godhead is back of you—the wisdom of God, the power of God, the love of God, and the grace of God—and you are as absolutely sure and safe as God is. Peter says, "And who is he that will harm you, if ye be followers of that which is good?" (1 Pet. 3:13). To obey the will of the Lord is the secret of all safety and security. And Romans 8:28 says, "We know that all things work together for good to them that love God, to them who are the called according to his purpose."

When we take God's will as ours, we do not destroy ours. There is no war between the two wills, no resentment that ours has been put in harmony with God's. The apostle Paul knew that if God willed that he not go to Corinth, that would have been his will too. Submitting to God's will is not only safe but it is also the secret of peace and serenity.

President Lincoln was once told by an associate, "I am very anxious that the Lord should be on our side." "Oh," said Mr.

Lincoln, "that does not give me the least trouble in the world, sir. The only question is whether we are on the Lord's side. If we are on the Lord's side, we are perfectly safe." It was that kind of faith that made Stephen, the first martyr, smile, and his face light up like the face of an angel, when he was on trial for his life before the council at Jerusalem.

When you yield your will to God you do not destroy your will. You put your will into harmony with His. You open your heart to His leading, and your life becomes the channel through which God flows and pours all the stream of His almighty power. Let it be the prayer of your life to go as you are led, when you are led, where you are led.

When Paul wrote the Corinthians that he was coming to them if the Lord willed, he was declaring that the Lord would gradually and eventually disclose that will to him. Because he saw the need, he wanted to go quickly. But just how quickly, only circumstances determined by God's will would gradually reveal.

We, too, must be willing to await the gradual disclosing of God's will. He doesn't always disclose it immediately. It is very much like that sheet that Peter saw coming down from heaven, in his vision on the housetop. It came down at the hour of prayer, and it ascended again when the hour of prayer was over, and all it revealed to Peter was his immediate duty. "While Peter thought on the vision, the Spirit said unto him, Behold, three men seek thee. Arise therefore, and get thee down, and go with them, doubting nothing; for I have sent them" (Acts 10:19, 20). That vision didn't tell Peter what his duty was next month or next year, but what his duty was just then and there.

Any work in which we are engaged that causes us a great deal of anxiety and fret and sleepless nights is probably not God's work at all. It is something we are doing because of our ambition, our appetite, our greed, our selfishness, or our desire to get on in the world. For if it were God's work we were doing, and we were just putting our hands to God's work, why should we worry about it? Isn't that a kind of impertinence? Isn't God able to take care of His own work? The man on the battlefield who has supreme confidence in the commanding officer and follows him into the thick of the fight doesn't consider himself responsible for the issues of the battle. He knows that there is a competent hand regulating the whole matter, and all he has to do as a soldier is to follow where his leader goes, and strictly to obey his commands.

It is God's will that I should cast
  All care on Him each day;
He also bids me not to cast
  My confidence away.

My soul, what folly then is thine,
  When taken unawares,
To cast away thy confidence,
  And carry all thy cares!
        —Author Unknown

Guidelines for Determining God's Will

Does following God's will always lead to success? It all depends on what we mean by success. As Christians, we should never equate success with the world's expectations. What the world counts as success, God may call failure; and what man considers failure, God may count as success.

For instance, when Stephen, newly consecrated to the work of God, and just beginning to make headway in his ministry and witness, fell under the rocks hurled at him by his enemies, most men might have said, "What a sad failure, to have his life cut off at the very beginning!"

But there was a young man standing by, looking at that face radiant with God's inner light, on whom it made an indelible impression. He was Saul of Tarsus, and it is very possible that the beginning of his conversion could be traced back to the impressions implanted in his mind when he looked upon the first of the martyrs for Christ. Was Stephen's death an indication that his life had ended in failure? For all we know, Stephen may have died to give the Church Saul of Tarsus as Paul, the apostle to the Gentiles.

When Paul and Silas journeyed to Philippi, a city of Macedonia, in answer to a vision God gave them in the night, and were thrown into prison, with their feet made fast in the stocks, most people might have thought, "Well, their mission certainly is a failure. They must have mistaken their calling." But when at midnight Paul and Silas were singing God's praises, and God answered by an earthquake that shook the prison and released every man's bands, what was the result? The jailer and his family became the firstfruits to Christ of that midnight hour, and what man counted failure, God in heaven counted success.

And when Paul went to Rome and was chained to a soldier of the Praetorian guard, and when every morning a new soldier was chained to him, until the whole Praetorian guard had had Paul under custody, most people might have said, "What a pity that a powerful preacher like Paul should have an audience of only one man a day, and a different one every day at that." But Paul could say, "God has enabled me to preach the gospel to the whole Praetorian guard." And who knows how much the conversion of pagans in Rome may be attributed to Paul's being chained to the soldiers of the Praetorian guard?

When Paul wrote to the Corinthians, "I will come quickly to you, if the Lord wills," what he meant was that as soon as he learned what God's will was, he would do it quickly. We should allow no delay in carrying out God's will, once He has made it known to us. There are some Christians who have a sort of vague intention of doing God's will, but they think the doing of it can be postponed to a time in the far future. It's perfectly proper to wait until we clearly understand what God's will is, searching meanwhile to know that will and earnestly desiring to find it. But the moment that will is made plain to us, it's impossible to be too much in a hurry to fall into line with God's purpose.

The signs that God gives to indicate His will may differ in each of our lives. However, there are certain principles that should be followed carefully, to protect us from making mistakes. Here they are:

Consider the Word of God. God will never give us any light outside of that Word. If He says, "Repent," "Believe," "Be baptized," "Do not forsake the assembling of yourselves together," we need no further light on these matters.

Consider the promptings of conscience. If our conscience compels us to a certain course, and we have compared its promptings with the will of God as declared in the Scriptures, and they prove to be in agreement, there can be no doubt where our duty lies.

Consider the outward call. Is there a door opened before us for service? Is a path plainly set before us, and does God seem to point providentially to that path?

Consider the inward call. How do our hearts respond as we ponder what the will of God is? How do our hearts respond to the voices of the Word and of our conscience and to the outward call of God's providences?

If these four fail to make God's will clear, then we are to *use our rational judgment, our God-given intelligence*. God has given us our reasoning powers in order that we may determine questions of duty. Suppose you think God is calling you to a work for which you have no qualifications or strength. Then you may seriously question such an impression, for God would hardly call a blind man to be an artist, or a deaf man to sing in the choir, or a paralytic to be an itinerant evangelist.

And lastly, but most importantly, we must use *our spiritual judgment*. We should weigh the question before us in the scale of the whole soul. We should notice how in prayerful moments of intimate communion with God the question appears to us, and how it strikes us in carnal moments when we are tempted to be worldly-minded. We must trust the judgment of the soul when it is nearest to God.

What's Your Excuse, Christian?

Why was Paul so eager to go to Corinth quickly, if that should prove to be God's will? He gives the answer in the last part of 1 Corinthians 4:19, "And [I] will know, not the speech of them which are puffed up, but the power." He wanted to learn by personal observation what the real situation was among them.

In the phrase "And I shall know," the Greek word is *gnṓsomai*, meaning knowledge gained from experience. Actually, the word "know" here is equivalent to "recognize" or "distinguish." In effect Paul was saying, "I am going to recognize what is what, and I'm not interested in the speech of those that are puffed up, but the power."

The word translated "speech" in Greek is *lógon*, meaning also "logic, reason, expression." I believe what Paul was determined not to recognize among the Corinthians was their logical explanations for their non-Christian behavior. He knew they would be ready with intelligent and philosophical excuses for all their wrongdoing. "I am not going to accept them," he made clear to them even before he went among them. He then explains he is going to reject such sophistries because they are the words of those who are puffed up with a sense of their importance. His feeling was that no matter how intelligent and logical the words of a proud person seem, they are not worth listening to.

In order to understand Paul's attitude, we must look back at verses 8 to 13 of this chapter. He said to the Corinthians, "Now ye are full, now ye are rich, ye have reigned as kings without us. . . ." And he contrasts his own life as an apostle, which was one of persecution and privation: "For I think that God hath set forth us the apostles last, as it were appointed to death: for we are made a spectacle unto the world, and to angels, and to men. We are fools for Christ's sake, but ye are wise in Christ; we are weak, but ye are strong; ye are honourable, but we are despised. Even unto this present hour we both hunger, and thirst, and are naked, and are buffeted, and have no certain dwellingplace; and labour, working with our own hands: being reviled, we bless; being persecuted, we suffer it: being defamed, we intreat: we are made as the filth of the world, and are the offscouring of all things unto this day."

How could the Corinthian Christians hope to outface him with excuses, after having read all this? Theirs was a life of ease and compromise; his was one of difficulties and faithfulness. "I know that you will try to excuse yourself," he is saying in effect. "You will speak arrogantly, out of your pride." To be selfish is bad enough. But to interpret selfish prosperity as the blessing of God, and to be proud of it, as the Corinthians did, was something Paul couldn't tolerate. "I won't swallow all that," is what Paul meant. The Corinthians were ready to tell Paul that they really had no opportunity to sacrifice; there was no need. I wonder what excuses our own generation of church people will render to God for living like kings and doing so little for others? I am not speaking of all, of course, but honestly, just how much are we willing to sacrifice for the cause of Christ?

I recently came across a poem called "Selfish Ambition" that expresses very clearly what I'm trying to get across:

> I wanted to walk in the beaten path
> That was trod by the feet of men.
> I wanted to thrive by the sweat of my brow,
> And rove in the valley of gain.

But the Master said,
  " 'Twas not thus I walked, nor lived;
If so, I lived in vain."

I wanted to live with a selfish will;
  My logic was surely sane.
No thought had I for a hungry world
  Nor for those who suffered pain.
But the Master said,
  " 'Twas not thus I lived, nor gave;
If so, I gave in vain."

I wanted to climb to a lofty height,
  To be known by the fame of men.
No care had I for the souls of men,
  Nor for death at the end of the lane.
But the Master said,
  " 'Twas not thus I lived, nor died;
If so, I died in vain."

And so my all to Him I gave
  In consecration deep. For me
He loved and lived and gave and died.
  Then self died out of me.
—Zech Ford Bond

Profession Versus Possession

The apostle Paul was a believer in that old saying, "What you are speaks so loudly I can't hear what you say." Although the saying was coined long after his day, he said practically the same thing to the Corinthian Christians in 1 Corinthians 4:19 when he told them he would recognize "not the speech of them which are puffed up, but the power."

What is this power? The Greek word is *tḗn dúnamin*, "miraculous manifestations," and here it stands in contrast to the words of the puffed up or proud. It means "energy, deed, activity." It can also mean the change in a person's life as a result of the operation of the grace of God. When a person receives Christ, he doesn't merely confess his faith with his mouth, but his whole life is transformed by the Holy Spirit.

As A. W. Tozer says:

> The truth received in power shifts the basis of life from Adam to Christ, and a new set of motives goes to work within the soul. A new and different Spirit enters the personality and makes the believing man new in every department of his being. His interests shift from things external to things internal, from things on earth to things in heaven. He loses faith in the soundness of external values; he sees clearly the deceptiveness of outward appearances; and his love for and confidence in the unseen and eternal world become stronger as his experience widens. . . . [T]he gulf between theory and practice is so great as to be terrifying. . . . Wherever the Word comes without power its essential content is missed.
>
> Is justification from past offenses all that distinguishes a Christian from a sinner? Can a man become a believer in Christ and be no better than he was before? Does the gospel offer no more than a skillful Advocate to get guilty sinners off free at the day of judgment? . . . The power of the gospel changes him, shifts the basis of his life from self to Christ, faces him about in a new direction, and makes him a new creation.
>
> The moral state of the penitent when he comes to Christ does not affect the result, for the work of Christ sweeps away both his good and his evil, and turns him into another man. The returning sinner is not saved by some judicial transaction apart from a corresponding moral change. Salvation must include a judicial change of status, but what is overlooked by most teachers is that it also includes an actual change in the life of the individual. And by this we mean more than a surface change; we mean a transformation as deep as the roots of his human life. If it does not go that deep, it does not go deep enough (A. W. Tozer, *The Divine Conquest*, 34–37).

Paul was not going to be taken in by the words of the proud Corinthians but was going to look for evidences of the power of the Holy Spirit in their lives. And from the tenor of all that he wrote them, that power, which is the evidence of the effectiveness of the gospel, was missing.

"Man is like an onion," said A. T. Pierson, "layer after layer, and each a layer of self in some form. Strip off self-righteousness and you will come to self-trust. Get beneath this and you will come to self-seeking and self-pleasing. Even when we think these are abandoned, self-will betrays its presence. When this is stripped off, we come to self-defense just as the Corinthians did—the word of the puffed up. And last of all, self-glory. When this seems to be abandoned, the heart of the human onion discloses pride that boasts of being truly humble."

Charles Kingsley said in his "Recipe for Misery: If you wish to be miserable, think about yourself; about what you want, what you like; what respect people ought to pay you; and then to you nothing will be pure. You will spoil everything you touch; you will make misery for yourself out of everything good; you will be as wretched as you choose."

Can you suppose that the Corinthians were truly happy in their pride and bristling self-defensiveness? Paul's words must have stung deep and brought a feeling of shame that they tried to throw off by rationalizing their guilt and thinking up high-sounding philosophical phrases to justify their conduct.

Spurgeon writes: "The shops in the square of San Marco were all religiously closed, for the day was a high festival. We were much disappointed, for it was our last day, and we desired to take away with us some souvenirs of lovely Venice, but our regret soon vanished, for on looking at the shop we meant to patronize we readily discovered signs of traffic within. We stepped to the side door and found, when one or two other customers had been served, that we might purchase to our heart's content, saint's day or no saint's day. After this fashion too many keep the laws of God to the eye but violate them in the heart. The shutters are up as if the man no more dealt with sin and Satan, but a brisk commerce is going on behind the scenes."

<u>LESSONS</u>:

1. The Corinthians' pride was revealed in their rejection of second-stringers. They wanted to contend directly with Paul, not with Timothy or one of Paul's letters. This common rejection of non-charismatic or popular leaders is a grievous sin. We should remember that even Samuel required direct revelation from God to recognize the chosen one (1 Sam. 16) among the more prominent looking candidates.
2. Paul's "I will" ("come to you shortly") was immediately qualified with "if the Lord wills." And so should we teach our tongue in general (James 4:15). There is pure joy in willful resignation to the Lord's will. Should our wills conflict, as perhaps in the death with which we will one day glorify God (John 21:19), it is enough that He will personally carry us.
3. God's will is unfolded to us in stages, much as it was to Abraham and Peter. We may be commanded to go, without knowing fully where we are going. Peter was told to go, doubting nothing, with the man God had commanded—that was it! (Acts 10:19, 20).
4. God's will is not worldly success. Because what men esteem God considers abominable (and vice versa, Luke 16:15), it is natural for unbelievers to consider the dedicated lives of believers to be failures.
5. God's will is expressed primarily in His Word. After this, we have the negative promptings of our enlarged (i.e., more sensitive) consciences, opened doors or windows of opportunity set before us, the desires of our hearts as they delight in the Lord (Ps. 37:4), and our God-given reason and spiritual discernment.
6. Paul differentiated "the words" from "the power" of the self-authenticating, Corinthian leaders. The dichotomy between words and power is not absolute, since the gospel itself, a set of propositions about Christ, is the power of God unto salvation. What Paul ultimately is comparing is what he laid out in the first chapter: the wisdom (words) of the world and the wisdom (words) of the gospel (God's truth). The different sets of words abiding in the Corinthian leaders and their converts would be fully apparent in divergent attitudes and actions.

1 Cor. 4:20 | How You Can Have Power

For the kingdom of God is not in word, but in power.

Restored in the Image of God

Why was the apostle Paul so scornful of the "words" of the proud Corinthians? Was it not because he was looking for the practical effects of the gospel upon the lives of the people? That's what he means by "power" in 1 Corinthians 4:20: "For the kingdom of God is not in word, but in power."

What does he mean by this statement? First of all, the kingdom of God stands for the kingship, kingly rule, reign, the rulership of God in the life of man. It is expressed by the Greek word *basileía,* which refers to God's sovereignty or lordship over the world that He made, but particularly over humanity. The term "kingdom of heavens, or the heavens" means virtually the same thing. The latter term occurs mainly in the gospel of Matthew, which is primarily addressed to the Jews. These people were so concerned lest they transgress the third commandment and take the name of God in vain when they spoke of the kingdom of God that they preferred to say "the kingdom of heaven, or the heavens." In Matthew 19:23, 24 the two terms are used interchangeably: "kingdom of heaven . . . kingdom of God."

When God created man He imparted to him His own image and likeness. That was a way of saying that our first parents, before they were driven out of the Garden of Eden, were like the God who made them, in that they possessed the power to lead a good life, as well as the gift of freedom to live by that power or to lose it by following the way of sin. Unfortunately they chose the way of disobedience, which was sin against God, and thus lost the power to do good. The fruit of the forbidden tree may have been sweet, as the pleasures of sin generally are, but after they had eaten came the knowledge that they were sinners. Thus began the pitiful story of rebellion against God, with all the misery and suffering that it entailed.

The Lord gave the Jewish nation the Law to deter them from evil. He allowed them to have human kings, such as David, who was the ideal king of Israel. Have you ever caught the full significance of Mark 2:23–28, which tells of the Lord and His disciples going through the cornfields on the Sabbath? Apparently they were hungry and began to pluck the grain. The Pharisees turned to Jesus and said, "Why do they on the Sabbath day that which is not lawful?" Work was not permitted by Jewish law on the Sabbath, and plucking grain fell into this category.

The Lord's answer was most significant in revealing the superiority of David, King of Israel, over the Law. Referring to an event recorded in 1 Samuel 21:1–6, He said: "Have ye never read what David did, when he had need, and was hungred, he, and they that were with him? How he went into the house of God in the days of Abiathar the high priest, and did eat the shewbread, which is not lawful to eat but for the priests, and gave also to them which were with him?"

Why did the Lord bring this up? David as the ideal King of Israel was regarded as foreshadowing the Messianic King. This incident clearly showed that David as King could set himself above the Law. How much more, then, could Jesus, who came to be King of kings and Lord of lords? What the Law could not produce—the ideal life God intended for man when He first created him, to be free to choose evil and yet to choose only good—the Lord Jesus came to accomplish.

Consider also Mark 10:2–12, where the Lord is asked about divorce. He does not take sides with Moses in Deuteronomy 24:1, 3, but goes back to the account of creation and points out that God's original intention was the lifelong union of one man with one woman—an intention man failed to carry out. What the Lord is actually asserting is that He is going to restore God's original purpose for man in creation.

Power over sin was not possible after man's fall, even with the giving of the Law. Sad experience forces us to acknowledge that the enacting of rules or laws cannot make people righteous. The Law makes clear what constitutes sin or transgression, but it cannot produce the innate righteousness that makes it possible for people to carry out its commands. It may deter them through fear of punishment, but it has no power to change the nature of the individual. This is why laws, and police to enforce them, are not the real answer to crime. They can contain crime to some extent, but they are impotent to transform the criminal—sinner—transgressor—call him what you will.

Christ came to introduce the kingdom of God, or the gospel, which is not merely a deterrent power but a transforming and regenerating power. That's why Paul, in writing to the Corinthians, says, "For the kingdom of God is not in word, but in power."

An unknown poet has expressed it this way:

> So let our lips and lives express
> The holy gospel we profess;
> So let our words and virtues shine
> To prove the doctrine all divine.

The Power to Live a Righteous Life

The kingdom of God and the gospel are synonymous. This is made clear in Mark 1:15, where John the Baptist is announcing the coming of Jesus' public ministry. "The time is fulfilled, and the kingdom of God is at hand," he says, and immediately adds, "repent ye, and believe the gospel." When is it possible for God really to reign in the human heart and life? Only when the sinner repents and allows Christ to give him new life—the birth from above of which He spoke to Nicodemus (John 3:1–15).

This is called the gospel, or *euangélion,* "good news," because it tells us, not of man's involuntary subjugation by God, but of God's change produced in man so that the rulership or sovereignty—kingdom (*basileía*)—of God over him is not an occupation by a monarch but the loving, protective care of a Father. A Christian, that is, one who has been restored to God through the new birth, is not afraid or resentful of God's sovereignty but rejoices in it. This is why the kingdom of God is not only "power," but also, as Romans 14:17 says, "righteousness, and peace, and joy."

Thus power to live a righteous, peaceful, joyful life and to do good was not wholly restored to man till the coming of Jesus Christ. Great men and women, by their faith and prayers, did much to prepare the way for a new life of power over sin and evil, but not till the day of Christ and the new age He ushered in was that power fully restored. It came, like the strong arm of help, to assist fallen man in his effort to regain his foothold and become once more a child of God. The apostle Paul expressed it in the familiar words of 2 Corinthians 5:19: "God was in Christ, reconciling the world unto himself, not imputing their trespasses unto them; and hath committed unto us the word of reconciliation."

The gospel that Christ preached was the good news of the beginning, at least, of the re-establishment of God's original plan and purpose for man, that he should dominate over sin instead of being dominated by it. Christ justified us through His death; in other words, He took our place as the guilty sinner paying the penalty for sin, which is death. But Christ also changes us so completely that we become averse to sin. We no longer run after sin, although sin never ceases running after us.

Throughout the Old Testament, whatever earthly rulers were rightly or wrongly exercising sovereignty, we see that the real King of Israel (and of the world) is God. He may and does work through deputies, but no one can share His ultimate authority. Yet the frequent triumph of evil-doers and the misery of the righteous often made this fundamental Jewish conviction difficult to sustain. They felt that God must have put off some of His authority, and that He must one day assert His creative sovereignty again; and men longed for the coming of that "day"—a day which the prophet declared would surely come.

The fundamental message of Jesus' proclamation was that that day had now dawned. The things that many prophets and other righteous men had long desired to see and hear were now present before the eyes and in the ears of Jesus' disciples (Matt. 13:16ff.; Luke 10:23f.). God's reign is here, or at least is so near at hand that already the signs of its activity are manifest; and men must make some response to the claims that it lays upon them.

The signs of God's rule were present in the work and words of Jesus Himself; they are proclaimed alike in His miracles and in His parables. They were not empty words but they were power. "For the kingdom of God is not in word, but in power." It's interesting to note that in the Greek text of this verse there is no verb. It does not read, "For the kingdom of God *is* not in word, but in power." It simply says, "For the kingdom of God not in word, but in power." There is no chronological limitation to this declaration. It was, is, and always shall be true. It is the permanent characteristic of the kingdom of God.

It "is not in word." What does that mean? The Greek for "word" is *lógō,* which also means "logic and expression." It is not something pertaining to mere human intelligence and its expression through human utterance. Here *lógō,* "word," stands in contrast to *dunámei*, "power, energy." The reference is not to the fact that men should act rather than speak. It is to the fact that the work of man is valueless in comparison with the power of God.

Observe what Paul said previously, in verse 19—that he was not going to recognize the word of the proud. He was referring to the words of the Corinthians in regard to what they were or were not doing. They thought they were something special when actually they were falling far below God's norm for the Christian Church. Paul reminded them that what counted in their lives was the power of God—the power of the kingdom of God. It is a contrast between the word and power of man—which are ineffective—and the Word of God which is the power of God unto salvation. Paul expressed it in Romans 1:16 when he said, "For I am not ashamed of the gospel of Christ [that's the kingdom of God]: for it is the power of God unto salvation [i.e., which results in salvation—the change and transformation of sinful man]."

The Word of the Proud

People who are proud of their abilities have a tendency to use them selfishly. They take credit to themselves for the gifts God has given them, and exploit them for their own benefit.

In 1 Corinthians 4, the apostle Paul exposes the selfishness of the Corinthian Christians when he says, "Now ye are full, now ye are rich, ye have reigned as kings without us" (v. 8). That they had more than others is evident from the context. But instead of humbly rendering back to God what they were well able to give, they held on to it as though it was the result of their own unaided achievement. That's why Paul asked them the penetrating question in verse 7, "For who maketh thee to differ from another? and what hast thou that thou didst not receive? now if thou didst receive it, why dost thou glory, as if thou hadst not received it?"

Selfishness is the daughter of pride. But spiritual pride is a great hindrance to spiritual growth. Paul called the Corinthians "babes" because of their spiritual immaturity. "And I, brethren, could not speak unto you as unto spiritual, but as unto carnal, even as unto babes in Christ" (1 Cor. 3:1). They were gifted people, rich and eloquent, but there was something lacking in their characters.

A young preacher frequently talked with a wise old farmer. One day the question under discussion was, "What is the greatest hindrance to spiritual growth and happiness?" The preacher said, "Surely it is failure to renounce our sinful self." "No," said the farmer, "the greatest hindrance is failure to renounce our righteous self."

Man's desire is to blow himself up out of proportion. This sin is confined not merely to the unregenerate but is also one that often afflicts those who have experienced the new birth. The Corinthians to whom Paul wrote were believers. They had renounced their former sinful practices, but they had become puffed up with the notion that their righteousness was attributable to their own efforts. It was to the Laodicean church that the Lord said, "Thou sayest, I am rich, and increased with goods, and have need of nothing; and knowest not that thou art wretched, and miserable, and poor, and blind, and naked" (Rev. 3:17). Apparently the Corinthians talked a great deal about themselves in somewhat the same spirit as the Laodicean Christians, and that was something Paul couldn't stand. "I will come to you shortly, if the Lord will," he says in 1 Corinthians 4:19, "and will know, not the speech of them which are puffed up, but the power."

The proud are full of words. Actually in this verse the Greek text uses *tón lógon*, "the word," for what is translated "the speech." Now notice Revelation 3:17, which I just quoted: "Because thou sayest, I am rich, etc." The verb in Greek here is akin to *lógos;* it is *légeis*, referring to an expression of the mind—*lógos* (*légō*, verb)—as contrasted with *laliá* (*laléō*, verb), which is mere babbling not necessarily accompanied by thought. The Corinthians knew what they were saying. It was premeditated boasting. They prided themselves on their consecration yet gave little in comparison to what they kept for themselves. Like Peter they uttered words, but when it came to performance it was a different matter.

> Beware of Peter's boastful words,
> Nor confidently say,
> "I never will deny Thee, Lord,"
> But "Grant I never may."

There are many people who would not kill a mouse without publicizing it, but Samson killed a lion and said nothing about it. Say much of what the Lord has done for you. Say little of what you have done for the Lord.

Remember the account of Ananias and Sapphira in Acts 5? They had a parcel of land that they were going to sell, and they said they would give all the proceeds to the Lord. But when it came to actual performance they gave only part, declaring it to be the whole. They were show-offs who were punished for their sin of lying to the Lord. They had spoken words in pride. Isn't it comforting that the Lord doesn't strike those of us dead today who are full of proud utterances, but whose acts are not commensurate with our words? If God acted uniformly in such matters, there would be few of us around, I'm afraid.

Apparently the Corinthian Christians were saying to Paul, "Come over and you'll hear of what we are doing." Paul responded, "I'll come to you quickly, if God wills, but I'm not going to recognize 'the word' of you who are puffed up." He could have known the power of their lives at a distance.

It reminds me of Aesop's fable about the traveler who was entertaining some men in a tavern with an account of the wonders he had done abroad. "I was once at Rhodes," said he, "and the people of Rhodes, you know, are famous for jumping. Well, I took a jump there that no other man could come within a yard of. That's a fact; and if we were there I could bring you ten men who would prove it." "What need is there to go to Rhodes for witnesses?" asked one of his hearers. "Just imagine you are there now and show us your leap."

Thus Paul intimated to the Corinthians, "I do not have to come to listen to your words. You can prove the quality of your life by what you do, and I will know it from where I am."

Thy Kingdom Come

Some people have been perplexed by the Lord's statement in Mark 9:1, "Verily I say unto you, That there be some of them that stand here, which shall not taste of death, till they have seen the kingdom of God come with power" (see also Matt. 16:28, Luke 9:27). This does not refer to the future kingdom—the culmination of what has begun with the first coming of the Lord—but to the coming of the kingdom as the power of Christ to save man. What our Lord was saying was that these people would see His power manifested through His crucifixion and resurrection. These words were part and parcel of Christ's prophecy concerning His forthcoming passion and triumph. That was the demonstration of the power of God's Kingship.

The kingdom of God is the dominant theme of the recorded teachings of the Lord Jesus. It is most strikingly presented in His parables. Some of these are described as parables of the kingdom. For example, in the Parable of the Seed Growing Secretly recorded in Mark 4:26–29, the stress is on the fact that the germination and growth of a seed is a process with which man has nothing to do.

The parable of the Mustard Seed (vv. 30–32) contrasts the proverbially tiny mustard seed with the large plant that grows from it. The kingdom of God resembles these processes; there is the power of God behind them, like the elemental power that forces a blade of grass through the earth. The ministry of the Lord Jesus corresponds to sowing time rather than to harvest; at present the kingdom of God is germinal rather than complete. Its consummation is as sure as the harvest, but that time is not yet (see the Parable of the Sower, Mark 4:3ff.).

The presence of this germinal kingdom of God challenges the men among whom it stands, and calls for a decision while there is yet time, before the final harvest makes it too late. The members of the kingdom of God are not the so-called righteous (Mark 2:17), the proud and self-satisfied Pharisees, but repentant sinners (see the Parable of the Great Supper, Luke 14:16–24; the Parable of the Pharisee and the Publican, Luke 18:9–14; and the Parable of the Two Sons, Matt. 21:28–31).

Thus, the kingdom of God, as it is presented in the teaching and work of Jesus, is essentially God's kingdom and not ours. It is something that proceeds from God, not something men build. It is not a utopia or a new social order, and it is not a mere disposition within men's hearts. It is an act of God Himself; it is His initiative in breaking the power of evil.

But, just because in the ministry of Jesus the kingdom was present in germinal rather than finished form, men still have their part to play: they must make a response to God's offer of

His kingdom. The kingdom of God has come so near as to provoke an unavoidable crisis. It is now up to men to draw near to the kingdom of God, and their response to it is shown by their attitude to the Lord Jesus Christ Himself. For it is in the person and deeds of Christ that God's reign has actively begun, that the assault against evil, physical and spiritual, has been launched. Men's acceptance or rejection of God's kingdom is thus inevitably expressed by their attitude to the Lord Jesus. This truth was clearly seen by the Pharisees and by Caiaphas; no mere technical dispute or personal quarrel gave rise to their determination to destroy Him. Jesus Christ had come to do what their Law could never accomplish—to restore God's damaged and perverted creation to its original destiny in perfect obedience to His will.

Although the kingdom of God as power to save began with the Lord Jesus, God's plan of fully restoring the world to its original state is still to come. Christ is going to finish the work He started. God's reign is still to be established; and it is in this sense that Jesus bids His disciples pray, "Thy kingdom come." In the absolute sense, God's kingdom will not come until the return of the Lord in absolute power, no longer to save but to bring punishment and retribution.

It is generally in this latter sense that the expression, "kingdom of God," is used in the New Testament, outside the Gospels, as denoting that kingdom which is the reward and goal in heaven of the Christian life here below. The kingdom of God began with the Lord Jesus as the power to save individuals, and it will come fully as the Lord returns in power to restore His whole creation to Himself.

Jesus is coming to earth again—
  What if it were today?
Coming in power and love to reign—
  What if it were today?

Coming to claim His chosen Bride,
All the redeemed and purified,
Over this whole earth scattered wide—
  What if it were today?

Faithful and true would He find us here
  If He should come today?
Watching in gladness and not in fear,
  If He should come today?
Signs of His coming multiply;
Morning light breaks in eastern sky;
Watch, for the time is drawing nigh—
  What if it were today?

Power to Overcome Fear

The Greek word for "power" in 1 Corinthians 4:20 is *dúnamis.* Some years ago, when an inventor developed a highly explosive substance, he used this Greek word to coin a name for it: dynamite. That's what "power" is, in the New Testament meaning of the word. As Christians, we have received this great power to live a victorious life against sin. It's not our own power but the power of God within us. It's power to live above circumstances instead of allowing them to toss us about like a football. It's power to live as poor men for Christ's sake when we might have had the opportunity and ability to be rich.

When Paul made his intended visit to the Corinthians, he didn't want to listen to their proud words but "to know the power," he said in verse 19. "For the kingdom of God is not in word, but in power" (v. 20). In other words, if God is King of your life, that will not result in boastfulness but in performance.

When Paul speaks of the transforming power of God, he calls it "the power," to distinguish it from all other kinds of influence. It was the power he himself had experienced as he traveled on the road to Damascus. It was an overcoming force that neutralized his Pharisaism and resistance to Christ. This power of Christ manifested itself in the transformation of proud Saul, who was persecuting the Christians, to Paul, the humble and persecuted believer who was ready to suffer anything for the sake of Christ whom he had previously despised. And this power manifested itself in his ministry of preaching the gospel as "the power of God unto salvation to every one that believeth" (Rom. 1:16).

Paul realized that this power was not only "unto salvation" but was God's endowment to the believer to enable him to overcome sin and live like Christ. What amazing changes it wrought in his life, and it can do the same in ours. Consider that Hindu woman who was converted by hearing the Word of God. She was terribly persecuted by her husband, and a missionary asked her, "How do you react to his cruel treatment?" Smiling, she replied, "Sahib, I try to cook better food for him. When he speaks unkindly to me, I answer softly. I want to show him that when I became a Christian I became a better wife and mother." In time a change took place in her husband. He had been able to withstand the preaching of the missionary, but he could not withstand the practicing of his Christlike wife. She had the joy of winning him to Christ.

When the apostles received the power of the Holy Spirit, what difference did it make in their lives? What kind of enablement does the power of God bring to men? It enables them to quit certain sins and wrong practices and acquire virtues and practices that are characteristics of a transformed life.

What a man loses by receiving such power can be summed up in one word: fear. He is no longer afraid to do what is right in God's sight although he knows it may cost him something. Paul expressed the difference that God makes in a person's life in 2 Timothy 1:7, "For God hath not given us the spirit of fear, but of power, and of love and of a sound mind." Where God's power is, fear is absent. There was real danger that Timothy would suffer persecution in Ephesus as a result of his Christian testimony, and be tempted to deny the faith (J. D. Jones, *The Unfettered Word*, 124). He was known as Paul's friend, and Paul was in jail for Christ's sake. That's why Paul wrote to Timothy, "Be not thou therefore ashamed of the testimony of our Lord, nor of me his prisoner: but be thou partaker of the afflictions of the gospel according to the power of God" (2 Tim. 1:8).

When this power comes upon you, fear of witnessing disappears, and a desire to sacrifice and suffer for Christ's sake emerges. Unfortunately, that was not what happened to the Corinthian Christians. They neither sacrificed nor suffered for Christ. They were fearful that to do so would result in their being in want. But as for Paul and Timothy, their testimony was "For God hath not given us the spirit of fear, but of power, and of love, and of a sound mind."

The Greek word translated "fear" in this verse *is deilías* (*deilía,* nominative), which is better rendered as "cowardice." When the power of Christ comes upon us through His Holy Spirit, we cease to be cowards. God supplies us with the courage to stand up to the world and to Satan instead of compromising. Cowardice always weakens the Christian. Fearfulness leads to impotence, as J. D. Jones reminds us:

> The man who distrusts himself is paralyzed by his distrust and accomplishes nothing. "I was afraid," said the man in the parable [Matt. 25:25]. . . . [A]ll his strength [was] drained away by his own hesitancies and timidities (*Ibid.*, 126).

John Newton wrestled with this problem and came up with the following declaration of faith:

> Why should I fear the darkest hour,
> Or tremble at the tempter's power?
> Jesus vouchsafes to be my tower.
> Against me earth and hell combine,
> But on my side is power divine:
> Jesus is all, and He is mine.

Power That Changes Lives

The characteristic of the Spirit-filled Christian is power. Christians should be dynamos. Christ promised His disciples, "Ye shall receive power, after that the Holy Ghost is come upon you" (Acts 1:8). That's what happened at Pentecost. The 12 disciples had kept themselves locked in the upper room for fear of what the enemies of the gospel would do to them. When the Holy Spirit came upon them, they lost that fear. They flung the doors open and went forth to preach the gospel.

The apostle Paul felt that the Corinthian Christians should have lost their fear of privation, defamation, and persecution. But they preferred ease to sacrifice. Isn't that true of most Christians today? They give so little room to God's Holy Spirit. They do so little and yet become so proud and puffed up. If Paul were to look down upon us today, he'd say, "I don't want to hear the words of the puffed up ones but to know the power."

The Holy Spirit is the One who makes the difference between an ineffectual life and a power-filled one. Take Peter as an example. He was a miserable coward at one time. With the rest of the disciples he forsook Christ and fled from the garden. Three times he denied that he knew Christ. He was afraid of having to suffer for Him. But what a difference Pentecost made! He stood up before vast crowds and fearlessly proclaimed the gospel. In Acts 4:13 we read, "Now when they saw the boldness of Peter and John, and perceived that they were unlearned and ignorant men, they marveled."

When you have this power, you acquire an intuitive knowledge of the unknown and the unseen. The difference between the Corinthians and Paul was a matter of values. The Corinthians thought chiefly of the comfort of material things, while Paul was willing to forego these when necessary because he thought of himself primarily as a citizen of heaven. He didn't care as much about the applause of men as he did about the approval of angels, and most of all God. "For we are made a spectacle unto the world, and to angels, and to men" (1 Cor. 4:9). In other words, when men make fun of your self-sacrificing dedication to Christ, angels praise you. The cowardly Christian can hear only the ridicule of men. He knows nothing of the praise of angels.

The power of the Holy Spirit gives knowledge of the unseen spiritual realities that the coward has no eyes to see. The fearful believer (what a contradiction of terms!) sees only the cross, while the courageous Spirit-filled Christian can see the resurrection. Power makes soldiers brave and enables them to envision the victory beyond the battle. If you cannot see God in the difficulties of life, you lack the power of which Paul spoke.

John Henry Jowett has beautifully expressed what characterizes this life of power.

> Another element in a forceful character is heat, the fire of an unquenchable enthusiasm. . . . The Acts of the apostles is a burning book. There is no cold or lukewarm patch from end to end. The disciples had been baptized with fire, with the holy, glowing enthusiasm caught from the altar of God.
>
> They had this central fire, from which every other purpose and faculty in the life gets its strength. This fire in the apostles' soul was like a furnace-fire in a great liner, which drives her through the tempests and through the envious and engulfing deep. Nothing could stop these men. Nothing could hinder their going. 'We cannot but speak the things that we have seen and heard.' 'We must obey God rather than men.' This strong imperative rings throughout all their doings and all their speech. They have heat, and they have light, because they were baptized by the power of the Holy Ghost (John Henry Jowett, *Things That Matter Most*, 251).

Paul told the Corinthians that when he came to them he would know the power. How can you know power? By experiencing its force. When you are empty this power fills you. When you are weak it strengthens you. When you are pushed and restrained you know it. When the disciples received the Holy Spirit at Pentecost, there was activity, there was noise, there were tongues of fire, there was speech, there were people repenting of their sins as a result of each one hearing the gospel in his own tongue. When you have this power it not only affects your own life but the lives of others.

The life of Paul was one that demonstrated the power of God. His ministry was unique. We read of no one else doing what he did, going from nation to nation, entering a city without knowing a single face, leaving it containing hundreds of men and women who would thank God throughout eternity that they had ever seen him. He entered Corinth a stranger and left it having brought into being a church of believers, despite the fact that it was one of the most sinful cities in the world. After visiting Thessalonica for only three weeks, he wrote: "Our gospel did not come to you in word only, but also in power. . . . and ye became imitators of us and of the Lord. . . . Ye turned to God, to serve a living and true God, and to wait for his Son from heaven" (1 Thess. 1:5, 6, 9, 10).

Lessons:

1. The kingdom of God is essentially God's restored, gracious sovereign rule over the human heart. This power produces very specific thinking, acting, and emoting that cannot be parroted.
2. The restoration power is not the motivating forces of reward and punishment found in the Law, but transforming, regenerating power that renews the mind and will. Thus, a man in Christ is a new creature, ordained to good works and a righteous life (Eph. 2:10). We become averse to sin as the Lord lives His holy life in us.
3. The kingdom of God is not in worldly wisdom but in the power of the words of the gospel. If you reduce your opponents propositions to contradiction, you will not thereby win him to Christ. There is a Logic (*Lógos*, John 1:1, 18) that is the Truth (John 14:6) but this is not the "logic" of the world, which begins with wrong premises and ends

with wrong conclusions. Paul no doubt has Greek speculative thinking in mind here. This will never match the *Lógos* of God, to Whom the gospel, which is the power of God unto salvation (Rom. 1:16) points.

4. Pride is a form of self-centeredness that denies in word, deed, and attitude the Giver of all things, Who makes us differ(ent). The proud are blowhards, full of empty words, exalting themselves beyond the truth. They believe foolishly that they are independent of God.
5. The power of the kingdom of God was manifested in Christ's first coming through miracle after miracle, the transfiguration, and finally His resurrection and ascension into glory. The parables show that the power of the kingdom is the full extension of the salvation of men between Christ's first and second comings. The history of the ingathering of the spirits of the elect into the church, culminating in the final resurrection and ingathering of their bodies.
6. The King of kings brought the kingdom of God near to men. Men and women must now enter the gates through faith in Christ, specifically in His atoning blood. All the Father has done in Christ has raised the level of accountability. Those who are owned by the gospel must preach it; those who hear, receive it.
7. The gospel is a power that both converts and sanctifies, that is, enables the believer to live a holy, godly life before God.
8. This power is contrasted with all the fears of the natural man—from everyday timidity to the fear of death. When the Spirit of God is within us, we are no longer cowards, compromising with the anti-Christian values of the world. We are bold and unstoppable.
9. Some specific fears eradicated by the Spirit of God are the natural fears of privation, defamation, and persecution. In these areas, the wealthy, leisurely Corinthians had not matured, which is why Paul makes his dramatic contrast between their affluence and the apostles' deprivation.
10. The sacrificing believer, while ridiculed by men and demons, is applauded by a cloud of witnesses, including "the spirits of the just made perfect" (Heb. 12:23) and the elect angels, whom we entertain unawaringly (Heb. 13:2). The power-words of the gospel to convert and sanctify so remarkably compare with the vain, useless and arrogant words of Babel.

1 Cor. 4:21 | *Apply Proper Discipline When Needed*

> *What will ye? shall I come unto you with a rod, or in love, and in the spirit of meekness?* (*1 Cor. 4:21*).

Accepting Rebuke in the Right Spirit

When you see something wrong going on in a Christian church, what ought you to do about it? Is it the Christian's responsibility to rebuke a fellow believer?

In the 4th chapter of 1 Corinthians, Paul spoke out strongly against the attitude of the Corinthian Christians, contrasting their selfish and proud affluence with the apostolic example of personal sacrifice for the sake of the gospel. "You have enriched yourselves," he says in verse 8, "while we go hungry and thirsty." He wanted to counsel them in a way that would cause them properly to evaluate the priorities of the Christian life.

One of the most difficult decisions we have to make is what to put first, second, third, or last in our lives. Paul was determined to put Christ first. The Corinthians apparently had not done this. This troubled Paul, since he had adopted them as his spiritual children (see v. 15).

What really upset Paul about the behavior of the Corinthians was that they seemed proud of their selfish attitudes. It's bad enough to be selfish, but to be proud of it compounds the guilt.

Paul attributed the worsening of such attitudes to the fact that he was not personally in Corinth to teach them. Lack of adequate teaching was apparently greatly to blame. That's why he decided to send Timothy to Corinth. He wanted to go himself and told them he would do so shortly, if the Lord willed.

The kingdom of God had become empty theory to the Corinthians instead of a demonstration of the power of the Holy Spirit. As a spiritual father, Paul sternly warned them that when he came he would rebuke them and set things right among them. At the beginning of this chapter, Paul had defended himself against the criticism of the Corinthians. Now he goes on to exercise his apostolic authority of discipline. The Corinthians did not want to accept his discipline, denying him the right to exercise the authority of an apostle since he was not one of the original Twelve Disciples chosen by Christ.

In 1 Corinthians 9 Paul defends his apostleship by saying, "Am I not an apostle? am I not free? have I not seen Jesus Christ our Lord? are not ye my work in the Lord? If I be not an apostle unto others, yet doubtless I am to you: for the seal of mine apostleship are ye in the Lord" (vv. 1, 2).

In 1 Corinthians 4:21, therefore, Paul is not acting as an individual believer rebuking fellow believers but in his divinely appointed office as an apostle. He is acting as the Corinthians' spiritual father. He is not even seeking the corporate action of the church, as he does in the next chapter. In a family, the father exercises his disciplinary privilege without seeking the agreement of the rest of the family

Paul indicates that the correction he desired to bring about could be accomplished in either of two ways: through punishment, by using the "rod," just as a father does when spanking his son; or through the persuasive power of words. Do you want me to come and spank you, or to counsel you in love? is his thought here. The choice, apparently, would be determined by their attitude. This indicates that both ways are permissible to the leader of the flock, depending on which will be more fruitful. In Paul's case, the attitude of the Corinthians would determine which method he would use. Isn't that comparable to how we parents act? Sometimes we find it necessary to spank, and at other times a word of reproof proves sufficient.

That the Corinthians needed correction, Paul had not the slightest doubt. Of course, they would deny this. But as an apostle he had made the diagnosis and was determined to apply the remedy. How foolishly we sometimes act in the spiritual realm. When a doctor tells us there is something wrong with our physical bodies, we recognize his expertise and accept the treatment he prescribes. We don't react with piqued pride when he tells us how we can have a blemish removed from our bodies. We willingly pay the price the physician asks to free us from a wart or other mark of disfigurement. Why, then, should we turn away with wounded pride from any mirror that presumes to throw back to us a reflection of our moral blemishes?

When it comes to our spiritual health, we want to make our own diagnosis and apply our own rules. We act like petulant babies, thrusting away the medicine that would make us well, because we find it unpalatable. We become angry with the wise spiritual leader and counselor who presumes to point out how we are harming ourselves and others by our unchristian behavior. We're like the King of Israel who said of Micaiah the prophet, "But I hate him; for he doth not prophesy good concerning me, but evil" (1 Kgs. 22:8).

Nevertheless, the King was persuaded to call for Micaiah; and the friendly servant who went to call him warned him to speak "that which is good," lest he incur the King's wrath. But Micaiah replied in the spirit of a true prophet of God, "As the Lord liveth, what the Lord saith unto me, that will I speak" (1 Kgs.

22:14). That was the spirit of the apostle Paul in exercising his authority in the church, as conferred upon him by Christ.

Lack of Discipline Means Lack of Love

When you love someone very much, it's hard to have to rebuke that person for a fault that is harming him and others. In the first place, you may be afraid he'll reject your words and love you the less. Something like that must have been going through the apostle Paul's mind as he felt it necessary to correct the faults that were harming the testimony of the Corinthian church.

Paul didn't want to estrange himself from the Corinthians and cause them to hate him. He knew the words of wisdom found in Proverbs 9:7–9: "He that reproveth a scorner getteth to himself shame: and he that rebuketh a wicked man getteth himself a blot. Reprove not a scorner, lest he hate thee: rebuke a wise man, and he will love thee. Give instruction to a wise man, and he will be yet wiser: teach a just man, and he will increase in learning." In the light of those words, Paul wanted to make sure of the best way to administer necessary reproof. Reproof is sometimes unskillfully administered and at other times unfaithfully withheld. Paul did not want to pursue either course. He wanted skillfully to administer needed rebuke.

Another admonition with which Paul was familiar is found in Proverbs 13:24: "He that spareth his rod hateth his son." If the rod is necessary, one should not hesitate to administer it. Paul loved the Corinthians as his own spiritual children. He would have been more popular among them had he been indifferent to their wrong ways. But he wouldn't have been faithful in the execution of his fatherly love. The father who avoids the application of the rod because it's easier not to incur the possible resentment of his son is actually a selfish father. Parents who are in the habit of giving their children everything they ask, and of permitting them to disobey without punishment, really do not love their children as much as they think they do. "He that spareth his rod hateth his son." To call it love is to be deceived by one of Satan's lies. The man who gravely tells his child what is wrong, and, if the wrong is repeated, strictly chastens him—that man really loves his child, and sacrifices his own ease for the child's highest good.

Paul considered the Corinthian Christians rough diamonds in need of grinding and polishing. The Koh-I-Noor diamond, when it came into the Queen of England's possession, was a misshapen lump. It was necessary to have its corners cut off and its sides reduced to symmetry. But no unskillful hand was permitted to touch it. Men of science were summoned to consider its nature and capacities. They examined the form of its crystals and the consistency of its parts. They considered the direction of the grain and the side on which it would bear pressure. With their instructions, the jewel was placed in the hands of an experienced lapidary, and by long, patient, careful labor its sides were ground down to the desired proportions. The gem was hard and needed a heavy pressure. It was precious and needed every precaution that science and skill could suggest to get it polished into shape without cracking it in the process. The effort was successful. The hard diamond was rubbed down into forms of beauty and yet sustained no damage by the greatness of the pressure to which it was subjected.

"Jewels, bright jewels," in the form of spiritual children were the heritage God gave to Paul as a spiritual father. God may permit us to play the same role as spiritual parents to our children, or to the children of God in the Church, in the case of pastors and teachers. Let us recognize in either case that children are unshapely and need to be polished; they are hard, and cannot be reduced to symmetry without firm handling; they are brittle, and so liable to be permanently damaged by the wrong kind of pressure, but they are stones of peculiar preciousness and, if they are successfully polished, they will shine as stars forever and ever, giving off the glory they reflect from the Sun of righteousness. Those in whose care and trust God has placed these diamonds in the rough should neither strike them unskillfully nor let them lie uncut and unpolished.

While there should be a strong manly love to wield the rod firmly, there should also be a farseeing wisdom to judge in view of all the circumstances, whether and when the rod should be applied. A parent must study carefully both his child's character and his own.

There's no inherent virtue in bodily pain to heal a moral or spiritual ailment. Much depends on the adaptation of punishment in kind and measure to the particular form of the child's misbehavior. If a child is seldom or never so wayward as to need the rod, then seldom or never let the rod be applied. But be careful not to determine or proclaim beforehand that you will never resort to corporal punishment, lest you be setting your wisdom against the law of the Lord.

The rod and love are not antagonistic. It's not necessary to banish one in order to live under the rule of the other. Love keeps the rod, and lays it on when needful. Our Father in heaven chastens every child whom He loves, and does not spare for their crying. Genuine parental love on earth follows the divine example.

Less Talk and More Walk

A Quaker had a bundle of hides stolen from his warehouse. He began to wonder what steps he should take to prevent a repetition of such an act. Instead of putting the machinery of the law in motion, he inserted the following ad in the newspapers: "Whoever stole a quantity of hides on the 5th of this month is hereby informed that the owner has a sincere wish to be his friend. If poverty tempted him to take this false step, the owner will keep the whole transaction secret, and will gladly put him in the way of obtaining money by means more likely to bring him peace of mind."

A few nights later, when the family were about to retire to rest, a man knocked at the door of the Quaker's house, and he carried with him a bundle of skins. "I have brought them back," he said. "It is the first time I ever stole anything, and I have felt very bad about it." "Let it be the last, friend," said the Quaker. "The secret still lies between ourselves." He spoke to the man faithfully and affectionately about the folly of dishonesty, and of the claims of the gospel. He also took him into his employ and the man became a changed character, living an exemplary life from then on.

Paul was hoping something like that would happen in the case of the proud Corinthians—that his single word of admonition would really suffice. He had no desire to go to them in a punitive spirit but in a spirit of love and kindly counsel. Where "a word to the wise is sufficient," there is no need of stronger measures. Wielding the rod should be the last resort, only after verbal persuasion has failed to bring about the desired results.

Later on, in 2 Corinthians, we see that Paul's hopes were realized. His words stung the Corinthians to a zealous purging of the sin in their midst, so that they almost went to the other extreme of being too harsh with the sinning members. Paul had to admonish them about this, also, and urge them to comfort the repentant and downcast sinner lest he be "swallowed up with overmuch sorrow" (2 Cor. 2:7).

His purpose in all this was that the "power" of God might be manifested in the Corinthian church rather than the bombast of "great swelling words." Surely this is what is needed in the Church today: less talk and more walk. Would you like to see results in your service for Christ? Whether you're a pastor, a Sunday school teacher, or simply a lay person in the home or the business world, you need the power of God to make your witness effective. This power must first of all be manifested *in* you before it can flow out *from* you.

How do you secure this power within? There's no mystery about it; God's Word makes it very simple. You believe in Christ as the Son of God and receive Him into your heart by faith. That results in your salvation from sin and deliverance from eternal condemnation. But to have His power, you must be "attached" to Him as a branch is attached to a vine. The branch has no life or fruit-bearing power apart from the vine, and you can have none apart from a constant abiding in Christ—relinquishing your so-called right to self-determination in complete submission to His will and plan for your life.

That's what the apostle Paul did, and his name rings down the corridors of time as the most fruitful and power-filled witness of the early Church.

The Christian who wants to be greatly used of God must first count the cost and decide whether he is willing to pay it. As Jesus Himself said: "Whosoever doth not bear his cross, and come after me, cannot be my disciple. For which of you, intending to build a tower, sitteth not down first, and counteth the cost, whether he have sufficient to finish it? Lest haply, after he hath laid the foundation, and is not able to finish it, all that behold it begin to mock him, Saying, This man began to build, and was not able to finish" (Luke 14:27–30).

Paul accepted that challenge, saying in Philippians 3:7, 8, "What things were gain to me, those I counted loss for Christ. Yea doubtless, and I count all things but loss for the excellency of the knowledge of Christ Jesus my Lord."

Here is a prayer of dedication by an unknown author that the apostle Paul himself could heartily make his own. Can you?

"O Lord, I present myself to Thee: my will, my time, my talents, my tongue, my property, my reputation, my entire being, to be—and to do—anything Thou requirest of me. Now, as I have given myself to Thee, I am no longer my own, but all the Lord's. I believe that Thou wilt accept the offering I bring. I trust Thee to work in me all the good pleasure of Thy will. I am willing to receive what Thou givest, to lack what Thou withholdest, to relinquish what Thou takest, to surrender what Thou claimest, to suffer what Thou ordainest, to do what Thou commandest, to wait—till Thou sayest, 'Go.' "

LESSONS:

1. The kingdom of God as power was not fully evident in the Corinthians' possessive attitudes toward worldly goods and status; so Paul wrote to remind them that Christ had come to save them fully from these inner dispositions.
2. This he did not as a stern, Mosaic disciplinarian, but as a caring father. However, he did offer them the choice of a father's rod or a father's love and meekness, in either case carrying the full weight of his apostolic authority. In this way, he even counseled the Corinthians to prepare a right spirit for his correction. We should learn to accept discipline from God as well as good (Job 2:10).
3. Here the rod, a harsh, conditional love that always punishes disobedience, is contrasted with *agápē*: ". . . shall I come . . . with a rod, or in love? . . ." Regardless which option the Corinthians preferred, they would have to concede that they were disobedient in their many concessions to the glory of the world. To take the rod would admit a reason for it; to take *agápē* would equally admit the presence of sin in the very unconditionality of the love.
4. Spiritual but immature children are like "diamonds in the rough." Destined in the long run to be conformed to the image of Christ and shine forever like the stars, they arrive at this goal with a lot of tough grinding and polishing.
5. In addition to his apostolic authority, Paul wrote and visited the Corinthians with the full weight of his life and spiritual maturity. He was living the very life of sacrifice he was calling them to enter. No wonder his words caused this carnal church to repent.

Bibliography

Bennett, Rev. William J. E. *Lecture-Sermons: on the Distinctive Errors of Romanism.* London: W. J. Cleaver, 1842.

Coates, Thomas. *The Chapel Hour.* Saint Louis, MO: Concordia Publishing House, 1950.

Conzelmann, Hans. "*Skótos.*" In *Theological Dictionary of the New Testament,* edited by Gerhard Kittel, edited and translated by Geoffrey W. Bromiley, vol. VII, 423–45. Grand Rapids, MI: Wm. B. Eerdmans Publishing Company, 1964.

Cremer, Hermann. *Biblico-Theological Lexicon of New Testament Greek*, 4th ed. Edinburgh: T & T Clark, 1895.

Davies, Llynfi. "Paul's Refashioning." In *Christian World Pulpit*, 118:22, 23. London: The Christian World Ltd., 1930.

Gillies, John. *Memoirs of Rev. George Whitefield.* New Haven: Horace Mansfield, 1834.

Gray, William A. *Laws and Landmarks of the Spiritual Life.* London: Charles H. Kelly, 1895.

Greenhough, J. G. *The Mind of Christ in St. Paul.* London: Hodder and Stoughton, n.d.

Greenven, Heinrich. "*Zētéō.*" In *Theological Dictionary of the New Testament,* edited by Gerhard Kittel, edited and translated by Geoffrey W. Bromiley, vol. II, 892, 893. Grand Rapids, MI: Wm. B. Eerdmans Publishing Company, 1964.

Hammond, Rev. T. C. *One Hundred Texts of the Society for Irish Church Missions.* London: The Society for Irish Church Missions, n.d.

Hanse, H. "*Loidoréō.*" In *Theological Dictionary of the New Testament,* edited by Gerhard Kittel, edited and translated by Geoffrey W. Bromiley, vol. IV, 293, 294. Grand Rapids, MI: Wm. B. Eerdmans Publishing Company, 1964.

Hobbs, David. "Things Secret and Revealed." In *Christian World Pulpit,* 45:10–12. London: The Christian World Ltd., 1894.

Holden, J. Stuart. "The Law of Divine Concealment." In *Christian World Pulpit*, 98:78–80. London: The Christian World Ltd., 1920.

Hutton, John A. "Fools for Christ's Sake." In *Christian World Pulpit,* 105:85–87. London: The Christian World Ltd., 1924.

Johnson, Herrick. "God's Great Praising Day." In *Churchman's Pulpit,* 1:490–92. London: Francis Griffiths, 1911.

Jones, J. D. *The Unfettered Word.* London: James Clarke & Co., 1912.

Jowett, John Henry. *Things That Matter Most*, I, 242. New York: Fleming H. Revell Company, 1913.

Lenski, R. C. H. *The Interpretation of I and 2 Corinthians*. Minneapolis, Minnesota: Augsburg Publishing House, 1963.

Liddon, H. P. *Advent in St. Paul's: Sermons Bearing Chiefly on the Two Comings of Our Lord*. 2 vols. London: Rivingtons, 1889.

Liddon, H. P. "Righteous Judgment." In *Christian World Pulpit*, 30:369–71. London: The Christian World Ltd., 1886.

Liddon, H. P. "Stewards of the Mysteries of God." In *Sermon Outline Bible, Acts 7—1 Corinthians*, ed. by W. Robertson Nicoll. 291, 292. Grand Rapids, MI: Baker Book House, 1958.

Liddon, H. P. "Humility and Truth." In *Sermons Preached before the University of Oxford*, Second Series, 1868–1882, 4th edition, 18–37. London: Rivingtons, 1887.

Masterman, J. H. B. *Sunday Teachings: The Collects, Epistles, and Gospels*. London: Society for Promoting Christian Knowledge, 1940.

Parker, Joseph. *Detached Links: Extracts from the Writings and Discourses of Joseph Parker, D.D.* Compiled by Rev. Joseph Lucas. London: Richard D. Dickinson, 1873.

Preisker, Herbert. "*Épainos*." In *Theological Dictionary of the New Testament*, edited by Gerhard Kittel, edited and translated by Geoffrey W. Bromiley, vol. II, 586–88. Grand Rapids, MI: Wm. B. Eerdmans Publishing Company, 1964.

Robertson, Archibald and Plumber, Alford. "A Critical and Exegetical Commentary on the Second Epistle of St. Paul to the Corinthians." In *International Critical Commentary*. Edinburgh: T. & T. Clark, 1956.

Seiss, Joseph A. *Lectures on the Epistles for Sundays and the Chief Festivals*. 2 vols. Philadelphia: Lutheran Bookstore, 1885.

Spurgeon, C. H. *An All-Round Ministry*. Great Britain: The Banner of Truth Trust, 1960.

Stalker, James. "Man's Self-Knowledge." In *Anglican Pulpit Library*, 1:169–72. London: James Mackenzie Ltd., n.d.

Sumner, Samuel. "Christian Mysteries." In *Samuel Sumner Sermons*, 84–105. London: William Ball, Aldine Chambers, Paternoster Row, 1837.

Tozer, A. W. *The Divine Conquest*. Westwood, NJ: Fleming H. Revell Co., 1964.

Trench, Richard Chenevix. *Synonyms of the New Testament*. Grand Rapids, MI: Wm. B. Eerdmans Publishing Company, 1953.

Lexicons, Encyclopedias, and References for Greek Readers, from Classical and Koine Greek to Modern Greek

Byzantiou, S. D. *Lexikón tēs Hellēnikēs Glōssēs* (*Lexicon of the Hellenic Language*). Athens: Koromēlá, A., 1852.

Dēmētrákou, D. *Lexikón tēs Hellēnikēs Glōssēs* (*Lexicon of the Hellenic Language*). Athens: Dēmētrákou, 1954.

Enkuklopaidikón Glōssologikón Lexikón (*Encyclopedic Glossological Lexicon*). Athens: Morfōtikē Hetaireia, n.d.

Enkuklopaidikón Lexikón Eleutheroudáki (*Encyclopedic Lexicon*). Athens: Eleutheroudákis, 1927.

Kalaráki, Michaēl and Nikólas Galanós. Iōánnou toú Chrusostómou Tá Hápanta (Complete Works of John Chrysostom). n.p. 1899.

Liddell, Henry George, and Robert Scott. *Greek–English Lexicon,* as Translated and Enriched by Xenophōn P. Móschos and Michaēl Kōnstantinídes. Athens: John Sideris, n.d.

Megálē Hellēnikē Enkuklopaideía (*Great Hellenic Encyclopedia*). Pursos (Pyrsos), Athens: Hēlios, n.d.

Neōteron Enkuklopaidikón Lexikón Hēlíou (*New Encyclopedic Lexicon "Hēlios"*). Athens: Hēlios, n.d.

Papaoikonómou, George L. *Lexikon Anōmálōn Rhēmátōn* (Lexicon of Irregular Verbs). Athens: Kagiáphas, n.d.

Stamatákou, J. D. *Lexikón Archaías Hellēnikēs Glōssēs* (*Lexicon of the Ancient Hellenic Language*). Athens: Pétrou Dēmētrákou, 1949.

Works by Spiros Zodhiates

Conquering the Fear of Death. Grand Rapids, MI: Wm. B. Eerdmans Publishing Co., 1970.

A Richer Life for You in Christ. Ridgefield, NJ: AMG Publishers, 1972.

Was Christ God? Grand Rapids, MI: Wm. B. Eerdmans Publishing Company, 1970.

Getting the Most Out of Life. Ridgefield, NJ: AMG Publishers, 1976.

Speaking in Tongues and Public Worship. Chattanooga, TN: AMG Publishers, 1997.

A Revolutionary Mystery. Chattanooga, TN: AMG Publishers, 1997.

The Behavior of Belief. Grand Rapids, MI: Wm. B. Eerdmans Publishing Company, 1959.

The Beatitudes. Chattanooga, TN: AMG Publishers, 1998.

List of Abbreviations

acc. (accusative)

act. (active)

aor. (aorist [2 aor. for second aorist])

a.t. (author's translation)

cf. (compare)

ch. (chapter)

comp. (composition)

dat. (dative)

e.g. (for example)

etc. (and so forth)

ff. (following)

fut. (future)

gen. (genitive)

i.e. (that is)

imper. (imperative)

imperf. (imperfect)

indic. (indicative)

inf. (infinitive)

KJV (King James Version)

MT (Majority Text)

mid. (middle)

neut. (neuter)

n.d. (no date available)

N.p. (no publisher available)

NASB (New American Standard Bible)

NIV (New International Version)

NKJV (New King James Version)

nom. (nominative)

p. (page), pp. (pages)

part. (participle, participial)

pass. (passive)

pers. (person)

perf. (perfect)

pl. (plural)

pres. (present)

pron. (pronoun)

Sept. (Septuagint)

sing. (singular)

TR (Textus Receptus)

UBS (United Bible Society)

usu. (usually)

v. (verse), vv. (verses)

vol. (volume)

Guide to the Transliteration and Modern Pronunciation of the Greek Alphabet

Capital Letter	Small Letter	Greek Name	Trans- literation	Phonetic Sound	Example
Α	α	alpha	*a*	a	as in father
Β	β	bēta	b	v	as in victory
Γ	γ	gamma	*g*	y	as in yell (soft gutteral)
Δ	δ	delta	*d*	th	as in there
Ε	ε	epsilon	*e*	e	as in met
Ζ	ζ	zēta	*z*	z	as in zebra
Η	η	ēta	*ē*	ee	as in see
Θ	θ	thēta	*th*	th	as in thin
Ι	ι	iōta	*i*	i	as in machine
Κ	κ	kappa	*k*	k	as in kill (soft accent)
Λ	λ	lambda	*l*	l	as in land
Μ	μ	mē	*m*	m	as in mother
Ν	ν	nē	*n*	n	as in now
Ξ	ξ	xi	*x*	x	as in wax
Ο	ο	omicron	*o*	o	as in obey
Π	π	pi	*p*	p	as in pet (soft accent)
Ρ	ρ	ro	*r*	r	as in courage
Σ	σ,ς*	sigma	*s*	s	as in sit
Τ	τ	tau	*t*	t	as in tell (soft accent)
Υ	υ	ēpsilon	*u*	ee	as in see
Φ	φ	phi	*ph*	ph	as in graphic
Χ	χ	chi	*ch*	h	as in heel
Ψ	ψ	psi	*ps*	ps	as in ships
Ω	ω	omega	*ō*	o	as in obey

*At the end of words

SPECIAL RULES FOR THE TRANSLITERATION AND MODERN PRONUNCIATION OF THE GREEK LANGUAGE

COMBINATIONS OF CONSONANTS

Small Letter	Greek Names	Trans-literation	Phonetic Sound	Example
γγ	gamma + gamma	*gg*	g	as in go
γκ	gamma + kappa	*gk*	g	as in go
γχ	gamma + chi	*gch*	gh	as in ghost

DIPHTHONGS (DOUBLE VOWELS)

Small Letter	Greek Names	Trans-literation	Phonetic Sound	Example
αι	alpha + iōta	*ai*	ai	as in hair
αυ	alpha + ēpsilon	*au*	af, av	as in waft or lava
ει	epsilon + iōta	*ei*	ee	as in see
ευ	epsilon + ēpsilon	*eu*	ef, ev	as in effort or every
ηυ	ēta + ēpsilon	*ēu*	eef, eev	as in reef or sleeve
οι	omicron + iōta	*oi*	ee	as in see
ου	omicron + ēpsilon	*ou*	ou	as in group
υι	ēpsilon + iōta	*ui*	ee	as in see

BREATHINGS (Occur only with initial vowels)

(᾿) Smooth, not transliterated or pronounced.
When words begin with vowels, it may occur at the beginning of words with every vowel or double vowel (diphthong). ἔργον—*érgon*, work; εὐχή—*euchḗ*, vow.

(῾) Rough = h.
When words begin with vowels, it may occur at the beginning of words with every vowel or double vowel (diphthong). No distinction in pronunciation from the smooth breathing. To indicate the rough breathing we use "h" in the transliteration.

(ῥ) Rho = r.

(ὑ) Ēpsilon = u.
When these begin a word, they always have the rough breathing. There they are transliterated rh, hu, respectively. ῥέω—*rhéō*, flow; ὑπομονή—*hupomonḗ*, patience.

Scripture Index

Romans

1 Corinthians

2 Corinthians